Implications of the Global Financial Crisis for Financial Reform and Regulation in Asia

Implications of the Global Financial Crisis for Financial Reform and Regulation in Asia

Edited by

Masahiro Kawai

Dean and CEO, Asian Development Bank Institute, Tokyo, Japan

David G. Mayes

BNZ Professor of Finance, Director Europe Institute and NZ Governance Centre, University of Auckland, Adjunct Professor, University of Canterbury, New Zealand and Visiting Professor, University of Buckingham, UK

Peter J. Morgan

Senior Consultant for Research, Asian Development Bank Institute, Tokyo, Japan

A JOINT PUBLICATION OF THE ASIAN DEVELOPMENT BANK INSTITUTE AND EDWARD ELGAR PUBLISHING

Edward Elgar

Cheltenham, UK • Northampton, MA, USA

Published by
Edward Elgar Publishing Limited
The Lypiatts
15 Lansdown Road
Cheltenham
Glos GL50 2JA
UK

Edward Elgar Publishing, Inc.
William Pratt House
9 Dewey Court
Northampton
Massachusetts 01060
USA

A catalogue record for this book
is available from the British Library

Library of Congress Control Number: 2011932874

MIX
Paper from
responsible sources
FSC® C018575

ISBN 978 0 85793 471 0

Typeset by Servis Filmsetting Ltd, Stockport, Cheshire
Printed and bound by MPG Books Group, UK

Contents

Figures

Tables

Contributors

Charles Adams is Visiting Professor, Lee Kuan Yew School of Public Policy, National University of Singapore, Singapore.

Jonathan A. Batten is Professor of Finance, Hong Kong University of Science and Technology, Hong Kong, China.

Yoon Je Cho is Professor, Graduate School of International Studies, Sogang University, Seoul, Republic of Korea.

Santiago Fernández de Lis is Director, International Department, Afi (Analistas Financieros Internacionales), a consultancy and think-tank based in Madrid, Spain.

Mariko Fujii is Professor of Economics and Finance, Research Center for Advanced Science and Technology, University of Tokyo, Tokyo, Japan.

Alicia García-Herrero is Chief Economist for Emerging Markets, Banco Bilbao Vizcaya Argentaria; Visiting Professor, University of Hong Kong; and Advisory Board member, Hong Kong Institute for Monetary Research, Hong Kong, China.

Warren P. Hogan was Professor of Economics, University of Sydney, Australia from 1968–1998, and earlier, Professor and Dean, University of Newcastle, Australia. He died in December 2009 following a short illness and period of hospitalization.

Muneesh Kapur is Director, Department of Economic and Policy Research, Reserve Bank of India, Mumbai, India.

Masahiro Kawai is Dean and CEO, Asian Development Bank Institute, Tokyo, Japan.

David G. Mayes is BNZ Professor of Finance, Director Europe Institute and NZ Governance Centre, University of Auckland, New Zealand; Adjunct Professor, University of Canterbury, New Zealand; and Visiting Professor, University of Buckingham, UK.

Rakesh Mohan is Senior Fellow, Jackson Institute for Global Affairs and Professor in the Practice of International Economics and Finance,

School of Management, Yale University, New Haven, CT, USA. He is also former Deputy Governor, Reserve Bank of India.

Peter J. Morgan is Senior Consultant for Research, Asian Development Bank Institute, Tokyo, Japan.

Michael G. Plummer is Development Division Head, Trade and Agriculture Directorate, Organisation for Economic Co-operation and Development (OECD), Paris, France.

Michael Pomerleano is Adviser, World Bank, Washington, DC, USA.

Mark M. Spiegel is Vice-President, International Research and Director of the Center for Pacific Basin Studies, Federal Reserve Bank of San Francisco, CA, USA.

Peter G. Szilagyi is Lecturer in Finance, Judge Business School, University of Cambridge, UK.

Larry D. Wall is Financial Economist and Senior Policy Adviser, Research Department, Federal Reserve Bank of Atlanta, GA, USA.

Adalbert Winkler is Professor, Frankfurt School of Finance & Management, Frankfurt, Germany.

Preface

The 1997–1998 Asian financial crisis highlighted several shortcomings in Asian financial markets, most notably the underdevelopment of domestic bond markets and deficiencies in corporate governance, transparency and financial regulation. Since then, Asian financial markets have made considerable progress in both development and regulation. Asian markets have now reached levels of development common in other economies with similar income levels. Markets are also becoming more integrated regionally, although not near the levels prevailing in Europe. Some of these changes have been the result of important initiatives undertaken to remedy deficiencies brought to the fore by the 1997–1998 crisis, including the Asian Bond Markets Initiative and the Asian Bond Fund project.

The global financial crisis of 2007–2009 posed a new set of challenges for Asian economies, while highlighting a lack of progress in some areas since the Asian financial crisis. This time the crisis originated in the developed economies – primarily the United States – that had large and sophisticated financial systems, but nonetheless allowed the build-up of systemic financial risks. Asian economies, for the most part, were not directly involved in the crisis, and were hit mainly by falls in exports and a loss of liquidity. Their economic and financial fundamentals had improved substantially since the time of the Asian financial crisis. Their financial systems were still relatively underdeveloped in terms of their reliance on sophisticated financial products such as collateralized debt obligations and credit default swaps, while their financial regulators were much less influenced by notions of self-regulating markets, and hence much more willing to impose prudential norms on lending behavior. Asian financial firms held relatively few toxic assets compared with their American and European counterparts. Asian economies also had much less exposure to short-term foreign currency debt than in the period before the Asian financial crisis, and had built up substantial foreign exchange reserves.

The purpose of this book is to identify the challenges imposed by the global financial crisis and suggest policy recommendations for addressing them. These challenges fall into four major areas: (1) preventing financial crises; (2) responding to financial crises if they do occur; (3) managing international capital flows; and (4) deepening and integrating financial markets to provide an alternative source of funding to foreign capital flows. Improving regional economic and financial surveillance and strengthening regional liquidity safety net mechanisms against future financial shocks can significantly contribute to achieving financial stability and supporting domestic demand growth. The global financial crisis illustrates the importance of implementing a framework for macroprudential financial supervision and regulation – through the creation of a powerful systemic stability regulator – that includes effective mandates and prudential tools. Steps to improve microprudential regulation and reduce the procyclicality of financial regulation are also important. Frameworks for monitoring innovative financial products and systemically important financial institutions need to be developed. Crisis response can be improved by: (1) having a coordinated set of financial authorities that, between them, cover all phases of the crisis; (2) ensuring there are credible *ex ante* means of handling failures in all financial firms, particularly those that operate across borders; (3) implementing an effective deposit insurance system; and (4) improving resilience against shocks by substantially enhancing regional mechanisms, among others, through an Asian financial stability dialogue.

Managing volatile international capital flows remains a key problem for most emerging Asian economies. Judicious use of capital controls can contribute to stabilizing such flows. A further deepening and integration of its financial markets, especially bond markets, could help support the region's long-term growth by helping to recycle Asia's high savings for investment in worthy projects in the region, particularly when capital flows from other regions are volatile. Deeper and more integrated financial markets can also provide an extra layer of protection against the withdrawal of foreign capital from the region during economic downturns.

Regional institutions can contribute to financial stability as well. The completion of the Chiang Mai Initiative Multilateralization agreement and the establishment of an Association of Southeast Asian Nations +3 Macroeconomic Research Office could significantly contribute to creating an Asian monetary fund to monitor international risks and provide hard currency liquidity when needed. The creation of an Asian financial stability dialogue could also further the cooperation of fiscal, monetary and financial authorities in the region. Further development of Asian bond markets (through the Asian Bond Markets Initiative and Asian Bond Funds) and a newly created Credit Guarantee and Investment Facility could provide important support to countries seeking to increase investment for growth, whether for infrastructure or other types of private investment. Development of a market for bonds denominated in an Asian currency unit could also contribute to widening the regional bond market.

An Asian infrastructure investment fund could facilitate regional infrastructure investment.

Meeting these challenges will help to put Asian economies on a path of sustainable growth that relies more than previously on domestic sources of savings and final demand. By contributing to smaller global imbalances, such policies can also promote stable growth and less systemic risk in the world as whole, not just in Asia. Finally, they will enable Asian economies to have a greater role in the reform of the global financial architecture.

Early versions of the chapters in this book were presented at the conference on Global Financial Crisis: Financial Sector Reform and Regulation, held on 21–23 July 2009, and organized by the Asian Development Bank Institute (ADBI). The chapters benefited from comments made by discussants and other conference participants. I greatly appreciate the efforts of the excellent team of authors and participants. Professor David Mayes of Auckland University, Dr Peter Morgan of ADBI and I provided overall guidance as co-editors of the book.

Masahiro Kawai
Dean and Chief Executive Officer
Asian Development Bank Institute

Abbreviations

ABCP	asset-backed commercial paper
ABF1	Asian Bond Funds 1
ABF2	Asian Bond Funds 2
ABMI	Asian Bond Markets Initiative
ABS	asset-backed security
ACRAA	Association of Credit Rating Agencies in Asia
ADB	Asian Development Bank
ADBI	Asian Development Bank Institute
AEC	ASEAN Economic Community
AFSD	Asian financial stability dialogue
AIG	American International Group
AMC	asset management company
AMRO	ASEAN+3 Macroeconomic Research Office
ASEAN	Association of Southeast Asian Nations
ASP	ASEAN Surveillance Process
BIS	Bank for International Settlements
BOE	Bank of England
BOK	Bank of Korea
CAMELS	capital adequacy, asset quality, management, earnings, liquidity and sensitivity to market risk
CDO	collateralized debt obligation
CDS	credit default swap
CEE	Central and Eastern European
CGFS	Committee on the Global Financial System
CMI	Chiang Mai Initiative
CMIM	Chiang Mai Initiative Multilateralization
CRR	cash reserve ratio
EBRD	European Bank for Reconstruction and Development
ECB	European Central Bank
ECU	European Currency Unit
EME	emerging market economy
EMEAP	Executives' Meeting of East Asia Pacific Central Banks
ES	expected shortfall
ESRB	European Systemic Risk Board

EU	European Union
EUROFIMA	European Company for the Financing of Railroad Rolling Stock
FC	foreign currency
FDI	foreign direct investment
FMM	Finance Ministers Meeting
FRA	forward rate agreement
FSB	Financial Stability Board
FSC	Financial Supervisory Commission
FSF	Financial Stability Forum
G7	Group of Seven
GDP	gross domestic product
IAS	international accounting standards
IBRD	International Bank for Reconstruction and Development
IFC	International Finance Corporation
IMF	International Monetary Fund
ITC	investment and trust company
JBIC	Japan Bank for International Cooperation
KAMCO	Korea Asset Management Company
KDIC	Korea Deposit Insurance Company
KIS AB	Kommuninvest I Sverige Aktiebolag
LC	local currency
LCFI	large and complex financial institution
LGD	loss given default
LIBOR	London Interbank Offered Rate
LOLR	lender of last resort
MBS	mortgage-backed security
MOFE	Ministry of Finance and Economy
NBFI	non-bank financial institution
NPL	non-performing loan
PAIF	Pan-Asia Index Fund
PRC	People's Republic of China
R&I	Risk and Investment Inc.
RFI	Reuters Fixed Income
RMBS	residential mortgage-backed security
S&P	Standard & Poor's
SBS	Superintendencia de Banca, Seguros y AFP
SEC	Securities and Exchange Commission
SEE	Southeastern European
SLWG	Squam Lake Working Group
SRC	systemic risk council
UK	United Kingdom

USA	United States of America
VaR	value at risk

Note: Throughout this book the term 'billion' refers to 1000 million and 'trillion' refers to 1000 billion.

1. The global financial crisis and its implications for financial sector reform and regulation in Asia

David G. Mayes and Peter J. Morgan

1.1 INTRODUCTION

Although Asian countries have done a great deal to improve their resilience to financial shocks, and have come through the global financial crisis of 2007–2009 relatively well as a result of their unpleasant experiences just over a decade ago in the Asian financial crisis, they have not in general been severely tested. In 1997–1998, many countries experienced foreign exchange as well as banking crises. This time, Asian countries in general have both greater foreign exchange reserves and more flexible monetary policies and currency regimes so they can absorb shocks more readily. Nevertheless, the economic consequences of the crisis have been severe, especially in countries such as the Republic of Korea (hereafter Korea) and Japan that are significant exporters of investment and durable consumer goods. Moreover, other countries, which thought they had excellent crisis management systems, have found themselves in severe difficulty. The problems resulting from the recent global crisis have both provided new challenges and advanced the benchmark for international best practice. The purpose of this book is to identify the new lessons that have emerged from the crisis and explore how the resulting policy recommendations might best be implemented in Asia.

This chapter provides an overview of the policy analyses and suggestions in the following chapters, which were initially presented at a conference organized by the Asian Development Bank Institute on the implications of the global financial crisis for financial sector reform and regulation in Asia.[1] Section 1.2 reviews what can be done at the national level to improve a country's ability to avoid shocks turning into crises, while Section 1.3 considers what can be done to improve the management of any crises that do occur so that the losses involved can be minimized and the countries swiftly returned to healthy economic growth. Section

1.4 then evaluates what more can be done jointly among the countries in the region in light of the changes that are likely to be implemented at the global level. Section 1.5 offers some concluding thoughts.

The main focus in each section is on the changes that might be made in the regulation of financial markets, both in the institutions that the authorities use to achieve their objectives, and in the tools and policies that are used in implementation. This crisis has revealed very sharply that action is required both at a systemic (macroprudential) level and in the handling of individual financial institutions (microprudential supervision). This book is thus complementary to works on financial stability in Asia that deal primarily with managing against external shocks. A good recent example is Mendoza (2009), which provides a list of some 38 instruments that could be used to advantage in increasing financial stability. There is some overlap in areas such as the development of capital markets, but in the main the discussions run in parallel.

1.2 WAYS OF AVOIDING OR MITIGATING FUTURE CRISES

It is not possible to avoid crises altogether and, indeed, there is likely to be a trade-off between reducing the chances of a crisis occurring and lowering the overall rate of economic growth. Calvo (2009) sets out the conditions under which occasional crises may actually be therapeutic and achieve the structural change that more gentle pressures fail to. The magnitude of the output losses resulting from the global financial crisis underlines the desirability of avoiding crises, but not at the expense of increasing the risk of future crises. There thus needs to be a balance between crisis avoidance and crisis management, although the present crisis has led to a general wish to do more in both areas. Crisis management techniques, and the structure of the safety net in particular, can contribute positively or negatively to the likelihood of future crises. The great willingness in some countries to avoid bank failures, although this has involved substantial use of taxpayers' money, will of itself encourage banks and their stakeholders to take more risks than they might otherwise. While Asian countries may have avoided this temptation, their resolve has not been substantially tested on this occasion. As a result, banks might well infer that despite what may have been said in advance, authorities in these countries may also turn out to be willing to take action to avoid bank failures. Moral hazard is thus not something that merely operates within borders, it can have an influence across borders as well.

1.2.1 Rationalization or Unification of Regulatory Structure

In many countries, regulatory structure is as much a function of history as it is of a careful allocation of objectives and tasks to individual institutions that ensure not merely that all aspects of the problem are covered (Kawai and Pomerleano, Chapter 2), but that there are no confusing overlaps and that the incentives of all those involved are clearly aligned to the task of preserving financial stability. As Wall (Chapter 3) points out, the issues are perhaps best illustrated in the United States (US), where, on the one hand, a plethora of regulatory institutions contributed to the emergence of the worst financial crisis in the world in over 50 years, yet on the other hand, regulators were able to handle a large number of problem banks swiftly and smoothly, with no threat to stability, no use of public money, and with limited losses to the private sector. The problematic resolutions and the requirements for large-scale bailouts of failed financial institutions occurred primarily in the non-bank sector where tools were not available.

Asian countries can learn from the mistakes of others revealed in the present crisis, and from their own experience of the Asian financial crisis of just over a decade ago. Indeed, perhaps the greatest lesson is that even with direct experience of problems, countries have been slow to implement change. Sweden, for example, developed proposals for handling problem banks as long ago as 2000, driven in part by its own crisis in 1992. Nevertheless, it did not implement them until it discovered that it could not handle distress in one of the very smallest banks in the country in 2006, before the main crisis broke.

There are six main tasks of the regulatory structure:

- prudential regulation and supervision of individual financial institutions;
- monitoring of systemic risks and action to maintain macroprudential stability;[2]
- providing short-term liquidity assistance to solvent banks;
- swiftly handling problems in troubled banks at limited cost;
- limiting the losses to ordinary people who do not have the means of protecting themselves; and
- coordinating the activities of the various parties involved to ensure coherence and the avoidance of gaps in the system.

It is universally accepted that the central bank is the institution that should provide liquidity assistance to the market and to solvent individual institutions, but to do that it needs to have adequate information from the supervisory authority about the state of such banks so that it avoids lending to the insolvent. Similarly, it is largely accepted that central banks should be the focus of macroprudential policy, although, as discussed in section 1.2.3, there is a lot to be said for a collaborative role involving supervisors as well.[3] Clearly there are several different ways of providing the necessary information, starting with the central bank also being the supervisor, down to separate organizations with a clear duty to exchange information. As Hsu and Liao (2010) point out, this range of solutions is already being applied in the People's Republic of China; Hong Kong, China; Singapore; and Taipei,China, with all models appearing to be successful, although they have not been severely tested. The People's Republic of China operates with a central bank and separate regulators for banking, insurance and securities. Taipei,China also has separation between the central bank and financial supervision, but there the supervision of the financial sector is undertaken by a single authority. In Hong Kong, China, the Hong Kong Monetary Authority is also responsible for banking supervision (although not for other financial sectors). Finally, Singapore has a completely integrated structure, with the Monetary Authority of Singapore being responsible for all functions. It is thus not so important which structure is used, but that the chosen structure enshrines clear relationships between the authorities.

The main question to be answered in this context is whether it is easier to resolve conflicts of interest internally within an individual institution, or externally among institutions. If the internal route is followed, then it is important to make sure that the conflicts are resolved transparently by the top decision-making body and not inconsistently at a variety of lower levels. Thus, it is common to assign responsibility for monetary and financial stability to different deputy governors in a central bank. However, as the present crisis has demonstrated, a basic incentive for regulators to undertake their task effectively is also required.

1.2.2 Ways of Improving Microprudential Monitoring

The improvement of microprudential regulation and supervision has attracted widespread attention in the present crisis because, on the one hand, such regulation has failed to detect problems or act early enough, and on the other hand, it has actually contributed to the problem by creating perverse incentives for banks. It is clear that the normal range of indicators of difficulty, as illustrated by the CAMELS[4] ratings in the US, can be of variable efficacy, but something comprehensive of this type that is regularly updated and reviewed provides the best chance of detecting a problem. For any such range of indicators to be effective, they must sometimes indicate problems when there are none if they are to be sensitive enough to catch almost all problem cases early. The cost of a few investigations that turn out to be unnecessary, however, is a small price to pay.

Until now, much weight has been placed on capital buffers, both in the advice of the Basel Committee on Banking Supervision, and in its implementation in the Capital Requirements Directive of the European Union (EU). However, the use of capital triggers alone for early intervention is not helpful as they cut in far too late. Capital triggers work well as a backstop for prompt corrective action, ensuring that the authorities do not delay in implementing solutions for problem banks. The incentives for forbearance are strong, so while considerable discretion is desirable over which techniques to use in any particular situation, clear rules are needed for how rapidly the authorities should act, as resolutions take several weeks to put in place. Both sets of requirements and the powers to act thereon are required. Thus, sufficient information is needed to be able to act early enough, and there must be a requirement to implement actions to resolve the problem rapidly before it develops too far.

The primary concerns have been: (1) that banks should hold more capital, as previous buffers have proved inadequate to allow banks to recover; (2) that banks should also have liquidity buffers so that they can withstand the drying up of financial markets for a significant period; and (3) that they should not become so leveraged so as to lessen the need for drastic asset sales when prices are artificially depressed in a crisis. These have all been reflected in the new Basel 3 recommendations (Basel Committee on Banking Supervision 2010). Clearly, central banks will always be there as lenders of last resort to ensure that confidence is maintained in the system as a whole in the event of market problems, but the rationale for buffers is to reduce the fragility of the system and buy time for solutions to be worked out in the event of difficulty. The prevailing Basel rules encouraged banks to shift problems off their balance sheets, but in practice there was still exposure to risk, especially to their reputations if their off-balance-sheet vehicles failed, and hence one can expect that authorities will be keen to make sure that this misleading shifting does not occur in the future (Plummer, Chapter 8).

1.2.3 Macroprudential Surveillance and Regulation

The present crisis has not only revealed that macroprudential supervision has been weak in many countries, but also that the relationship between macroprudential and microprudential supervision has not worked well. The key feature of macroprudential regulation is that it draws attention to movements in the market as a whole that can be a threat to systemic stability, even if, at the individual institutional level, the problem might not be so clear. For example, the growth and extent of collateralized debt obligations (CDOs) in the US should have been seriously worrying, as should have been the extent of the exposure of non-US financial institutions to CDOs. Wall (Chapter 3) argues that there is a danger in overestimating what macroprudential supervision can achieve, but that it must at least have the tools necessary to act. Currently, those responsible for macroeconomic stability can do little more than warn the government and the financial system of emerging dangers. Kawai and Pomerleano (Chapter 2), therefore, put improved macroprudential architecture at all levels – global, regional and national – at the top of their list for action.

Two major areas for action need to be addressed. The first is the structure of the financial system. It needs to be strengthened so that it can withstand major shocks, both by eliminating having institutions whose failure could disrupt the system, and by compelling institutions to put in place plans for handling the failure of core suppliers in a manner that does not disrupt the system (this theme is developed further in section 1.3.1). The second is to make available discretionary tools that can be used to supplement the automatic countercyclical stabilizers mentioned above. Such tools can take the form of loan-to-value ratios for lending or even reserve requirements (Mohan and Kapur, Chapter 6).

One important step that can be taken is to assign specific responsibility for handling systemic risk. Adams (Chapter 10) advocates the establishment of a systemic risk council. Such a council would be of a very high level and would not only be responsible for monitoring and coordinating, but also for ensuring that both pre-emptive and corrective macroprudential measures are undertaken by the responsible agencies. While such a council could be driven by one of the main agencies, such as the central bank, there are advantages in it being independent so that conflicts of interest are reduced. Cho (Chapter 9) makes a similar proposal, and identifies one of the main tasks of a crisis management team as being 'triage' – there needs to be a common diagnosis and an agreed response, especially regarding communication, across all agencies. Kawai and Pomerleano (Chapter 2) support the same notion, citing the National Economic Action Council in Malaysia as a successful example, while Cho points out that during the Asian financial crisis of 1997–1998 Korea held an emergency economic policy coordination meeting chaired by the President and created a Financial Supervisory Commission to carry out actions. One advantage of having such a council, rather than simply assigning responsibility to the central bank, is that it leaves the bank able to continue to run an independent monetary policy.

1.2.4 Ways of Reducing Procyclicality

It has become clear that capital adequacy regulation, particularly under Basel 2, can contribute considerably to increasing the amplitude of the financial and economic cycle. In rising markets, capital values increase and little effort is required to meet capital requirements that are constant through the cycle. However, in downturns, not only do losses mean that new capital is required, but capital values themselves fall and the cost of raising capital increases. This means that banks may have to contract lending in order to preserve adequate capital, thereby adding to the difficulties for the real economy at a time when it is already under pressure. In addition, under Basel 2, credit ratings, whether internally or externally generated, played an enhanced role in determining capital requirements. However, ratings also tend to follow a cyclical path, in part because the track record of the rated institution plays an important part in the determination of its rating.[5] Taken together, these factors can amplify the cycle. This was clearly an unintended consequence of Basel 2, yet one that had been pointed out for some time before it came into effect (Peura and Jokivuolle 2003).

There are also much longer-standing reasons why the financial system tends to exacerbate cycles in the real economy (Fernández de Lis and García-Herrero, Chapter 4), and knowledge of these should have led regulatory authorities to implement a system that was countercyclical in character much earlier. The reasons include the fact that 'good times' are likely to lead to a more relaxed attitude to risk (as memories fade the longer it has been since people were exposed to a downturn), and that herd behavior exacerbates swings and encourages overlending. Another aspect is that bonus systems encourage risk taking in the up phase as people make provision for the possibility that they will lose their jobs in the contraction.

Considerable thought has therefore gone into how these pressures might be offset. Monetary policy already tends to lean against the economic cycle, for example. The simplest response is to introduce a countercyclical element into the determination of capital ratios, raising them when growth picks up and allowing them to diminish as growth eases. Given that this involves increasing capital when it is cheap but not having to do so when it is scarce, this conveys an immediate benefit. Such changes can probably be made without the need for new legislation in many countries. Basel 3 includes provisions for such buffers, but they do not have an explicit form for general implementation at present. Fernández de Lis and García-Herrero (Chapter 4) describe a different approach, currently employed in Spain and more recently introduced in Peru and Colombia, whereby provisioning for bad loans is procyclical. In Spain, whenever lending increases more rapidly than normal, provisioning needs to increase more than proportionately on the grounds that rapid increases are likely to be accompanied by a decrease in the quality of lending. In a downturn, such provisions can then be used as defaults increase, without the need to increase capital in such difficult times.[6] Thus, the provisions reflect the behavior of the individual banks. In Peru, the process is related to cyclical fluctuations in gross domestic product (GDP) and, therefore, constitutes a part of macroprudential stability.[7]

Asian countries have made some use of similar countercyclical provisions in the past. Hong Kong, China, for example, has used loan-to-value ratios that become more cautious the faster the asset price underpinning the loan increases. Andritzky et al. (2009) suggest a wide range of countercyclical measures that could be applied, in particular taking into account the asymmetric problems of liquidity that occur when the economy turns down and doubts about loan quality lead to a withdrawal from markets and the freezing out of marginal participants. Such liquidity issues can most readily be addressed simply by ensuring a substantial liquidity cushion and matching funding sources to cash flow needs.[8] This approach has already been introduced in New Zealand (Reserve Bank of New Zealand 2009). More realistic stress tests that take account of the freezing of markets will help in determining the necessary level of preparedness. Leverage ratios will also tend to limit procyclicality.

A further concern relates to accounting methods. The use of fair value accounting can be highly procyclical if values are derived from impaired markets when the economy turns down. Not only does there tend to be overvaluation in the more euphoric phase, but also artificially low valuation in the downturn. It would be highly retrograde to return to the use of historical values or other systems that ignore market realities, and valuation methods that operate through the cycle (for example those using models) make far more sense. However, accounting rules themselves tend to make it more difficult to introduce provisioning in excess of what is known based on historical values (incurred losses) (Fernández de Lis and García-Herrero, Chapter 4).

1.2.5 Regulation of Innovative Financial Products and Specific Investor Groups

The Asian region has not rushed to adopt the sorts of derivative instruments, such as CDOs and credit default swaps, that caused such difficulties in the US when there was doubt about the value of the underlying loans (Fujii, Chapter 5). There are, therefore, few immediate concerns over how they should be handled as the later stages of the crisis unfold (Morgan 2009). However, many of these instruments are valuable means of hedging and spreading risk, and their adoption in the region, once the present crisis is over, will help in the deepening of markets and the management of risk. In this section, therefore, the need for such products and the implications for their regulation, along with other potentially destabilizing market actions that help to hedge and spread risks, will be considered.

For example, mortgage-backed securities have formed a stable source of housing finance in Australia for nearly 30 years.[9] Loan portfolios are all of a high quality and have not strayed into the subprime area[10] or moved off balance sheet. Other countries that have stayed with the less exotic and more transparent asset-backed securities have also enjoyed stable markets. In reaction to the crisis, there has been a rethink to ensure that, in future, the aspects of securitization that have led to instability are offset. In the first place, the concern is that all of those involved should retain proportionate exposure until the principal underlying the security has been paid back. In the past, many of those involved have collected their fees up front and have had no exposure to any subsequent deterioration in quality. Thus, agents, originators and rating agencies, for example, should receive their remuneration according to the performance of their portfolios (Joint Shadow Financial Regulatory Committees 2009). This will help all parties to ensure the quality of the assets. Fujii (Chapter 5) notes that in 2009 the US proposed that originators and sponsors be required to retain an economic interest in a 'material portion of the credit risk of securitized credit exposures' and that 'compensation of market participants' should be aligned 'with longer term performance of underlying loans' (US Treasury 2009: 13). This would go a long way to achieving the required outcome, especially in combination with the standardization of many products. Asian countries could, for example, agree on common features for mortgage-backed securities (Fujii, Chapter 5).

The anomalous treatment of asset-backed securities under the Basel regime and associated accounting procedures that encouraged banks to move such assets off their balance sheets should be ended. While some agents were able to collect their remuneration up front, many banks discovered that reputation risk meant that they were exposed to losses in the special investment vehicles they had set up to take mortgage-backed securities off their balance sheets. A concentration by financial markets on standardized products would make these products more transparent and easier to price. Indeed, they could become more readily traded on exchanges and gain stability from the existence of central counterparties. Hence, if these straightforward measures are taken, mortgage-backed securities could be developed to advantage across the region, assisting in the financing of standardized loans and reducing borrowers' dependence on banks without introducing any unwelcome instability into financial markets.

Authorities around the world have had concerns about the potentially destabilizing effects of the speculative activities of investor groups such as hedge funds. Their concerns have stemmed from two issues: first, that such organizations are largely unregulated and little is known about them; and second, that they might present significant risks to financial stability. However, as the crisis has developed, it has become clear that hedge funds have presented few problems and, indeed, insofar as they have been holding some of the impaired assets that have shown major losses, they have in fact had a stabilizing influence as they have been able to absorb their losses and have not proven to be a source of contagion to the market as a whole.

Credit rating agencies have seen their reputations become severely diminished during the crisis. Confidence could be increased by greater transparency, but also by the income of rating agencies being linked to the performance of the assets they rate. The main rating agencies have been somewhat less active in Asia than might have been expected from the level of financial development in Asian countries, and regional rating agencies have only been emerging slowly. While this may have resulted in Asia having been less caught up in the misrating of securities that has been demonstrated in the present crisis, it also means that Asian financial assets have been more difficult to value. Hence, moving forward, Asian countries will want to see rating agencies develop, albeit within a new framework of confidence and without the conflicts of interest that have arisen from agencies acting as both advisers and raters (Plummer, Chapter 8).

1.2.6 Management of Capital Flows

The inflow of capital plays an important role in the continuing development of the Asian region. And the relaxation of controls plays an important role in enabling that flow. However, open economies are vulnerable to sudden stops and reversals, and need to be able to cope with rapid variation. Such variations can be reflected in prices as well as in quantities in an open environment, putting pressure on competitiveness in an upturn and leading to rapid depreciations and credit squeezes when the flows reverse. In the Asian financial crisis of 1997–1998, there was a double mismatch problem in that not only was the currency mismatched, but the inflow of funds had become mainly short term, despite the fact that it was financing longer-term projects. Hence, a sudden stop in lending had a disastrous effect as assets could not be realized rapidly, nor could existing loans be repaid.

Many Asian countries have sought to find a middle way through this problem (Mohan and Kapur, Chapter 6) by not abandoning all capital controls, sterilizing much of the capital inflow to avoid it generating inflation, and managing their exchange rates so that fluctuations are limited. To some extent, therefore, these flows are the consequence of trying to ensure competitiveness and rapid export growth. However, the range of possible responses is heavily affected by the degree of openness of each country. India, which is not particularly open, has been able to manage pressures rather more extensively, using reserve requirements, for example.

There is a question of the optimal sequencing of liberalization such that as much of the benefits from deeper capital markets as possible can be obtained without the downside of unwelcome fluctuation in competitiveness in industries with narrow margins. In many cases, the main competitors to Asian countries are other countries in the region, so the concern is to see only limited fluctuations in cross rates. In the present crisis, a number of Asian countries have introduced measures to discourage short-term capital flows in an attempt to increase stability without harming the prospects for future longer-term investment flows. At least in the run-up to the present crisis, Asian countries have, on the whole, managed to avoid the problem of extensive foreign currency borrowing by those whose incomes are largely in domestic currency.

1.3 WAYS OF IMPROVING CRISIS MANAGEMENT

It is clear that the state has an important role to play in the organization of crisis resolution and that the private sector is both unwilling and unable to perform much of this function efficiently. However, this role is very different from the state bailing out financial institutions with taxpayers' money. On the whole, bailouts occur because the authorities have no reasonable alternative, either because of inadequate powers or inadequate prepositioning.[11] To maximize the chances of maintaining financial stability, governments need a balance between effective crisis avoidance measures and well-formed crisis management regimes. However, it is easy to overdo the constraints and cause financial 'repression', under which the development of the economy is inhibited (Cho, Chapter 9).

There is no reason why Asia should require any special measures for crisis management, even though the constituent states face different problems. Perhaps the most obvious general requirements are that authorities need to be able to intervene early before losses mount; that they need to make sure losses are recognized so as to reduce the uncertainty that causes markets to freeze up; and that they need to have a wide range of tools for early intervention, particularly to be able to take over failing banks from their shareholders before all value is lost. Delay and indecision tend to make crises much worse.

Time consistency – that is, delivering on *ex ante* commitments – is important. Policy reversals are typical in financial crises. Despite prior assurances that this will not happen, authorities often show a willingness to bail out the first institutions that get into difficulty. If the crisis turns out to be worse than expected, authorities often discover that a switch back to a harsh policy is required if funds are not to run out. Such switches can have a disastrous effect on risk taking, willingness to achieve private sector solutions, and confidence (Calvo 2009).

Adams (Chapter 10) suggests that crisis management should be considered in three phases:

- stabilization and containment;
- asset write-downs and absorption; and
- rehabilitation and normalization.

In the first of these phases, the authorities typically try to buy time. They are not sure about the size of the problem, but wish to make it very clear that the problem will be handled without major disruption so that confidence is maintained. This is an extremely difficult task as such situations are characterized by uncertainty and, as Adams puts it, financial crises are by their nature 'messy and disorderly' and unpredictable. The present crisis has seen the introduction of a multitude of new measures that countries will want to add to their tool kits, ready to be deployed on future occasions. In general, it has proven possible to handle liquidity problems. The crisis has also highlighted the dilemma of whether to employ drastic measures early on and then ease up later, or to start more gradually, but risk finding that options have already been foregone.

However, it is not possible to suggest a single recipe for handling crises as not only do crises differ in character, but the institutional structures of countries also differ. As discussed in the case of crisis avoidance, it is essential that the authorities work closely together in their efforts both to bring the crisis under control and to resolve problems rapidly.

1.3.1 Coordination Issues

There is widespread agreement that some organization needs to be in charge of actions in a crisis if they are to be rapid, clear and effective. Any such organization will need very close working links with all parties involved: central bank, supervisory agency, deposit insurer and ministry of finance. An alternative is that each party addresses its own responsibilities and there is a coordinating committee that makes sure that all the issues are addressed in a coherent manner. Government by committee under such circumstances is likely to be difficult, but has been practiced successfully (as pointed out by Cho, Chapter 9) in the case of Korea. But there are difficulties with giving any one organization so much power, as decisions will tend to become politicized.

What is required to overcome time inconsistency is to make as much of the resolution of the problem as possible subject to rules of behavior that have been laid down outside times of crisis. Thus, for example, it has been possible for the Federal Deposit Insurance Corporation in the US to handle all but the very largest banks under existing rules. Indeed, it would have been able to handle more of the problem had the special resolution regime for banks extended to the other financial sectors where problems arose in the present crisis. The existence of such arrangements pushes back the frontier of where panic and crisis start. Hence, a major lesson from the present crisis (Adams, Chapter 10) is that the authorities should try to make sure that as little as possible lies outside their ability to treat it under 'normal rules'. This involves trying to abolish the idea of 'too big, too complex or too interconnected to fail', which will be developed in the next section.

1.3.2 Bank Recapitalization and Disposal Issues

Perhaps what is most worrying in the present crisis is the degree to which market discipline has failed to be effective. In part, this is because the concentrated structure of many banking systems makes it difficult to find suitable purchasers, but in the main, it is because appropriate incentives do not exist and because many of the larger banks have become too complex to be resolved.

These circumstances need to change and authorities need to put in place a plan that can cope with problems in any of the banks in their jurisdiction. In many respects, the onus is on the banks themselves to have structures that can be resolved. The Governor of the Bank of England has suggested that each bank needs to prepare a 'living will' that sets out how the institution could be resolved in a manner that allows its vital functions to keep operating so that markets are not disrupted and confidence in the system is maintained.[12] Confidence requires that depositors believe that even though a bank may get into difficulty, they will not face any material break in access to their funds and normal activity will not be interrupted.

Much of the problem revolves around the difficulty of assigning losses when a bank is resolved. It needs to be possible to write down the shareholders according to a valuation – to zero if necessary. The bank also needs to be recapitalized. In some countries subordinated debt can also be written down automatically, but an approach that has considerable merit is to ensure that a sufficient amount of the bank's debt is hybrid capital so that it can be converted from debt to equity in the event of a resolution without any need for obtaining the agreement of debtholders at the time (Wall, Chapter 3). The key feature of this arrangement is that it enables the vital functions of a bank to continue without interruption as a going concern even if existing shareholders are wiped out or their holdings are heavily diluted (Huertas 2010). New Zealand is in the process of building in such a scheme (the Reserve Bank of New Zealand's Creditor Recapitalization Project), whereby debtholders, including depositors, become the new owners of the bank. Such a debt-for-equity swap appears to be a somewhat more plausible approach than requiring contingent capital, whereby an insurer provides the necessary capital should the bank get into a certain degree of difficulty.[13] The problem in this case is that in a systemic crisis the burden on insurers may become too great because of simultaneous demands from several banks. If either of these approaches can be implemented, the need to rely on the taxpayer can be greatly reduced and nationalization can actually be the last resort.

There is a clear link between these concerns over resolution and the improvements in microprudential regulation discussed in section 1.2.2. It has become apparent to some authorities as a result of the present crisis that there are important differences between the sources of a bank's capital that affect its ability to stabilize the institution in the event of a shock. It is really only equity that can be used while the bank is still running. Hence, Basel 3 has substantially increased equity requirements.

It is usually very difficult to proceed to recapitalization without thoroughly addressing the question of the valuation of impaired assets (Adams, Chapter 10). Two techniques are normally employed. One is to support existing organizations so that assets are kept on the balance sheet, but subject them to some loss-sharing agreement. The other is to strip assets altogether from banks that are troubled and place them in asset management companies (AMCs) or 'bad banks'.[14] The former route stands a better chance of avoiding having the AMC pay over the odds for assets that cannot be valued rapidly, and increases the chances that the assets will be well managed. Otherwise, banks will try to offload all their worst assets at inflated prices and may harm lending to get the economy restarted, as AMCs are less likely to roll over loans and may be unable to offer new lending. On the other hand, keeping the problem assets in existing banks may keep those banks under pressure and not end the dangerous cycle of expected losses that result in the need to sell assets, which further depresses their price, which then requires further asset sales. The key task is to decide rapidly which banks do not need assistance, which have problems that can be addressed, and which simply require intervention and resolution.

1.3.3 Issues Related to Deposit Insurance

There has been increasing use of deposit insurance in Asia, and the Malaysian authorities have been among the leaders in implementing standards and principles for what their systems are to achieve. Nevertheless, the experience in Europe in the present crisis has emphasized five main failings in deposit insurance systems. First of all, the system may not be able to offer people sufficiently continuous access to their accounts. Hence, they rush to withdraw their deposits just as they would without insurance, and generate the sort of retail run that deposit insurance is designed to avoid. Second, coverage has been found to be inadequate and deposit insurance levels have been raised. Third, some funds have been unable to cope with the demands placed on them and, in the case of Iceland, the country as a whole could not support its fund sufficiently for all claims to be met. Fourth, some countries have found that they need to offer wider guarantees to creditors, spreading well beyond just depositors. In the case of Ireland this has resulted in such a large payout that the government fell and the solvency of the country as a whole was threatened – saved by a joint EU–IMF bailout. Lastly, there have been serious problems with the insurance of depositors in cross-border banks that have operated through branches in other EU countries. Asian countries therefore need to check their arrangements against current standards as set out by the International Association of Deposit Insurers (2009).

The resort to blanket guarantees, while largely costless and very effective if a crisis does not deepen and they are not in fact called upon, can – as Ireland has discovered – become very expensive and lack credibility if a crisis becomes very serious (Adams, Chapter 10). To some extent, countries may find it difficult to resist the call for such guarantees despite the moral hazard involved if their use in other countries becomes widespread. Here, a degree of prior coordination among Asian countries – say, as part of the proposed Asian financial stability dialogue (AFSD) – might help, but such commitments can often prove valueless in the heat of a crisis.

1.4 JOINT REGIONAL CONTRIBUTIONS TO BETTER CRISIS AVOIDANCE AND CRISIS MANAGEMENT

While individual countries can do much to improve their resilience to crises, many Asian countries are relatively small and will always be vulnerable to external shocks. There is thus an important role for increased regional cooperation. However, this increased financial interdependence for mutual benefit with respect to crises will also tend to offer benefits at any time. One example is the development of bond markets that will help develop sources for financing investment within the region to lessen dependence on exports. Section 1.4.1 considers the development of bond markets before the chapter moves on to consider the wider aspects of integration in section 1.4.2. Section 1.4.3 considers one specific proposal that has been widely floated: the idea of developing an AFSD that would help countries develop a common approach to problems. The final subsection, 1.4.4, evaluates ideas for greater regulatory cooperation.

1.4.1 Deepening Asian Bond Markets

In the decade since the 1997–1998 Asian financial crisis, Asian bond markets have substantially expanded in size. This is partly because of initiatives such as the Asian Bond Markets Initiative and the Asian Bond Funds, but also because of special factors such as the widespread issuance of sterilization bonds by governments. Nevertheless, these markets are still relatively undeveloped compared to the region's share of the world economy, especially in the case of private sector bonds. Further deepening could contribute to enhancing financial stability and promoting a rebalancing of growth toward domestic demand by helping to channel the high level of regional savings to investment projects (both public and private) and consumption within the region. Aside from problems of scale, Eichengreen and Luengnaruemitchai (2006) highlight several obstacles to the development of bond markets in the Asia and Pacific region and advocate various reforms to support financial markets, such as improving bankruptcy legislation, reducing the degree of corruption, strengthening securities market regulation, removing capital controls, and adopting international accounting standards. The very presence of capital controls, by keeping bond markets underdeveloped, reduces the apparent incentive to end those controls. In addition, there are regulatory reforms necessary to improve corporate governance (Nestor and Thompson 1999; Thompson and Poon 2000) and various blueprints for financial market development to be made (Jiang and McCauley 2004; Park and Park 2003).

Due to small market size, many bond issuers in Asia are still not covered by the major global credit rating agencies. This reduces the investor base, as many large Western institutional investors, such as pension funds, require that the bonds included in their portfolios be rated by international credit rating agencies. In addition, the presence of a significant government sector may crowd out corporate issuers. This is clearly linked to the underdevelopment of some private bond markets (for example in India, New Zealand, and Pakistan) (Batten, Hogan and Szilagyi, Chapter 12).

All these factors inhibit the size of the market, which, in turn, discourages market participants, leading to a kind of low-level equilibrium trap. Even in countries where the government has actively sought to develop markets, success has been hindered by the lack of proactive involvement of market participants. For example, see Korea's failure to develop a viable foreign bond trading and issuance market despite the best efforts of policymakers (Batten, Hogan and Szilagyi, Chapter 12).

Despite the efforts and the progress made in developing markets, there is substantial potential to expand Asian bond markets further. First, encouraging foreign bond issuance in local markets is likely to bring regional markets closer to global standards. Supranational corporations, such as the World Bank, can play a key role in developing the corporate bond market, as this market is almost entirely of high credit quality, comprising sovereign, supranational, and major international bank issuers (Batten, Hogan and Szilagyi, Chapter 12). As noted by Hoschka (2005), the presence of highly rated multinational corporations in a domestic local currency bond market may actually 'crowd in' local issuance, because multinationals are likely to be experienced in raising capital through this channel and can deepen the markets for their domestic counterparts (Spiegel, Chapter 11). In addition, foreign firms that raise funds in Asian markets with the intention of swapping these funds into other currencies can contribute to the development of cross-currency swap markets. This is desirable for local issuers that issue abroad and wish to hedge these issues to avoid exposure to currency mismatches (Spiegel, Chapter 11).

Second, governments can improve their debt management. Risk-free benchmarks are an integral and necessary requirement for pricing and hedging in the corporate bond market. Ultimately, the risk-free government bond provides the benchmark for credit spreads. Thus, it is critical to recognize that adequate liquidity must be maintained, irrespective of fiscal requirements (Batten, Hogan and Szilagyi, Chapter 12).

Improving financial infrastructure can also contribute. Globally, the great majority of bonds (88.2 percent) are fixed rate with simple pricing features. Issuers of such bonds will normally require the means to hedge the currency risk associated with local currency bond issuance. The long-term viability of this segment is thus closely linked to the presence of: (1) highly liquid foreign exchange and derivatives markets that facilitate risk management and transformation; (2) regulations that facilitate cooperation with market participants; and (3) benchmark issues and competitive pricing between markets (Batten, Hogan and Szilagyi, Chapter 12).

It is crucial to expand credit rating agencies' coverage of private issues by encouraging regional rating agencies and promoting activities by global rating agencies (Spiegel, Chapter 11). Global and regional rating agencies have their strengths and weaknesses, but the best strategy is likely to be one that encourages additional coverage by both. However, the conflicts of interest that have compromised the independence and impartiality of ratings must be addressed.

It is also important to develop a robust, stable and secure domestic financial system to encourage both issuers and investors. Many market imperfections in Asian markets are self-induced. For example, withholding taxes and legal constraints combine to segment markets from global capital (Jiang and McCauley 2004) and appear to be a major deterrent to investors. Reluctance by some currency authorities to permit overseas transactions in their currency is another barrier. Of course, financial deregulation entails risks, and needs to be implemented judiciously.

For many Asian countries, increases in bond market size as a share of GDP are unlikely to be sufficient to obtain the scale economies necessary to achieve the cost reductions that are adequate to compete successfully with offshore bond markets. Instead, the achievement of adequate scale economies is likely to require cooperation at the regional level. Their best prospect is some kind of regional currency basket that would mitigate the currency exposure of issuers, although not eliminate it entirely (Spiegel, Chapter 11). The example of European bond markets is instructive. Hale and Spiegel (2009) found that subsequent to the launch of economic and monetary union in Europe, there was a 35.3 percent increase in the probability of issuing in euros relative to pre-union national currencies among non-financial firms in international bond markets. Even before the adoption of the euro, the development of the European Currency Unit led to a rapid expansion of European Currency Unit-denominated bond issues in Europe. The adoption of an Asian currency unit might result in a similar increase in issuance within the region.

Finally, Asian countries will have to sustain progress in the regional harmonization of regulatory standards.

1.4.2 Sources of Gain from Regional Integration

The experience of Europe in the global financial crisis has shown the advantages of the mutual support of closer integration, but also the problems for an individual country arising from being hit by a harsh individual shock. The euro remained stable throughout the main part of the crisis, so countries avoided currency-induced instability that could otherwise have added to their problems. Those countries that have encountered serious banking problems have largely sown the seeds of their distress themselves, particularly through permitting overleverage and through insufficient regard for ensuring liquidity. The countries of the eurozone that previously had to pay wide interest rate spreads but have not faced such problems have largely been able to retain the gains of being part of a larger currency area. However, more recent experience has shown that countries with fiscal weakness, such as Greece, Ireland and, increasingly, Portugal and Spain, can still be vulnerable to markets even in a monetary union. Nevertheless, the eurozone member states have been prepared to put together emergency financing of 0.75 trillion euros to give the stressed countries time to restructure their finances.

Winkler (Chapter 7) argues that closer economic relations in the EU and beyond have offered clear benefits to the development of the region. These benefits relate not simply to an improved rate of growth, but also to an ability to withstand shocks. Economic and financial integration in Asia is at most at the level it was in Europe 20 years ago. There is, therefore, a prima facie case that closer regional relationships would assist Asia as well (Asian Development Bank 2004). However, it is important not to exaggerate the benefits. Some countries that have either adopted the euro (Ireland for example) or have euro-backed currency boards (that is, the Baltic States) have been particularly hard hit by the present crisis as they have not been able to depreciate their currencies in response to larger than average adverse shocks, and have hence experienced substantial real output declines. Furthermore, EU and European Economic Area countries have realized that their macroprudential preparedness as a region was weak and that their plans for handling cross-border problems, particularly where banks run across borders, were seriously deficient (de Larosière 2009). In 2010, proposals were made by the European Commission for European resolution funds to provide a buffer for large cross-border banks encountering problems. As a result, the European Commission set up the European Systemic Risk Board in January 2011, led by the European Central Bank, and plans to develop an enhanced European system of financial supervisors. These are only steps along a road, but they are developments worthy of note in the Asian region, as are the early steps in the process of financial integration. These developments would dovetail with the proposal for national systemic risk councils advocated by Adams (Chapter 10) (see section 1.2.3 above).

1.4.3 AFSD

One of the most important steps in regional cooperation is better information and analysis, to understand the extent of the financial interdependencies in the Asian region and to assess the challenges these pose and how they can best be addressed. Europe has one key advantage over Asia in this regard. At the outset, in 1956, the European Community set up a central organization, the European Commission, whose task it is to promote the process of integration. Other institutions have since been added, including most notably the European Central Bank. Corresponding Asian institutions, insofar as they exist, are small and have little power by comparison. Hence, to make substantial progress in improving regional financial stability, there needs to be a suitable driving force. Plummer (Chapter 8) promotes the idea of an AFSD (Kuroda 2008).

In the early stages, such an arrangement could focus on issues that would help advance the areas of common interest that have already been identified and that are largely being dealt with under separate initiatives, such as the management of volatile short-term capital flows. Plummer sees it initially focusing on improving early warning systems, being able to assist in negotiations on common exchange rate changes, and, perhaps, helping in crisis management. This is akin to the open method of coordination in the EU, whereby countries agree that certain common objectives should be targets for the medium term. It is each country's choice how far to go in implementing any of the agreements, but the role of the secretariat (the European Commission in the EU case) is to monitor progress and publish the results. When countries see themselves, in effect, in some form of league table, it may put peer pressure upon them. The problem with this arrangement is that it is easy for countries to implement measures that enable them to claim that they have undertaken the necessary actions, but it is quite difficult to see to what extent these actions are working in practice and whether the desired changes have really taken effect.

The principal question is how far an AFSD might proceed beyond simply monitoring, diagnosing potential threats and suggesting remedies. One of the problems revealed in the run-up to the present crisis is that some organizations, particularly the Bank for International Settlements, did diagnose various sources of fragility, but they had no powers to act upon them. Drysdale (2009) and others see an AFSD as being an immediate vehicle for getting Asian countries out of the recent crisis, with measures such as coordinated monetary easing, infrastructure investment, and a major expansion of the Chiang Mai Initiative to make it fully multinational, that between them would constitute a 'road map' for recovery. The establishment of the Association of South East Asian Nations +3[15] Macroeconomic Research Office in Singapore is an important step in this direction.

While an AFSD as outlined by Kuroda (2008) would not be aimed at the sorts of closer harmonization of financial markets and tools in member countries as developed in Europe and accelerated under the Lamfalussy process, Hsu and Liao (2010) suggest this is exactly the road it should take, with matching committees of Asian banking supervisors, Asian securities and futures supervisors, and Asian insurance and pension supervisors. They see these committees as identifying areas where common regulatory arrangements would be helpful. However, while they might be able to develop such recommendations, it will still be up to the individual countries to implement such change.

Plummer (Chapter 8) argues that an AFSD could play an important role in developing best practice for securities markets in the region and in encouraging the development of regional markets. This would not merely make it easier for investors to address a number of markets, but would also deepen the markets so that a yield curve over the range of maturities could develop. This would be a marked improvement over the rather fragmented present framework.

The structure of the proposed AFSD relates closely to the objectives of the Financial Stability Board at the international level. Its predecessor, the Financial Stability Forum, promoted the observance of standards and codes. An AFSD can thus be seen as a first step toward achieving greater financial stability in the region. It makes more sense to have an organization with a limited mandate that makes successful progress than to try to leap immediately to closer cooperation without the necessary political and popular support.

The Executives' Meeting of East Asia Pacific Central Banks has been playing an increasing role in helping Asian countries work together in recent years. While it may be overambitious to suggest that this might develop into an Asian Bank for International Settlements (Plummer, Chapter 8), nevertheless it presents a possible organizational basis for increasing cooperation. As yet, the organization does not have a developed secretariat, although participating central banks service its subcommittees and working groups. In some respects, the problem for Asia is that there are quite a number of different forums for cooperation, comprising different groupings of countries, rather than one with a major focus that has the resources and mandate to make a major impact.

1.4.4 Regulatory Regimes and Cooperation

Kawai and Pomerleano (Chapter 2) extend the analysis of macroprudential policy to the international level, not merely because many of the largest banks run across borders, and so expecting purely national arrangements to suffice for the resolution of such institutions is unrealistic, but also because many macroprudential issues are international and the lack of a central empowered actor means that they are not addressed, as national authorities cannot act alone. Kawai and Pomerleano fear that the actions undertaken thus far by the international community as the crisis has evolved are insufficient. While the new Financial Stability Board is an improvement on its predecessor the Financial Stability Forum, it is not likely to have the staff to undertake action on the scale required. National authorities will retain power and, hence, it will be difficult to get them to act without effective forms of compulsion. International attempts to handle cross-border banks have been successful in identifying the problems but not the solutions. Even in the EU, where the internationalization of the financial system is an explicit objective, they have not yet been able to address the problem.

1.5 CONCLUDING REMARKS

All countries have received a wake-up call from the present financial crisis. Fortunately, most in the Asian region have only been subject to an economic shock, but that has been very harsh for countries with large export sectors. However, the disturbing experience of other countries that thought they had good systems for crisis avoidance and management shows that it is essential for Asian countries to take this opportunity to review their financial regulatory systems. As a result of experiencing their own crisis only just over a decade ago, they have both strengthened their systems and instituted a range of buffers that insulate them far better than was the case in the 1990s. Nevertheless, both techniques and experience have moved on and there are new lessons to learn. Many of these lessons can be implemented at the national level, but some are regional issues and the experience of Europe suggests that there is a range of measures that can be implemented to improve the ability both to avoid crises and to withstand shocks. The development of frameworks for macroprudential policy, coordinated crisis management and resolution, and regional cooperation, as well as the deepening of local-currency bond markets, rank high among these. However, such measures will need to be coordinated with the ongoing work of international institutions, particularly the Basel Committee on Banking Supervision and the International Monetary Fund, not just to improve macroprudential and microprudential stability, but to provide cross-border insulation and action as well.

NOTES

1. The conference, entitled Global Financial Crisis: Financial Sector Reform and Regulation, was held in July 2009 in Tokyo.

2. Macroprudential stability is a concept that has emerged in recent years, which reflects the wish to see that the economy as a whole, and the financial system within it, operates in a manner that will ensure stability. It is a top-down perspective to complement the longstanding requirement that each individual financial institution should be operated prudently in a bottom-up contribution to the stability of the system. It reflects the very obvious evidence from recent experience that a bottom-up approach alone is seriously deficient.
3. And possibly the government, as it has the main tools through fiscal policy.
4. CAMELS is an abbreviation for capital adequacy, asset quality, management, earnings, liquidity and sensitivity to market risk.
5. Until recently, many countries had enjoyed over a decade without a serious downturn so there was little opportunity to judge accurately how many assets would fare in such circumstances.
6. Unfortunately, the length of the Great Moderation was sufficient that, by 2004, there was a strong argument that provisioning had become excessive and the system was eased. However, it now seems likely that there was insufficient provisioning for the present crisis as a result.
7. Fernández de Lis and García-Herrero (Chapter 4) argue strongly in favor of bank activity-related provisioning, simply because this, unlike GDP, is something the banks themselves can affect. Furthermore, the authorities have direct access to bank-related data, which are less likely to be revised than GDP and are available more frequently and quickly.
8. Parallel liquidity requirements were discussed by the Basel Committee when it was developing its original capital requirements. Unfortunately, the committee did not reach an agreement and so they were left out of the accord. This time around, liquidity provisions have been included in Basel 3.
9. The Joint Shadow Financial Regulatory Committees (2009) use Denmark as an example of a country with long-standing stable arrangements for securitizing mortgages. Covered bonds have also been widely used in Europe, although they present problems in some legal frameworks as they have priority over other senior debt holders.
10. In many respects, the idea of 'subprime' mortgages is peculiar to the US, where mortgages need to be categorized to enable their securitization. Minimum lending conditions are required for a mortgage to qualify for securitization by the federal home loan institutions, best known by their nicknames of Fannie Mae and Freddie Mac. Many countries regard lending to households who cannot meet such minimum conditions as imprudent and, hence, the market does not really exist. However, other imprudent lending can take place, as illustrated by Northern Rock in the United Kingdom lending more than the value of the house that secured the loan in the hope of a continuing rise in house prices.
11. Prepositioning requires that the authorities have in place before the crisis all the necessary facilities for rapid response. Thus, for example, if depositors are to be paid out rapidly, not only must it be possible to identify the insured deposits and their holders on an ongoing basis, but there must also be an adequate interface with the banks' computer systems such that funds can be transferred or paid out.
12. Wall (Chapter 3) refers to 'shelf bankruptcy', which is largely similar in concept. 'Living wills' are distinct from 'funeral plans'. The former is a plan for a troubled continuing bank to organize its own recovery, whereas the latter is a plan for the authorities to resolve a failed bank.
13. The Squam Lake Working Group (2009) has suggested that such a debt for equity swap should not be triggered by the problems of an individual institution, but only in circumstances where there is a general crisis. Where the problem is not system-wide, the individual institution should be handled by the normal special resolution regime as there will be other well-capitalized institutions in the market that can take on the troubled bank (whether before or after failure).
14. The number of techniques that can be applied is large (Adams, Chapter 10). An AMC can be created for each institution, for example, and even for different types of assets

within an institution. They can be privately run or owned by the state. Each technique has its supporters and critics.

15. Member countries are Brunei Darussalam, Cambodia, the People's Republic of China, Indonesia, Japan, Korea, Lao People's Democratic Republic, Malaysia, Myanmar, the Philippines, Singapore, Thailand and Viet Nam.

REFERENCES

Andriztky, J., J. Kiff, L. Kodres, P. Madrid, A. Maechler, A. Naraian, N. Sacasa and J. Scarlata. 2009. Policies to Mitigate Procyclicality. Paper prepared for a conference on Financial Sector Reforms and Regulations, Asian Development Bank Institute (ADBI), Tokyo, 21–23 July.

Asian Development Bank. 2004. Monetary and Financial Integration in East Asia, 2 vols, Basingstoke, UK: Macmillan.

Basel Committee on Banking Supervision. 2010. The Basel Committee's Response to the Financial Crisis: Report to the G20. Basel: Bank for International Settlements.

Calvo, G. 2009. Financial Crises: Tales for Regulators and Central Bankers. Keynote speech at a conference on Financial Regulation: Lessons from the Recent Global Crisis, Banco Central de Chile, Santiago de Chile, 17 August.

Drysdale, P. 2009. Getting East Asia's Act Together for the G20 Summit. Vox web site, 23 March. http://www.voxeu.org/index.php?q=node/3323.

Eichengreen, B. and P. Luengnaruemitchai. 2006. Why Doesn't Asia Have Bigger Bond Markets? In *BIS Papers No 30 – Asian Bond Markets: Issues and Prospects.* Basel: BIS.

Hale, G. and M. Spiegel. 2009. Who Drove the Boom in Euro-Denominated Bond Issues? Federal Reserve Bank of San Francisco Working Paper 2009-20. San Francisco, CA: Federal Reserve Bank of San Francisco.

Hoschka, T.C. 2005. Local Currency Financing: The Next Frontier for MDBs? ADB Economics and Research Department Working Paper 68. Manila: ADB.

Hsu, C.M. and C.F. Liao. 2010. Financial Turmoil in the Banking Sector and the Asian Lamfalussy Process: The Case of Four Economies. ADBI Working Paper 221. Tokyo: ADBI. http://www.adbi.org/working-paper/2010/06/28/3920.financial.turmoil.prc.banking.lamfalussy.process/.

Huertas, T. 2010. The Road to Better Resolution: From Bail-out to Bail-in. Paper prepared for a conference on The Euro and the Financial Crisis, Bank of Slovakia, Bratislava, 6 September.

International Association of Deposit Insurers. 2009. Core Principles for Deposit Insurance. Basel: International Association of Deposit Insurers.

Jiang, G. and R. McCauley. 2004. Asian Local Currency Bond Markets. BIS Quarterly Review. June.

Joint Shadow Financial Regulatory Committees. 2009. Making Securitization Work for Financial Stability and Economic Growth. Statement 20. Santiago de Chile, 17 August.

Kuroda, H. 2008. Asia's Contribution to Global Development and Stability. Closing remarks presented at the ADBI Annual Conference, Tokyo, 5 December.

http://www.adbi.org/speeches/2008/12/05/2760.closing.remarks.kuroda.asia.global.financial.crisis.conference/.

de Larosière, J. 2009. The High Level Group on the Financial Crisis: Report. Brussels: European Commission. http://ec.europa.eu/internal_market/finances/docs/de_larosiere_report_en.pdf.

Mendoza, R.U. 2009. A Review of Financial Stability Instruments for Emerging Market Economies. *CESifo Economic Studies* 55(2): 353–97.

Morgan, P. 2009. Unregulated Entities, Products, and Markets: Challenges for Monitoring and Regulation. ADBI Research Policy Brief 30. Tokyo: ADBI. http://www.adbi.org/research-policy-brief/2009/08/12/3260.unregulated.entities.products.markets/.

Nestor, S. and J. Thompson. 1999. Corporate Governance Patterns in OECD Economies: Is Convergence Under Way? Paper prepared for a conference on Corporate Governance in Asia: A Comparative Perspective, Organisation for Economic Co-operation and Development and Korea Development Institute, Seoul, 3–5 March.

Park, Y.C. and D. Park. 2003. Creating Regional Bond Markets in East Asia: Rationale and Strategy. Paper prepared for the Second Annual Conference of the PECC Financial Forum, Pacific Economic Cooperation Council, Hua Hin, Thailand, 7–10 July.

Peura, S. and E. Jokivuolle. 2003. Simulation-Based Stress Testing of Banks' Regulatory Capital Adequacy. Bank of Finland Discussion Paper 04/2003. Helsinki: Bank of Finland.

Reserve Bank of New Zealand. 2009. Liquidity Policy. Prudential Supervision Department Document BS13. Wellington: Reserve Bank of New Zealand.

Squam Lake Working Group. 2009. An Expedited Resolution Mechanism for Distressed Financial Firms: Regulatory Hybrid Securities. www.cfr.org/content/publications/attachments/Squam_Lake_Working_Paper3.pdf.

Thompson, E.R. and J.P. Poon. 2000. ASEAN After the Financial Crisis: Links between Foreign Direct Investment and Regulatory Change. *ASEAN Economic Bulletin* 17: 1–15.

United States Department of the Treasury. 2009. *Financial Regulatory Reform – A New Foundation: Rebuilding Financial Supervision and Regulation*. Washington, DC: US Treasury.

PART I

Financial Surveillance and Regulation to Prevent Crises

2. Strengthening systemic financial regulation

Masahiro Kawai and Michael Pomerleano

2.1 INTRODUCTION

With a few notable exceptions, central bankers, financial supervisors and regulators, other policymakers, international organizations, the private sector and academic economists failed to predict the global financial crisis and underestimated its severity. Such a dramatic failure of the entire financial community warrants soul searching: is it possible to prevent a systemic crisis? In this chapter, it will be argued that this is indeed possible and that the best way to prevent a financial crisis is to identify and act on systemic risk or sources of financial instability.

The devastating global financial crisis of 2007–2009 offers a set of lessons. The new lessons learned are more substantial than those learned in the past, as what were considered the best financial systems – those of the United States (US), the United Kingdom (UK), and continental Europe – all went wrong. The objective of this chapter is to explore how to spot signs of systemic risk and prevent a financial crisis. It will be argued that an effective framework for systemic stability regulation should be established in each country, but that such a national effort would not be sufficient without the US and the UK – hosts to global financial centers and where the crisis originated – making a full political commitment to systemic stability regulation.

The chapter is organized as follows. Section 2.2 discusses the importance of crisis prevention and argues that effective macroprudential supervision – a top-down approach complemented by bottom-up microprudential supervision – can effectively spot and prevent crises. Section 2.3 provides basic principles in establishing a systemic financial regulator from the perspectives of objectives and mandates, resources, implementation and structure. Section 2.4 reviews recent reform developments nationally and internationally to address systemic financial risk, and recommends that each country create a framework for systemic stability regulation or even an independent financial stability regulator. Section 2.5 concludes with recommendations for future action.

2.2 IMPORTANCE OF CRISIS PREVENTION

2.2.1 Policy Mistakes Behind the Global Financial Crisis

The root cause of the global financial crisis of 2007–2009 traces back to a build-up of excessive optimism – created by a long period of worldwide high economic growth, low real interest rates and subdued volatility of financial prices – as well as a flood of liquidity. With these benign macroeconomic and financial environments, investors around the world were prompted to search for yield and underestimated the risks of investment, especially those in new financial products. From this perspective, the International Monetary Fund (IMF) (2009a) summarized the causes of the global financial crisis in three dimensions: flaws in financial regulation and supervision; failure of monetary policy to address the build-up of systemic risk; and a weak global financial architecture.

Flaws in traditional financial regulation and supervision

Several excellent reviews of what went wrong in financial regulation (Group of Thirty 2009; Brunnermeier et al. 2009; de Larosière Group 2009) point to the fact that there were regulatory and supervisory deficiencies, including inadequate macroprudential supervision.

Essentially, national financial regulators and supervisors failed to see the large build-up of systemic risks. In the US, the regulatory and supervisory framework was highly fragmented; its scope was narrowly focused on insured deposit-taking institutions and did not cover all financial activities that posed economy-wide risks. As a result, the 'shadow banking' system grew among investment banks, mortgage brokers and originators, special investment vehicles, insurance companies and other private asset pools, as they had long been lightly regulated by a patchwork of agencies and generally had not been supervised prudentially.[1]

Due to the propensity to focus on individual institutions, supervisors around the world failed to recognize interconnections and links across financial firms, sectors and markets due to the lack of a macroprudential approach. Supervisors only focused on their own piece of the puzzle, overlooking the larger problem. Shin (2009) pointed out a fallacy of aggregation: 'mis-educated' supervisors and examiners were focused on individual institutions, without regard to the impact on the system. There is thus a growing realization that a macroprudential approach to supervision and an effective systemic stability regulator are needed to complement microprudential measures.

Failure of monetary policy to contain financial imbalances

The IMF's analysis (IMF 2009b) points out that a key failure during the boom was the inability to spot the big picture threat of a growing asset price bubble. Equally, monetary policy did not take into account building systemic risks. Clearly, the US Federal Reserve underestimated the build-up of financial imbalances coming from housing price bubbles, the high leverage of financial institutions, and interconnections between financial markets. The US Federal Reserve may well have assumed that even if the asset price boom collapsed, the impacts on the financial system and the economy could be mitigated by lower interest rates.[2]

In theory, tighter prudential regulation could have been mobilized to contain systemic financial risk, but in practice, before the authorities realized it, huge systemic risks had accumulated below the regulators' radar, in the shadow banking system. Given the failure of prudential supervisory action to prevent a build-up of systemic risk, the central bank, as a macro-financial supervisor, should have reacted to credit booms, rising leverage, sharp asset price increases, and the build-up of systemic vulnerabilities by adopting tighter monetary policy.

Weak global financial architecture

There were deficiencies in the global financial architecture – the official structure that facilitates global financial stability and the smooth flow of goods, services and capital across countries. There are three issues.

First, global institutions – like the IMF, the Bank for International Settlements, and the Financial Stability Forum (now the Financial Stability Board, FSB) – failed to conduct effective macroeconomic and financial surveillance of systemically important economies; that is, they did not clearly identify the emerging systemic risk in the US, the UK and the eurozone, send clear warnings to policymakers, or provide practical policy advice on concrete measures to reduce the systemic risk.[3] Their analysis clearly underestimated the looming risk in the shadow banking system, interconnections across financial institutions, markets, and countries, and global macroeconomic–financial links.

Second, there was considerable discussion of global payments imbalances during 2002–2007. The IMF in particular warned repeatedly, particularly through the newly established multilateral consultation process, that global imbalances posed a serious risk to global financial stability. However, the global imbalance discussion may have diverted policymakers' attention away from US 'domestic' financial imbalances toward 'global' imbalances, the risk of dollar collapse and the need to revalue the currency of the People's Republic of China, the renminbi.

Third, the crisis has revealed the ineffectiveness of fragmented international arrangements for regulation, supervision and resolution of internationally active financial institutions. The problem became particularly acute when such institutions showed signs of failing. Although home-country authorities are mainly responsible for resolving insolvent institutions, host-country authorities were often quick to ring-fence assets in their jurisdictions because of the absence of clear international rules governing burden-sharing mechanisms for losses due to failure of financial firms with cross-border operations.

2.2.2 Principles of Crisis Containment

The most fundamental approach to a financial crisis should be to prevent one from taking place in the first place. Once a crisis breaks out, however, efficient crisis management and resolution policies become important.

The key principle should be: 'Crisis prevention is better than cure'. This entails the prevention or mitigation of the build-up of vulnerabilities that could lead to systemic risk and eventually a financial crisis. The major preventive mechanisms should include: (1) establishment of effective regulation and supervision that monitors and acts on economy-wide systemic risk; (2) a sound macroeconomic management framework (for monetary, fiscal and exchange rate policies) that can counteract the build-up of systemic vulnerabilities such as asset price bubbles; and (3) creation of a strong international financial architecture that can send pointed early warnings and induce effective international policy coordination to reduce systemic risk internationally. In the prevention exercise, the macroprudential approach is becoming increasingly important.

Once a financial crisis breaks out, it is necessary to adopt comprehensive policy measures so that the crisis does not magnify or prolong itself. Crisis management tools include: (1) provision of timely and adequate liquidity; (2) rigorous examination of financial institutions' balance sheets, including through stress tests; (3) support of viable but ailing financial institutions through guarantees, non-performing loan removal and recapitalization; and (4) adoption of appropriate macroeconomic policies to mitigate the adverse feedback loop between the financial sector and the real economy, reflecting the specific conditions and reality of the economy. An important challenge is how to ensure that such management policies do not create moral hazard problems.

Finally if a financial crisis evolves into a full-blown economic crisis, with systemic damages to the financial, corporate and household sectors, it is vital to resolve the problem quickly. Crisis resolution measures include: (1) use of mechanisms for restructuring financial institutions' impaired assets and, hence, corporate and household debt; (2) use of well-functioning domestic insolvency procedures for nonviable financial institutions; and (3) use of international mechanisms for resolving non-viable internationally active financial institutions, including clear burden-sharing mechanisms. Without a clearly defined regime for the resolution of financial institutions domestically and internationally, the crisis management process can create international conflict, resulting from such actions as the ring-fencing of foreign bank assets.

The nature of a crisis resolution mechanism affects crisis management policies and the degree of moral hazard for financial institutions. It will be argued below that a systemic stability regulator with sufficient powers should be established at the national level and focus on all three dimensions: crisis prevention, management and resolution. Given that the role of the global stability regulator – the IMF and the FSB – may be limited, the role of a national stability regulator will be critical.

2.2.3 Macroeconomic and Financial Surveillance and Macroprudential Supervision

Several excellent reports that have addressed the need to improve financial regulation and supervision from systemic perspectives agree on the following:[4] the financial regulatory frameworks around the world have paid too little attention to 'systemic risk'; current financial regulations have tended to encourage procyclical risk taking, which increases the likelihood of financial crises and their severity when they occur; and current regulations do not deal adequately with 'large complex financial institutions' – financial intermediaries engaged in some combination of commercial banking, investment banking, asset management and insurance – whose failure poses a systemic risk or 'externality' to the financial system as a whole (Haldane 2009). They also point to the danger induced by implicit 'too big to fail' or 'too interconnected to fail' problems.

The traditional bottom-up supervision addressing the soundness of individual institutions is founded on the assumption that making each bank safe will make the whole system safe. The focus on individual institutions and the inadequate attention paid to the overall system evident in this approach explains how global finance has become so ripe for contagion without sounding regulatory alarms. Crisis prevention necessitates taking a macroprudential approach to complement the existing microprudential supervisory rules. The objects of systemic oversight should be broader, including the corporate and household sector, as well as macroeconomic elements such as capital flows and external debt.

Essentially, the aim of macroprudential supervision is to preserve systemic financial stability by identifying vulnerabilities in a country's financial system and calling for policy and regulatory actions to address those vulnerabilities in a timely and informed manner to prevent a crisis. In contrast to microprudential supervision, which takes a 'bottom-up' approach that focuses on the health and stability of individual institutions, macroprudential supervision takes a 'top-down' approach that focuses on the economy-wide system in which financial market players operate, and helps assess sources of risks and incentives. It requires the integration of detailed information on banks, non-bank financial firms, corporations, households and financial markets.

2.3 SYSTEMIC STABILITY REGULATION: PRINCIPLES

It is proposed in this chapter that each country should establish an effective, powerful systemic stability regulator that is in charge of crisis prevention, management and resolution. Using the methodology first presented by Carmichael and Pomerleano (2002) to address the role of a systemic stability regulator, this section presents a rigorous framework that systematically reviews the following four components:

- Objectives and mandates – that is, what the stability regulator expects to achieve.
- Resources – that is, the political backing, legal support, and human and financial resources required to enable the stability regulator to carry out its objectives and mandates effectively.
- Implementation – that is, the instruments, tools and techniques that the stability regulator uses to achieve its objectives.
- Structure and organization – that is, the organizational structure of a stability regulator that is able to perform the delegated financial stability responsibilities in the most effective way.

2.3.1 Clear Objectives and Mandates of a Systemic Stability Regulator

Regulatory objectives and mandates are what the systemic stability regulator expects to achieve. When a systemic crisis takes place, financial authorities are forced to be intensively involved in managing and resolving the crisis. However, those actions take place after the onset of a crisis. One of the most important functions of the systemic stability regulator is to monitor, anticipate and intervene prior to a crisis. Such an approach and methodology would aim to preserve systemic financial stability by spotting vulnerabilities in a country's financial system, so that, if necessary, actions could be taken in a timely and informed manner to prevent a build-up of systemic risk and an eventual crisis from occurring. The role of the systemic stability regulator would be to strengthen, not displace, examinations and supervision focused on individual institutions.

The major objectives and mandates can be summarized as:

- Monitoring systemic risks – such as large or growing credit exposure to real estate – across firms and markets.
- Assessing the potential for deficiencies in risk management practices, broad-based increases in financial leverage, or changes in financial markets and products, creating systemic risk.
- Analyzing possible spillovers between financial firms or between firms and markets – for example through the mutual exposures of highly interconnected firms.
- Identifying possible regulatory gaps – including gaps in the legal regime governing the insolvency of financial institutions – that pose risks for the system as a whole.
- Curtailing systemic risks across the entire financial system encompassing corporations, households and capital inflows, as well as making arrangements for crisis management and financial institution resolution – through legislative action, prudential measures, advising on monetary policy, and intervention in individual institutions.
- Issuing periodic reports on the stability of the financial system.

The stability regulator needs to have a clear mandate addressing expectations and responsibilities. It must conduct a macrofinancial surveillance and take a macroprudential approach to supervision that addresses risks to the financial system as a whole in an effort to enhance economy-wide financial stability and prevent systemic crises. This would include the monitoring of corporate finance and household debt, which have implications for monetary policy and financial stability, as well as international banking flows, which bear on systemic stability due to the risks of sudden stops.[5]

The stability regulator would also organize the immediate response to a crisis, the strategy for coordinated financial and corporate sector restructuring, and the orderly resolution of failed corporations and financial institutions. The stability regulator is thus charged with express responsibility for containing systemic risks in the financial system.

2.3.2 Sufficient Regulatory Resources to Fulfill Responsibilities

The systemic stability regulator needs sufficient political, legal, legislative, human and financial resources to carry out its objectives and mandates effectively. It needs substantial analytical capabilities and resources to identify the types of information needed, collect the required information, analyze the information obtained, and develop and implement the necessary policy, supervisory and regulatory response. The stability regulator should be allowed to obtain information from assessments and programs of the central bank (if the central bank does not have the full responsibility of systemic stability regulation) and other financial supervisors whenever possible. It further needs broad authority to obtain information – through data collection and reports or, when necessary, examinations – from a range of financial market participants, including banking organizations, securities firms and key financial market intermediaries.

In some countries, the stability regulator might be able to rely on private companies (for example, credit bureaux and rating agencies) to collect corporate data or might assign this responsibility to bank supervisors. To collect the necessary data, the stability regulator would have to operate in a system that provides the capacity to enforce compliance or exact a commensurate penalty when companies are found to be in violation of laws. This includes the authority to craft an orderly resolution of systemically important financial firms and benchmarks to limit leverage. Essentially, the stability regulator would require knowledge and expertise across a wide range of financial firms and markets to offer a comprehensive and multifaceted approach to systemic risk.

2.3.3 Effective Implementation by the Systemic Stability Regulator

The systemic stability regulator should possess the entire implementation arsenal – the instruments, tools and techniques to be used to achieve its objectives and mandates. These include macroprudential supervisory tools to reduce systemic risk, such as the ability to impose capital and liquidity requirements, limit leverage ratios, loan-to-value ratios and debt-to-income ratios, as well as set the policy interest rate and introduce (or revise) legislation concerning insolvency regimes for non-viable financial firms.

The systemic stability regulator would need to set the standards for capital, liquidity and risk management practices for financial firms, given the importance of these matters for the aggregate level of risk within the financial system. A comprehensive list of macroprudential measures is discussed in Borio and Shim (2007). Table 2.1 offers a partial list of such measures.

Table 2.1 Macroprudential supervisory measures

Competition regulation
- Reduction of the 'too big to fail' or 'too interconnected to fail' problem through imposing size limits on firms

Market conduct regulation
- Enhanced transparency and competition

Financial firms
- Higher standards for capital requirements and risk management for systemically important financial institutions
- Limits on financial firms' leverage, such as setting maximum leverage ratios and/or credit growth
- Efforts to mitigate procyclicality through automatic countercyclical provisioning, such as a form of dynamic provisioning
- Limits on sectoral exposure, for example to corporations, households, hedge funds, among others

Households
- Loan-to-value (LTV) restrictions for mortgages
- Limits on consumer debt, such as debt-to-income ratios

Corporations
- Limits on leverage, such as debt/equity ratios
- Limits on tax advantages, such as disallowing interest deductibility for leverage exceeding a certain level or foreign currency-denominated debt

External
- Limits on external debt
- Limits on currency and maturity mismatches

Source: Authors' summary.

Borio and Shim (2007) suggest that macroprudential actions may be taken in a gradual, sequenced manner in the face of a build-up of vulnerabilities and systemic risk. For example, once a sign of built-up vulnerabilities is identified, a stability regulator would need to issue warnings. When vulnerabilities worsen but the problem is largely limited to a certain sector of the economy – such as commercial real estate and household mortgages – targeted tools could be mobilized, including sector-focused stress tests, tightening of lending and underwriting standards, and limiting of loan-to-value ratios and/or debt-to-income ratios. If the problem were to become more generalized and threaten systemic stability, then raising minimum capital requirements could be called for; and if the problem were built through markets and unregulated institutions, as opposed to banks, then tightening monetary policy by raising policy interest rates could be more effective.

Inadequate information, in part due to limited data capture – inadequate efforts and excessive parsimony in expenditures on human resources and databases – is possibly the biggest obstacle to adequate monitoring, analysis and macroprudential supervision.

2.3.4 Effective Organization of a Systemic Stability Regulator

The organizational structure of the systemic stability regulator must be designed in the most effective way possible to carry out the delegated responsibilities of financial stability. The focus of the stability regulator should be on the macrofinancial surveillance of the system, which is an analysis of an economy's macroeconomic and financial developments, as well as macroprudential supervision, which is a top-down approach that helps assess sources of economy-wide risks. Such an organization would require political independence, credibility and transparency, as well as an adequate level of staffing of individuals who possess knowledge, expertise and experience across a wide range of financial institutions and markets.

An important issue is whether the systemic stability regulator should be a single entity or a collective effort among different national financial authorities, each with a different specific responsibility. Key financial authorities include the central bank, financial supervisor(s) and the finance ministry. The central bank is critical to financial stability, both as the monetary policymaker that sets the policy interest rate in response to the emergence of systemic vulnerabilities or the outbreak of a crisis, and as the lender of last resort that protects a country's payments system. A finance ministry should also be involved in stability regulation as crisis resolution invariably entails fiscal outlays – whose costs should be made transparent and be accounted for explicitly in the fiscal budget.

First, a fully consolidated stability regulator, combining all the functions of central banking, financial supervision and regulation, and treasury – as in the case of Singapore – could be the ideal arrangement from the perspective of maintaining financial stability.[6] This option requires the establishment of a new national agency in charge of systemic stability regulation that absorbs all the macroprudential and monetary policymaking functions of other authorities. However, because of the heightened emphasis on central bank independence, this model is not a realistic option for many developed countries.

The second option would be for the central bank to play the systemic stability regulator function by taking over macroprudential supervisory and regulatory powers. However, an argument can be made that a central bank is not in the best position to take sole responsibility of maintaining financial stability – as this responsibility requires much broader expertise and regulatory experience than is typical in traditional central banking. This arrangement could also expose the central bank to the risk of political interventions once the eruption of a crisis requires management and resolution policies.

The third option would be to establish a coordinated systemic stability regulatory council, comprising the finance minister, the central bank governor and the head(s) of national financial supervisors. An independent, powerful working group that supports this council may be chaired by a reputable expert and include as active members finance and central bank deputies, as well as head(s) of supervisors and other relevant parties with authority to engage in crisis prevention, management and resolution. The working group would provide recommendations for policy actions to the council, which would make the ultimate decision. In this instance, a country's central bank may assume a secretariat role, given its usual advantages in analysis of macrofinancial surveillance for systemic stability.

2.4 ALTERNATIVE MODELS OF SYSTEMIC STABILITY REGULATION

2.4.1 Global Practices of Central Banks in Financial Stability

The role of a country's central bank is critical to promoting financial stability. There is a view that the central bank should be responsible for financial stability in addition to the usual responsibility of price stability. There are several reasons for making such a recommendation. First, in the US, full employment and price stability are the dual mandates conferred by Congress on the Federal Reserve in the conduct of monetary policy. Financial stability is an essential element in achieving those objectives. Second, there are important synergies between systemic stability regulation and monetary policy, as insights garnered from performing one of those functions inform the performance of the other. Third, close familiarity with private credit relationships, particularly among the largest financial institutions and through critical payment and settlement systems, enables the central bank to anticipate better how its actions could affect the economy. Finally, the lender-of-last-resort function of the central bank is a natural link between the central bank and the emergence and reduction of systemic risk.

Of the 83 economies covered by Čihák and Podpiera (2006) on the structure of financial supervision and regulation and the role of central banks in prudential supervision, 29 have an integrated prudential supervisor, 20 have supervisory agencies in charge of two types of financial intermediaries and 34 have multiple sectoral supervisors (see Table 2.2). The central banks of 49 economies (59 percent of the total) have the authority of banking supervision, and of these 49 countries, 41 (84 percent) are developing and

Table 2.2 Economies with single, semi-integrated and sectoral prudential supervisory agencies, 2009[a]

Single prudential supervisor for the financial system (year of establishment)		Agency supervising two types of financial intermediaries			Multiple sectoral supervisors (at least one for banks, one for securities firms, and one for insurers)	
		Banks and securities firms	Banks and insurers	Securities firms and insurers		
Australia (1998)	Malta* (2002)	Finland	Canada	Bolivia	Albania*	Italy*
Austria (2002)	Netherlands* (2004)	Luxembourg	Colombia	Bulgaria*	Argentina*	Jordan*
Bahrain* (2002)	Nicaragua* (1999)	Mexico	Ecuador	Chile	Bahamas, The*	Lithuania*
Belgium (2004)	Norway (1986)	Switzerland	El Salvador	Jamaica*	Barbados*	New Zealand*
Bermuda* (2002)	Singapore* (1984)	Uruguay	Guatemala	Mauritius*	Botswana*	Panama
Cayman Islands* (1997)	South Africa* (1990)		Malaysia*	Slovak Rep.*[b]	Brazil*	Philippines*
Denmark (1988)	Sweden (1991)		Peru	Ukraine*	China, People's Rep. of (PRC)	Poland*
Estonia (1999)	Taipei,China (2004)		Venezuela		Croatia*	Portugal*
Germany (2002)	United Arab Emirates* (2000)				Cyprus*	Russia*
Gibraltar (1989)	United Kingdom (1997)				Czech Republic[b]	Slovenia*
Guernsey (1988)					Dominican Republic*	Spain*
Hungary (2002)					Egypt*	Sri Lanka*
Iceland (1988)					France*	Thailand*
Ireland* (2002)					Greece*	Tunisia*
Japan (2001)					Hong Kong SAR*	Uganda*
Kazakhstan* (1998)					India*	United States*
Korea, Rep. (1997)					Indonesia*	
Latvia (1998)						
Maldives* (1998)	**Total – 29**	**Total – 5**	**Total – 8**	**Total – 7**	Israel*	**Total – 34**

Notes:

[a] The table focuses on prudential supervision, not on business supervision (which can be carried out by the same agencies or by separate agencies, even in the integrated model). Also, the table does not consider deposit insurers, even though they play an important role in banking supervision in a number of countries and can do so under any regulatory model.

[b] The authorities announced plans to integrate prudential supervision in their central banks in 2006.

[c] An asterisk (*) indicates that banking supervision is conducted by the central bank.

Source: Updated version of Čihák and Podpiera (2006).

emerging economies. Notably, in countries with multiple sectoral supervisors, central banks almost always have this supervisory authority.

In all Group of Twenty and main Asian economies, the central bank is in charge of price stability as well as payment system stability, and in some cases it is in charge of supervising and regulating securities and insurance firms – in addition to banks. Close to half of the central banks have financial stability committees and most of them publish financial stability reports. Also, the central banks of Saudi Arabia and Singapore hold the responsibility of macroprudential supervision, while the majority of the world's central banks do not.

2.4.2 Recent Reform Developments in the US, the UK and the European Union

National efforts to address systemic risk and promote financial stability are proceeding in the US and the UK, while regional efforts are being made in the European Union (EU). Many central banks are receiving significant new responsibilities for macroprudential supervision. Several arguments have been put forward for justifying why central banks are receiving a prominent role in macroprudential supervision, including: (i) financial supervision offers insights into the condition of financial institutions that is essential in the conduct of monetary policy; and (ii) central banks are inextricably involved in the financial stability function through their lender-of-last-resort function. Yet assigning such a task to central banks has raised concerns and objections. Several arguments have also been put forward for opposing central banks receiving the financial stability mandate. First, there is an innate contradiction in taking enforcement action against an individual institution (for example Lehman Brothers) while protecting financial stability. Second, the financial stability mandate might at times require actions that may distract central banks from their core price stability task.

US stability reform

In the US, the Dodd–Frank Act was signed into law in July 2010, and is designed to minimize the threats from financial firms that are so big or interconnected that they pose a 'systemic risk' to the overall economy. It also sets forth a plan to wind down troubled nonfinancial firms, blunting the impact that the failure of those companies could have on the economy. Dodd–Frank makes it easier for regulators to dismantle a failing firm. It sets up a council of regulators charged with identifying systemic risks and gives the government and the Federal Reserve sweeping powers over financial firms at home and overseas.

The legislation established the Financial Stability Oversight Council, which is led by the Treasury Secretary and also includes the Chairman of the Federal Reserve and the heads of key regulatory agencies (Securities and Exchange Commission, the Commodity Futures Trading Commission, the Federal Deposit Insurance Corporation, the Office of the Comptroller of the Currency, the Federal Housing Finance Agency, and the National Credit Union Administration). One state insurance regulator and one state bank regulator also get a nonvoting seat.

A key part of this task is identifying firms that 'could pose a threat to financial stability', i.e., firms that are considered 'too big to fail'. Financial firms would be placed in this category if the council deems that 'material financial distress at the company could pose a threat to financial stability or the economy'. The council would identify these firms and ask their respective regulators to tighten oversight.

Although commendable, there are some concerns as to whether the council would be able to play an effective role:

- While the council brings all regulators to the table, it does not cover other systemic risks that are prone to arise in the US economy, such as corporate and commercial real estate and consumer debt overhangs or the level of government debt.
- Despite its mandate, the council does not have authority to take binding decisions and does not have an explicit process for authorizing the use of fiscal resources subject to congressional scrutiny. It might end up relying on the used (and abused) clause of the Fed 13(3), which invokes 'unusual and exigent' circumstances.
- The council has adequate tools to develop 'heightened prudential standards' for individual institutions, but it is not clear that it has the tools needed to address systemic risks, such as the excessively indebted consumer sector through 'heightened prudential standards', including changing the deductibility of interest or imposing system-wide ratios of loan to value.

One of the key problems during the financial crisis was how to unwind troubled nonbank financial firms, such as American International Group, Bear Stearns and Lehman Brothers, which posed a threat to the economy. Traditional bankruptcy procedures would be drawn out, which could endanger the overall financial system. In addition, banking regulators did not have the legal authority to 'resolve' a nonfinancial firm. Dodd–Frank aims to solve this dilemma. The Federal Deposit Insurance Corporation would be able to take over a failing firm so that taxpayers would not have to foot the bill for a bailout.

A troubled firm's shareholders and creditors would be responsible for bearing the costs of its resolution, but the government would also establish a Systemic Resolution Fund within the Treasury Department to help cover any additional costs. Financial firms with more than $10 billion in assets would be required to repay any taxpayer money used to seize or wind up their competitors.

UK stability reform

The government in the United Kingdom (UK) overhauled the regulatory system. It broke up the Financial Services Authority (FSA) into the Prudential Regulation Authority (PRA) and a Consumer Protection and Markets Authority, and moved the PRA to the Bank of England (BoE) as its subsidiary. The government has been proposing to disband the FSA and establish an independent business-conduct regulator, the Financial Conduct Authority (FCA), which has been provisionally titled the Consumer Protection and Markets Authority. In addition, an independent Financial Policy Committee (FPC) was created within the Bank of England.

The PRA will supervise deposit-taking financial firms and insurance companies and promote the stability of the UK financial system, thereby supporting the new objectives of the BoE and its new FPC. The reason for this drastic overhaul is that the government believed that the tripartite system – comprised of BoE, FSA and Her Majesty's Treasury – failed to prevent the financial crisis, leading to massive state intervention in the banking system and the deepest recession in the post-WWII era.

As a result of this regulatory change, the BoE will have statutory responsibilities for financial stability – in addition to price stability – and be in charge of macroprudential supervision. Essentially, this move transformed the BoE into a key systemic stability regulator, signifying a return to pre-1998 financial services regulation in the UK. The FPC, which will function along the lines of the BoE's Monetary Policy Committee, is responsible for maintaining financial stability by monitoring systemic risks and vulnerabilities that threaten the financial system as a whole, and acting in response.

EU stability reform

The financial crisis prompted the European Union to reinforce the structure of EU-wide financial supervision resulting in the creation of the European System of Financial Supervision (ESFS) in January 2011. The new ESFS was considered essential in helping to detect any risks to financial stability and set up an efficient early warning system. Moreover, the new structure was designed to meet the objective of a single, stable market for financial services by bringing together all the national supervisory authorities with shared and mutually reinforcing responsibilities.

The ESFS comprises the European Systemic Risk Board (ESRB) and the three European Supervisory Authorities for banking, securities, and insurance (EC 2010). The ESRB is responsible for EU-level regulation and supervision of macroprudential risk and supports the creation of EU-level colleges or agencies to supervise systemically important cross-border banks and other financial firms, markets and instruments. The ESRB is an entirely new European body, with no precedent. It is responsible for macroprudential oversight and has three objectives:

- To develop a European macroprudential perspective to address the problem of fragmented individual risk analysis at the national level.
- To enhance the effectiveness of early-warning mechanisms by improving the interaction between microprudential and macroprudential analysis.
- To allow risk assessments to be translated into action by the relevant authorities.

The three European Supervisory Authorities (ESAs) – i.e., the European Banking Authority, the European Insurance and Occupational Pensions Authority, and the European Securities and Markets Authority – are designed to work together in a network, interacting with the existing national supervisory authorities. Their objectives are to strengthen microprudential supervision, that is, to promote the financial soundness of individual firms and to protect consumers of financial services. The new European network combines supervision of financial firms at the national level and at the EU level, so as to encourage regulatory harmonization as well as consistency in supervision and in implementation of the rules. One of the primary supervisory tools used by these authorities for analysis is the EU-wide stress test.

The ESRB may issue risk warnings that should prompt early responses to avoid the build-up of wider problems and the risk of a future crisis. If necessary, the ESRB may also recommend specific actions to address any identified risks. However, the ESRB does not have any binding powers to impose measures on member states or national authorities. It is conceived as a 'reputational' body composed of high-level members capable of influencing the actions of policymakers and supervisors by means of its moral authority. Nonetheless, recipients of recommendations will not be allowed to remain passive with regard to an identified risk and will be expected to react in some way.

On the positive side, the European approach is far more independent than (and not subject to the same political considerations as) the US Financial Stability Oversight Council, chaired by the secretary of the Treasury. On the other hand, it has a number of limitations:

- The ESRB does not adopt multidimensional, multidisciplinary, multi-agency approach to systemic risk, as central banks are very much over-represented in it. By virtue of providing the chair and secretariat functions, the European Central Bank (ECB) is likely to dominate other views and expertise on the ESRB in the decision-making process.
- Given the large size of the General Board, the process is unwieldy, which is why the Steering Committee was established. Central bankers dominate the Steering Committee, with seven out of 12 members.
- The board does not appear to have clear regulatory objectives and mandate, accountability, or clear processes covering crisis prevention, management and resolution.
- As with the ECB, accountability is defined purely in terms of reporting obligations to the European Parliament, with no sanctions or punishment available to be imposed on the ESRB and its members should their performance be inadequate.
- The ESRB has potential conflicts in terms of policies and instruments. The recent crisis has made it clear that fiscal resources need to be used in combating systemic distress. By relying on the ESRB, with a composition similar to the ECB and with no EU-wide fiscal authority, the safety of the banking system might conflict with the goal of price stability.
- Finally, the EU-wide model of bank supervision and bank restructuring is handicapped by a weak EU cross-border framework for crisis management and resolution due to multiple (and conflicting) proceedings and competencies. The lack of a cross-border resolution framework impedes the sharing of information and collaboration due to the risk of asset grab. Therefore, existing resolution tools are likely to be ineffective in real time during a crisis.

2.4.3 Alternative Models

There are several models for systemic stability regulation, including a fully integrated model, *à la* Singapore; a central bank-led model as in the new UK supervisory structure; and a coordinated 'council' model. Although the fully integrated model – that combines the finance ministry, central bank, and supervisory functions – could be ideal from the perspective of promoting financial stability, its establishment is now increasingly difficult due to the rising demand for central banks to be independent from the government and political process. The central bank-led model is gaining popularity, but it bears the risk of government interference, particularly in times of crisis management and resolution, threatening the independence of the central bank in its role of maintaining price stability. So a major challenge in this model is how to secure monetary independence of the central bank given the need for financial stability. However, in countries – particularly in many developing and emerging economies – where the central bank has had the traditional role of banking sector supervision, this model will likely remain viable.

A realistic approach for most developed countries would be to establish a 'council' model, despite the UK's decision to move away from this model. In the council model the national financial authorities (the central bank, supervisor(s), and finance ministry) work collectively, as if they formed a single systemic stability regulator, to perform the stability regulation function. There were frameworks for financial crisis management in the US, the UK and Japan in the pre-2008 period, and these frameworks did not seem to function properly. The 'council' model would require, in a sense, a substantial modification of these frameworks to address broader issues of crisis containment, including crisis prevention.

For such a 'council' approach to function successfully, the collective objectives and mandates as well as the division of labor among the authorities should be clearly defined; sufficient capacities and resources should be provided collectively; and all the necessary macroprudential tools should be made available for use. Most importantly, a culture of sharing information should be developed and there should be intensive day-to-day dialogue among the financial authorities.

The central bank has a comparative advantage in macrofinancial surveillance and may or may not have macroprudential authority (particularly tools). If the central bank does not have macroprudential tools, then it could still suggest that supervisor(s) take certain macroprudential actions (such as an increase in capital adequacy ratios, a reduction of loan-to-value ratios, and so on) to contain a build-up of systemic risk. Similarly, the supervisor(s) could suggest that the central bank alter monetary policy to contain systemic risk, and the central bank may make its independent decisions by taking into account all conditions affecting the future course of price inflation.

2.5 CONCLUSIONS

The starting point for this chapter is that a financial crisis is not an 'unknown unknown', though its precise timing and the magnitude of its severity might be. A crisis builds up over time in response to policy mistakes and investor herd behavior. While markets tend to be forgiving for a long time, the unsustainable imbalance is eventually corrected. By identifying and dealing with systemic risk – or sources of financial vulnerabilities – before it creates critical instability, policymakers could prevent a financial crisis. For this purpose, macrofinancial surveillance and macroprudential supervision are vital, and a systemic stability regulator – or relevant financial authorities under a collective framework for systemic stability regulation – must act to avoid the build-up of large vulnerabilities and imbalances in each jurisdiction. Past experience suggests that an inadequate effort to capture and analyze data is a key obstacle to conducting adequate macroprudential supervision.

Several models are possible to choose from in creating a systemic stability regulator, including a fully integrated model *à la* Singapore, a central bank-led model as in pre-1998 or post-2010 UK and a coordinated 'council' model that has yet to be tested. For most countries, a realistic approach would be to adopt the 'council' model, where: (1) all financial authorities (central bank, supervisor(s) and finance ministry) work in a coordinated manner, including by engaging in intensive regular information exchange and consultation; and (2) the central bank conducts macroeconomic and financial surveillance while the supervisors take macroprudential actions in addition to conducting microprudential supervision. It is highly desirable for supervisors to consolidate their supervision over banks, non-bank financial institutions and markets.

Even if such a framework for national systemic risk regulation is established, financial stability may be at risk without a global strategy to address financial crisis prevention, management and resolution. A successful international financial order can be constructed only with a binding set of minimum international standards. In the absence of such standards, the differences in national policies in accounting, information transparency, regulating leverage and capital standards will likely lead to a regulatory arbitrage race to the bottom, with the competition from more pliant jurisdictions undermining more stringent regulatory regimes, and 'exporting' financial instability.

In this sense, the Westphalian principles of sovereignty that govern international financial oversight are not suited to the realities of an interconnected financial system in the twenty-first century. If the financial authorities in major economies – such as the US, the UK and the eurozone

– do not make progress in the creation of a binding global financial order, the prospects for attaining global financial stability are limited. The financially integrated world would have to continue to live with regulatory fragmentation, with all of its attendant risk to stability. In order to be successful, the recent reforms at the global level – that focus on the newly created FSB – require that the US and the UK make strong political commitments to national and international financial stability regulation.

NOTES

1. Adrian and Shin (2009) estimate that the 'shadow banking' system was as large as US$10.5 trillion, comprising US$4 trillion in assets of the large investment banks, $2.5 trillion in overnight repurchases, US$2.2 trillion in structured investment vehicles and another US$1.8 trillion in hedge fund assets. This should be compared with US$10 trillion in assets held in the conventional US banking system, which meant that system leverage was at least double what was reported.
2. Wessel (2009) provided a well-documented and insightful account of the thinking of US policymakers during the crisis. The inescapable conclusion is that for a long time after the start of the crisis, central bankers – Bernanke, King, Trichet and their colleagues – did not see the crisis coming and for too long ignored the advice of those who did.
3. The IMF (2009a: 2) admitted that: 'official warnings both within and outside the Fund were insufficiently specific, detailed, or dire to gain traction with policymakers'. IMF surveillance often echoed the conventional view that advanced countries – such as the US and the UK – with relatively low stable inflation, together with profitable and well-capitalized banking sectors, could withstand the unwinding of the bubble in housing and capital markets.
4. These include: the Volker recommendations in the Group of Thirty report (Group of Thirty 2009); the Geneva Report on the World Economy (Brunnermeier et al. 2009); the de Larosière report (de Larosière Group 2009) on financial supervision and stability in the European Union (EU); and papers by a group from New York University's Stern School (for example Acharya and Richardson 2009).
5. In emerging markets, a corporate sector that is highly leveraged and unprofitable or that is prone to currency mismatches (as in Indonesia and the Republic of Korea in 1997) can lead to massive problems. See Kawai (2000).
6. Singapore has not had significant financial crises. Japan had a land price bubble in the late 1980s and a systemic banking crisis in the late 1990s, despite the fact that the finance ministry had the power to supervise and regulate banks and the central bank was not independent (see Kawai 2005). So the most important element of success or failure may not be in the organizational structure of such a systemic stability regulator, but in how it functions.

REFERENCES

Acharya, V.V. and M. Richardson, eds. 2009. *Restoring Financial Stability*. NYU-Stern Report. New York: John Wiley & Sons.

Adrian, T. and H.S. Shin. 2009. Money, Liquidity and Monetary Policy. *American Economic Review* 99(2): 600–605.

Borio, C.E.V. and I. Shim. 2007. What Can (Macro-) Prudential Policy Do to Support Monetary Policy? BIS Working Paper 242. Geneva: Bank for International Settlements.

Brunnermeier, M., A. Crockett, C. Goodhart, A. Persaud and H.S. Shin. 2009. *The Fundamental Principles of Financial Regulation*. Geneva, Switzerland and London, UK: International Center for Monetary and Banking Studies and Centre for Economic Policy Research.

Carmichael, J. and M. Pomerleano. 2002. *The Development and Regulation of Non-Bank Financial Institutions*. Washington, DC: World Bank.

Čihák, M. and R. Podpiera. 2006. Is One Watchdog Better than Three? International Experience with Integrated Financial Sector Supervision. *Czech Journal of Economics and Finance* 56(3–4): 102–126.

Commission of the European Communities. 2009. Proposal for a Regulation of the European Parliament and of the Council on Community Macro-Prudential Oversight of the Financial System and Establishing a European Systemic Risk Board. Brussels: Commission of the European Communities. http://ec.europa.eu/internal_market/finances/docs/committees/supervision/20090923/com2009_499_en.pdf (accessed 18 January 2011).

European Union. 2010. Regulation (EU) No. 1092/2010 of the European Parliament and the Council. Brussels: European Union. http://www.esrb.europa.eu/shared/pdf/ESRB-en.pdf?679d2670aa3cb14f20eadb68b45f021b.

Group of Thirty. 2009. Financial Reform: A Framework for Financial Stability. Washington, DC. www.group30/pubs/reformreport.pdf.

Haldane, A.G. 2009. Rethinking the Financial Network. Speech delivered at the Financial Student Association, Amsterdam, April.

International Monetary Fund (IMF). 2009a. Initial Lessons of the Crisis for the Global Architecture and the IMF. Washington, DC: IMF. http://www.imf.org/external/np/pp/eng/2009/021809.pdf.

International Monetary Fund (IMF). 2009b. *Global Financial Stability Report*. Washington, DC: IMF. http://imf.org/external/pubs/ft/gfsr/2009/01/pdf/chap3.pdf.

Kawai, M. 2000. The Resolution of the East Asian Crisis: Financial and Corporate Sector Restructuring. *Journal of Asian Economics* 11: 133–168.

Kawai, M. 2005. Reform of the Japanese Banking System. *International Economics and Economic Policy* 2(4): 307–335.

de Larosière Group. 2009. Report on Financial Supervision: High-Level Group on Financial Supervision in the EU (February). www.ec.europa.eu/internal_market/finances/docs/de_larosiere_report_en.pdf.

Shin, H.S. 2009. It Is Time for a Reappraisal of the Basic Principles of Financial Regulation. Vox web site, 31 January. http://www.voxeu.com/index.php?q=node/2949.

Wessel, D. 2009. *In Fed We Trust: Ben Bernanke's War on the Great Panic*. New York: Crown Business.

3. Enlisting macroprudential and market regulatory structures to strengthen prudential supervision

Larry D. Wall[1]

3.1 INTRODUCTION

Risk taking is an essential part of the financial system that contributes to economic growth around the world. Risk taking in the financial system is also crucial for the efficient allocation of risk within our societies. But this risk bearing should take place in the context of sound risk management. Individual firms must prudentially manage their own risks, and financial supervisors must prudently manage the risks posed by the financial system to society.

The consequences of inadequate risk management can be a financial crisis that spills over into the real economy. Several East Asian countries experienced the consequences of significant breakdowns in risk management at both the firm level and the supervisory level in the late 1990s. Many Asian countries drew the conclusion from this experience that rapid increases in asset prices and/or debt may endanger financial stability. Subsequently, many supervisory authorities in Asia – including those in Hong Kong, China; India; the Republic of Korea; and Thailand – tightened regulatory restrictions on residential mortgage lending to forestall rising price and debt levels (Vanikkul 2009).

The consequences of inadequate risk management are again being felt with the recent global financial crisis. This time, the weaknesses were primarily in the risk management of firms in some developed countries, with the Asian financial sector having little direct exposure. However, just as the affected policymakers in Asia drew lessons from the Asian financial crisis, so too will policymakers in countries currently struggling with weakened financial systems. Moreover, the lessons they draw from the current problems are likely to have an especially large impact on international standards.

The purpose of this chapter is to identify some of the breakdowns that occurred and evaluate some possible policy changes intended to strengthen financial sector risk management. The chapter considers some alternatives to strengthen both macroprudential supervision and market discipline.

The discussion of macroprudential supervision finds that macroprudential supervision was weak or absent in some of the key players. Many of the problems that arose could have been detected at an earlier stage by reviews of systemically important markets, starting with the initial underwriting and continuing through to the ultimate risk holders. In at least some cases, it may have been possible to take supervisory action that would have reduced the ultimate extent of financial instability. However, we should not expect too much of macroprudential supervision. As Cho (2009) noted, an agency with a broad mandate to deal with systemic risk issues cannot maintain political independence. By the time it is clear that market developments are moving to create significant risks of financial instability, it is likely that they are also providing substantial benefits to politically important constituencies. These constituencies are likely to demand that the agency's decisions be reviewed by politically accountable bodies that may overturn them for political reasons. Thus, macroprudential supervisors should be bold in seeking to understand the risks in the financial system, and modest about promising an end to financial instability.

Although prudential supervision is important, sound risk management starts at the firm level. A prerequisite for sound risk management at the financial institution level is that the institution's owners and managers bear the costs of bad management. If the government bears most of the risk of loss, not only will the managers lack adequate incentive to manage the risk, but the government is likely to insist on playing a major role in the firm's risk management. The problem with having the government take over risk management is that many efficiency gains that arise from a market-based economy will ultimately be lost if risk management is outsourced to the government.

Unfortunately, the recent crisis is likely to have the exact opposite effect on private incentives to manage risk. The experience has been that governments will provide bailouts if the troubled firm is sufficiently large or interconnected. The problem of how to reverse both the perception and the reality that the government is bearing the risk is difficult. There are some options, including deposit insurance reform, special resolutions, financial institution-prepared 'shelf bankruptcy' plans, and contingent capital. All these alternatives are likely to have a role to play in restoring market discipline.

The chapter is organized as follows: section 3.2 discusses macroprudential regulatory structures; section 3.3 discusses issues in establishing effective market discipline structures; and section 3.4 concludes.

3.2 MACROPRUDENTIAL STRUCTURES

Macroprudential supervision arises out of a combination of old practices and new perspectives. An important element of the old practices is the role of central banks in preserving financial stability. Padoa-Schioppa (2003) argued that the role of central banks in financial stability is part of their 'genetic code'. He noted that European central banks acted as lenders of last resort by the end of the nineteenth century.

Ryback (2006) argued that macroprudential regulation has re-emerged as a separate concern over the last 10–15 years for several reasons. One factor in the re-emergence was the Asian financial crisis of 1997–1998, which demonstrated that a nation's banking system could be exposed to a shock that is not readily observable by looking at individual banks. Another factor is that central banks came to appreciate that their capability to meet monetary policy goals depended not only on the stability of the banking system, but also on developments in the non-bank financial sector, especially bond markets.

The current round of financial instability has forcefully re-emphasized the weaknesses of the older approaches. A strong bank sector is a necessary condition for financial stability, but it is not a sufficient condition. Weaknesses in the non-bank financial sector are both a potential direct threat to financial stability and an indirect threat to stability through its impact on the banking system.

Given the desire to reduce the costs of financial instability and restrict moral hazard, there is increased interest in creating a macroprudential supervisor. This supervisor would have new powers to examine and regulate previously less-regulated financial firms, possibly combined with some regulatory power over firms already subject to microprudential supervision.

This section analyzes the role of macroprudential supervision in managing systemic risk. The messages are twofold: there is much that can and should be done, but there are limits, and promising to do too much could be worse than doing nothing. This section starts with some ideas on what is relatively easy, continues with a discussion of the more difficult tasks and concludes with some warnings about the current limits of what is feasible.

3.2.1 Macroprudential Information Gathering

Central banks are already gathering and processing some publicly available information as part of their regular financial stability reviews. This analysis is likely to improve over time as economists develop a better understanding of the causes of financial instability.

Macroprudential authorities should obtain broad powers to examine the financial system to understand linkages within the system and potential weak spots better. One of the first responsibilities of a macroprudential supervisor should be to address weaknesses in the financial system that could turn what should be an isolated problem into a systemic problem. That is, the macroprudential supervisor should make sure that the financial plumbing system is in good order. This includes payment and settlement systems, which are already a concern of the central banks in many countries. But it also includes issues associated with infrastructure for all types of financial transactions. A macroprudential supervisor also should have the authority to conduct thorough reviews of systemically important markets, including firms not subject to microprudential regulations, and impose regulations as necessary to address weaknesses.

A second area in which macroprudential supervision could improve on current practice is by developing a clear understanding of the major markets from the first transaction through to the ultimate bearer of the risk. The United States (US) residential real estate market provides an excellent example of how such an end-to-end analysis of markets could have identified weak practices that would combine to create a systemic problem.

A macroprudential supervisor that observed rapid growth in the use of new residential mortgage instruments to systemically material levels should have examined the process from loan origination through to the purchase by domestic investors. As discussed by Demyanyk and Van Hemert (2008), if that had happened in the US, a review at the origination level should have noted the growing dependence of many loans on home price appreciation to provide the borrower with a means of repayment. A review of the securitization process should have revealed that, in many cases, the processors were focused on maximum throughput of loans and conducted few or no quality checks on the loans. Finally, it might also have raised questions about some of the practices used by the ultimate holders of some residential mortgage-backed securities (RMBSs), in particular, their reliance on vehicles that were funded primarily with asset-backed commercial paper (ABCP) with little capital.

Following transactions through to the ultimate bearer of risk may also reveal concentrations of risk that would not be readily observable. For example, a review of the credit guarantee market (that is, credit default swaps and similar contracts) should have revealed the American International Group's (AIG) net position and the extent to which different counterparties had become exposed to AIG. Although the exposure of any individual counterparty to AIG might not be a cause for concern, the aggregate exposure of banks should have raised concerns about AIG's capability to honor its commitments in the event of a large drop in credit quality.[2]

Just as a microprudential supervisory focus is inadequate for understanding the risks to stability in an interconnected domestic financial system, a domestic focus to macroprudential supervision is also inadequate for understanding the risks to stability posed by an interconnected global financial system. The effectiveness of macroprudential supervision will be greatly enhanced to the extent that the supervisor understands the connections between domestic and international markets and institutions. The chain of events leading from mortgage loans in the US to the dramatic widening of London Interbank Offered Rate (LIBOR) spreads in 2007 helps to illustrate this point.

A domestic macroprudential supervisor in the US would have noted the dramatic rise in private label RMBSs, and an examination should have revealed some weaknesses in the underwriting. But a US macroprudential supervisor would also have observed that a substantial fraction of these RMBSs were being held by foreign investors, which could be taken to imply that these RMBSs would not pose a threat to US financial stability. The potential for these foreign investors suddenly to place greatly increased demands on the US dollar LIBOR market would not have been directly observable. Similarly, a macroprudential supervisor of a country whose banks were buying these RMBSs would have seen the build-up of holdings and their funding with very little capital and a large amount of ABCP. But most of these RMBSs were highly rated, and these banks, individually, had access to lines of credit and the LIBOR market. The macroprudential supervisor could not have seen that many European banks were holding their mortgage-backed security investments in similar structures so that if one of them lost the confidence of the ABCP market, most or all of them would need alternative sources of US dollar funding.

Although macroprudential supervision done right requires a view across country boundaries, a global supervisor with such scope is unlikely to be created anytime soon. This implies that macroprudential supervision cannot reach its potential unless national supervisors work with each other.

3.2.2 Macroprudential Regulation

There are some clear opportunities for a macroprudential supervisor to improve the regulation of the financial system. A macroprudential supervisor can extend powers already used by microprudential regulators to improve the financial systems' plumbing. A macroprudential supervisor can also bring a valuable perspective to the writing of microprudential regulations.

However, when promoting macroprudential supervision in the current environment, one must take care not to oversell its capabilities. Policymakers must be disabused of the idea that the existence of a macroprudential supervisor will guarantee that a country will never again suffer from financial instability. Expectations that the macroprudential supervisor will prevent financial instability are worse than misleading; such expectations will change incentives in ways that are likely to result in significant damage to the financial system.

Difficulty of regulating popular innovations

A particular problem for macroprudential regulation is innovation, both in the form of new instruments and the expanded use of old instruments by new clienteles. The risks and the benefits of existing instruments when used in the normal way by long-standing clienteles are likely to be understood by the suppliers, users and regulators. Moreover, these instruments have likely been tested in the legal system, and the relevant rules have largely been determined. However, there is likely to be a substantial amount of learning about innovations. In particular, the various types of risks associated with these instruments and their users may not be well understood until they have been tested in a more challenging environment. As a result, if such innovations are introduced during benign economic conditions, they may grow to the point where they raise systemic concerns without having their weak points tested.

A supervisor focused on macroprudential issues may not take an interest in such innovations until they grow to the point where the innovation poses a threat to financial stability. However, the fact that the innovation has grown so large that it could be systemically important suggests that its customers perceive the innovation to be valuable, and the suppliers of the product find it profitable. Many innovations also provide benefits to third parties. For example, innovations that lower the cost of residential mortgages are likely to benefit the construction and residential brokerage industries. All these parties are likely to raise political objections if the macroprudential supervisor attempts to significantly raise the cost of using this innovation or place substantial limits on its use.[3]

Whether a macroprudential supervisor will be able to withstand such political pressure depends on its political power and that of those opposing the new regulations. However, the supervisor will not necessarily gain prestige from preventing crises. Suppose that the supervisor is right about the need for the regulation, and adoption of the regulation prevents the innovation from causing a period of financial instability. Those that opposed the action may respond by claiming that a lack of instability shows that the regulation was unnecessary.

Pressure to overregulate innovations

A macroprudential supervisor that recognizes the political difficulty and costs of stopping innovations after they become systemically important is likely to be tempted to try to stop innovations before they become so popular. In this case, the problem is not of under-regulation but of over-regulation.

Suppose that for a particular innovation, the errors of under- and over-regulation are of roughly equal magnitude in terms of their impact. The impact of these errors on the macroprudential supervisor will not be equal. Errors in the form of under-regulation may become observable in the form of financial instability and lead to widespread criticism of the macroprudential supervisor. On the other hand, errors in the form of over-regulation that prevent an innovation from succeeding will not be readily observable because the beneficiaries of the innovation will not be able to see the benefits they might have received.

Wrong expectations may create moral hazard

A further danger to macroprudential regulation is that it increases investors' confidence that there will not be periods of significant financial instability, thereby increasing investors' incentives to take more risks. The impact of investors' concern about financial instability on their actions is illustrated by recent behavior. In 2006, many investors appear to have believed that there was at most a trivial risk of financial instability in the developed countries. This lack of concern, combined with low real interest rates, led many investors to seek higher returns. In some cases these returns were obtained by investing in higher-risk assets, and in others by investing in highly leveraged portfolios of seemingly safe assets funded largely with shorter maturity debt. Many of these positions proved dangerous to their holders' financial condition as markets became unstable. As a result, many investors have sought to shift their portfolios into safer assets and fund their positions with more equity and longer maturity debt.

The very act of creating a macroprudential supervisor could move attitudes toward a belief that financial instability is no longer a risk. Some (less sophisticated) investors may believe that the macroprudential supervisor will use its regulatory powers to stop potential systemic risk before it causes financial instability. Other (more sophisticated and more cynical) investors may believe that the creation of a macroprudential supervisor that oversees all parts of the financial system signals a willingness by the government to extend the safety net to any part of the financial system that might threaten financial stability.

3.3 MARKET DISCIPLINE STRUCTURES

The underlying basis of sound financial institutions and a sound financial system is sound risk management by financial firms. Neither microprudential supervisors nor macroprudential supervisors can oversee all the risk management decisions that are made by financial firms. But, market participants will price only the risks that they believe they are bearing. Unfortunately, what market participants often observe is that governments will step in to prevent the collapse of financial firms deemed too big to fail (or too interconnected to fail), with the side-effect of protecting many types of claims from taking any losses. What is required for effective market discipline is a credible system of imposing losses on the firms' investors.

Although exposing market participants to the risk of loss is critical to obtaining market discipline, there is a reason why governments around the world have often engaged in bailouts. Governments feel that they are being forced to pick the lesser of two evils: (1) withdraw the charter, impose losses on creditors and deal with the resulting financial instability; or (2) exercise forbearance and/or bail out the distressed firm. The problem from the supervisory perspective is that the supervisors had not been provided with tools to handle failure in a way that would preserve financial stability before the problems arose.

Thus, in order to reverse market expectations that some financial firms are too interconnected to fail, countries must develop and implement credible policies that allow critically undercapitalized financial firms to 'fail' without adverse consequences to the financial system. This section discusses the weaknesses in current systems for dealing with failing financial institutions and some possible solutions.

3.3.1 Deposit Insurance

Although market discipline depends on some creditors and counterparties of financial firms being exposed to risk, effective market discipline does not depend on all depositors, creditors and counterparties being exposed to risk. Indeed, exposing some creditors to the risk of loss may be counterproductive to the extent that it weakens the credibility of the government's commitment to resolve failing financial firms without a full bailout of creditors. In particular, exposing depositors with relatively low balances to risk does not add much to effective market discipline and weakens the credibility of commitments not to bail out all creditors. Few small depositors are likely to contribute to informed market discipline because few have the sophistication to understand the financial condition of large, complex banks. When threatened with loss, the reaction of retail customers is likely to be to withdraw from their bank (if possible) or exert political pressure for a bailout. Moreover, discipline from these depositors is typically not necessary because systemically important banks are generally dependent upon their capability to trade and enter into credit relationships with large and relatively sophisticated counterparties.

3.3.2 Special Resolution Regimes for Financial Institutions

If losses are to be imposed on uninsured investors at failed systemically important firms, the supervisors must have a credible mechanism for restructuring or winding down the firm without increasing financial instability. One common mechanism for restructuring and winding down firms is corporate bankruptcy.[4] Bankruptcy courts are designed to provide due process to the claims on different groups of creditors. This approach is workable when payments on the claims can be suspended while alternative methods of restructuring or liquidating the firm's longer-term assets are evaluated. However, a large part of the business of almost all systemically important financial firms is the payment of old claims, the receipt of funds that generates new claims, and entering into new financial contracts on a daily basis. If counterparties cannot be sure of their status, they will refuse to deal with a bankrupt financial firm, and that firm will be forced to stop operations almost immediately.

Domestic firms

One solution to the problem of applying the corporate bankruptcy code to financial firms is the creation of a special resolution regime in which financial experts are given the authority and time to restructure the financial institution. In the case of large or complex financial firms, the authorities are likely to control the failed institution temporarily, as happens with bridge banks in the US. Immediately after withdrawing the charter of the failed bank, US authorities can charter a new bridge bank that is under the control of the deposit insurer. The bridge bank then steps into the shoes of the failed bank, receiving some of the assets, all the insured liabilities, some of the remaining liabilities and some of the derivatives contracts from the failed bank. Those claims that are not transferred are paid out of the proceeds of the liquidation of the remaining assets plus the profit (if any) when the bridge bank is sold back into the private sector. The bridge bank then carries on the operations of the failed bank until those operations are either sold back into the private sector or wound down in an orderly manner.

In the US, the problem has been that the special resolution regime and bridge bank powers are limited to financial firms that are chartered as domestic insured depositories and certain government-sponsored financial firms. All other financial firms are subject to the general bankruptcy code. Thus, had AIG failed, it would have been resolved by the bankruptcy court. Moreover, this limitation extends to those parts of US banking groups that do not have a commercial bank charter. This split treatment of banks and their affiliates is a problem because large financial groups tend to operate as integrated entities with most parts of the group depending on other parts of the group for vital services such as information technology, liquidity management and risk management.

Although a special resolution regime would appear to be a straightforward solution to the problems posed by AIG, some important details remain. One unsolved issue is what the boundaries of special resolutions are. That is, which financial firms should be subject to special resolutions? This problem has two dimensions. First, should the special regime apply to all financial firms or only to some firms? And, if only to some firms, to which ones? Second, which resolution regime should apply when a systemically important financial firm is part of a group with large non-financial operations? This depends on the extent to which the financial and non-financial parts are operating as integrated entities. Separate resolution regimes may not be very efficient if the various subsidiaries depend on the same centralized provision of services or have integrated management structures.

International firms

The resolution of systemically important financial firms with cross-border operations faces all the problems associated with domestic firms plus the added problem that there is no global system for resolving internationally active firms. Hüpkes (2004) discussed several difficult problems related to restructuring or winding down systemically important financial institutions (SIFIs) operating across national borders.

One of these problems is that misaligned incentives preclude global solutions. Hüpkes (2004) pointed out that regulators are accountable to national legislatures for solutions that are optimal on a national level. Their mandate to protect their own national markets and their local creditors will very likely take precedence over solutions that take a more global approach. Rosengren (2009) pointed out one implication. Suppose that the home-country supervisor puts the parent operation into a receivership and tries to operate the group as a bridge financial institution. The bridge institution is unlikely to be able to continue normal operation of the firm because host-country supervisors will probably impose controls on the transfer of resources to protect creditors in their own countries. Similar problems may arise if the problem is at a systemically important subsidiary located in a host country.

The problems with resolving part or all of a cross-border SIFI have received some local and regional attention. Mayes (2006) discussed New Zealand's requirements that foreign-owned banking operations be run through subsidiaries and that these subsidiaries be capable of restoring operations within the value day if the parent cannot provide services. The problems with cross-border resolution are also being considered in the European Union, in which the single passport for financial services firms precludes a New Zealand-type arrangement (Mayes et al. 2008). However, we are a long way from an international framework that would allow the orderly restructuring of a global SIFI in a way that would not have an adverse impact on financial stability.

3.3.3 Custom Tailored Failure Plans

The issue of how to maintain financial stability in the presence of a distressed global SIFI cannot be deferred until there is a workable global agreement that provides a general mechanism for resolution. An alternative is to work out tailored solutions for individual SIFIs.

Hüpkes (2004) argued that not all the functions of SIFIs are systemically important to all the countries in which they operate. She recommends that the systemically important functions in each jurisdiction should first be identified. The authorities can then work on arranging a replacement for the important functions or for the systemically important parts to be detached and run separately.

Hüpkes (2004) also recognized that both these alternatives also have problems. The authorities may not be able to arrange for another financial institution to provide timely replacement of some systemically important services of the failed SIFI. Further, detachment can run into a variety of legal problems, some of which have parallels in the problems with resolving the SIFI as a group.

Rajan (2009) proposed that instead of supervisors trying to resolve a complex financial group on their own, the group should be required to develop a 'shelf-bankruptcy' plan to be used by the supervisors. This proposal would require that financial institutions track and document their exposures. The requirement to develop such a plan would give institutions an incentive to 'reduce needless complexity' (Rajan 2009: 79).

With only minor modifications, Rajan's (2009) proposal could be used to help implement Hüpkes' (2004) recommendation. First, financial institutions could be required to identify activities that they perceive as systemically important. Then the institutions could be required to provide more thorough plans for maintaining systemically important services. These plans could include an analysis of the extent to which replacement providers could step in, in a timely manner. The plans could also include detailed plans and supporting legal analyses for detaching other systemically important units.

A possible problem with Rajan's (2009) shelf-bankruptcy proposal, according to Thoma (2009), is that of the institution's incentives in preparing the plan. Rajan (2009: 79) recognized the problem with financial firms' incentives and would require that 'the mechanism would need to be stress-tested by regulators'.

Thus, a shelf-bankruptcy proposal has considerable potential and should receive careful consideration. This proposal is not a complete solution, but shelf-bankruptcy plans could be a big step toward better preparing for the failure of an SIFI.

3.3.4 Contingent Capital

A substitute for resolving a firm in bankruptcy proceedings or through a special resolution regime is to recapitalize the financial institution before it fails. Historically, the responsibility for this recapitalization has largely fallen on the government. An alternative is for the recapitalization to come from the private sector. However, private investors will generally participate only if their investment is expected to yield a positive return at the time it is made. This implies that it is generally too late to seek new private funds after a firm is clearly insolvent. However, investors would be willing to invest in such claims while the firm is still solvent, provided that they can expect to earn sufficiently high returns if the financial firm does well.

Culp (2002: 47) discussed a variety of structures that provide firms with such contingent capital that would allow a distressed firm to continue operation. He defined contingent capital as a contract in which the 'company pays an investor a fixed price or premium for the right (but not the obligation) to issue paid-in capital later'. The requirement that systemically important financial firms issue contingent capital is at the heart of several recent proposals.

Capital insurance

A proposal by Kashyap et al. (2008) would give financial institutions the option of replacing part of their capital with an insurance policy that is payable in the event of large losses to the financial system. In order for the policy to be able to pay off with certainty, the insurer would need to purchase Treasury securities that would be put into a custodial account for the duration of the policy.

A potential problem with an insurance-type system is that the managers could manipulate the criteria to trigger a payment on the insurance policy. Kashyap et al. (2008) addressed this risk by using a trigger that is based on losses in aggregate capital to financial institutions within some prespecified geographic region, excluding the institution that would receive the insurance payment.

Although the use of aggregate financial institution losses solves the moral hazard problem, it creates another problem in that the insurance provision could not be triggered by problems at one institution, no matter how important that institution is to financial stability. Thus, if the largest financial institution in a country dominated by two or three large institutions were to make a major risk management error not made by the others, no insurance payment would be triggered because the trigger excludes the institution that would receive the payment.

Reverse convertible securities

Convertible bonds are securities that convert into common stock at the option of the holder and are typically structured so that conversion is desirable when the firm is doing well. Reverse convertible securities are securities for which the conversion decision lies not with the holders of the securities, but with the firm's managers, or is based on prespecified triggers. Reverse convertible securities may be used as a form of contingent capital by requiring the security to convert to common equity when a firm's equity capital is low relative to its risk exposure.

Flannery (2005) considered the case for requiring banks to issue reverse convertible debt.[5] He noted that bank supervisors recognize the importance of market discipline from uninsured creditors, but that in order for this discipline to be exerted, banks must be allowed to fail, something that supervisors have proven 'very reluctant' to do with 'systemically important' financial firms (Flannery 2005: 171). Supervisors could require higher equity capital levels to reduce the probability of distress, but bankers argue that this would raise their cost of funding and make them uncompetitive.

As a substitute for requiring higher equity capital levels, Flannery (2005) proposed that banks be required to issue reverse convertible debt, as it would: (1) protect depositors and taxpayers while providing a transparent method of automatic recapitalization; (2) force shareholders to internalize the cost of the bank's risk taking; (3) not immediately take from the bank the tax shield of issuing debt; and (4) reduce the incidence of costly failures.

The trigger for the conversion in Flannery's (2005) proposal is the financial institution's capital ratio measure falling below some specified level, where capital is measured using its current stock price. His use of stock market prices in the trigger reflects concern about managers exploiting generally accepted accounting principles to avoid loss recognition. If triggered, these notes would convert into equity at the current share price, so the conversion does not provide gains to either the shareholders or bondholders.

The Squam Lake Working Group (SLWG) (2009: 4) proposed another version of reverse convertible securities: that the debt convert only if both of two triggering events occur: (1) a declaration by the regulators that the 'financial system is suffering from a systemic crisis'; and (2) a violation by the financial institution of one of the covenants in the reverse convertible security. The group argued that the advantage of the first trigger is that it disciplines financial institution management risk taking. Conventional debt offers a source of discipline that would be undermined if it 'conveniently' converted to equity whenever the institution was in distress. This way, the discipline of debt is retained unless the financial system is in distress. The second trigger addresses the problem that would arise if sound financial institutions were required to accept additional capital because of other institutions' losses. If such conversion occurred, the SLWG (2009: 4) argues that it would 'dull the incentive' of these well-managed institutions 'to remain sound'.

SLWG (2009) also discussed one important limitation of reverse convertible securities: these securities cannot guarantee that a financial firm will never fail. If a firm suffers losses in excess of its original common equity and its reverse convertible securities, it fails. This limitation applies more generally to all contingent capital proposals; these proposals can provide only a limited cushion against losses.

Tier 1 and Tier 2 reverse convertible securities

Tier 1 and Tier 2 capital can absorb losses that would otherwise be taken by the institution's creditors and/or government guarantors. Tier 1 capital should be able to absorb losses in the ordinary course of business. The use of Tier 2 capital means that the losses cannot be absorbed in the ordinary course of business, but as the most junior form of debt, it should lose all its value before any other creditor or the government takes a loss.

Thus far the only Tier 1 or Tier 2 capital that has fully achieved its purpose as a cushion to absorb losses is the common equity component of Tier 1 capital. The preferred stock component of Tier 1 capital has taken losses to the extent that dividends have been suspended at some institutions. However, for it to absorb losses beyond that point, it has to be converted to common equity.[6] Tier 2 capital has not absorbed losses because governments have not withdrawn the bank charters of systemically important banks.

However, both preferred stock and subordinated debt could fulfill their purposes if they were structured as reverse convertible securities. Such a conversion feature would work as follows for the parent financial firm.

Preferred stock would be converted on terms consistent with its role as Tier 1 capital. The preferred stock would convert to common equity at the current market price of common stock, as proposed by Flannery (2005). This conversion need not trigger any immediate change in the governance of the firm.

The primary trigger for the conversion would be when the firm's tangible common equity ratio dropped below some threshold. An additional fail-safe trigger would also be set using a capital adequacy ratio based on the market value of the firm's common stock.

Subordinated debt would convert on terms consistent with its role as an element of Tier 2 capital that should bear losses only in the event of 'failure'. As such, the subordinated debt would convert to common equity on terms intended to approximate that of a 'prepackaged bankruptcy', without the bankruptcy court.

If conversion is triggered, it is done so at a fixed ratio that would give the former subordinated creditors 99 percent of the outstanding shares. A new board of directors of the firm would be elected within 30 days of the conversion. The existing board members could run for re-election, but the new shareholders would be allowed to nominate new board members that would appear on the election ballot. The existing management of the financial institution would be required to tender its resignation at the first meeting of the new board.[7] The new board could accept the resignations without triggering any requirement that the firm make additional payments to the managers (such as change of control payments). As with preferred stock, the conversion of subordinated debt could be triggered by either the firm failing a tangible common equity or a market trigger.

One limitation of the Flannery (2005) and SLWG (2009) proposals is that they did not address the important difference between parent corporations and their subsidiaries. The conversion of reverse convertible debt into equity will reduce the proportion of shares held by the original owners. Such a change in ownership may have an undesirable side-effect on the subsidiaries in financial groups: reducing the rest of the group's incentives to work with that subsidiary. For example, if the group has central risk management, the risk managers may decide to transfer some risks out of subsidiaries that are wholly owned by the group and into a subsidiary that is only partially owned after the conversion of the reverse convertible securities.

A better alternative for implementing reverse convertible securities at a subsidiary level is to have the securities convert into the parent's common stock and have the parent then use the proceeds to purchase the subsidiary's stock. This alternative would provide for an increase in the subsidiaries' common stock without weakening the link between the subsidiary and its group affiliates.

Summary

If a systemically important financial firm becomes insolvent, the application of normal bankruptcy procedures risks creating financial instability. A special resolution regime would likely help, but it may not be adequate for firms with large cross-border operations. That suggests that there would be a high pay-off for implementing procedures using private funds to recapitalize the financial institutions before insolvency.

3.4 CONCLUSION

The recent experience demonstrated the necessity of good macroprudential supervision. Ideally, the macroprudential supervisors that come out of the current experience will be both bold and modest. They will be bold in their determination to understand the major risks facing their financial system, going wherever necessary to understand the nature and distribution of the risks. Given the global nature of the financial system, this boldness must extend to being willing to work with other macroprudential supervisors around the globe.

But all concerned also need to be modest in their expectations of what can be done. Macroprudential supervisors cannot guarantee an end to all financial instability, and trying to attain such a goal could be worse than having no macroprudential supervisor. A macroprudential supervisor trying to prevent all instability will have an incentive to limit severely the financial system's capability to innovate and to take risk. Further, when incipient instability appears, the macroprudential supervisor (and its government) will be under greater pressure to engage in bailouts to prevent or limit the instability.

The market discipline structure is also important. Supervisors cannot observe every financial decision made by systemically important financial institutions. The managers of financial institutions and their investors must have adequate incentive to manage their risk exposures to keep them within reasonable limits. In order for this discipline to occur, managers and investors must believe that they are at risk of loss from inadequate risk management.

The key to placing managers and investors credibly at risk is setting up procedures that would allow systemically important financial firms to fail without a significant adverse impact on the financial system or the real economy. In this respect, there is increased recognition of the merits of special resolutions procedures for systemically important financial institutions.

Even these measures are not likely to be adequate for handling a failing financial institution with substantial cross-border operations. Thus, serious consideration should be given to two additional measures: (1) to plan better for the resolution of systemically important groups by requiring the financial institution to develop a plan for its own resolution; and (2) to reduce the probability that a financial institution would become insolvent by obtaining contingent capital commitments while that institution is healthy that would recapitalize the institution if it becomes undercapitalized.

NOTES

1. This chapter is a condensed version of Prudential Discipline for Financial Firms: Micro, Macro and Market Structures, published as Asian Development Bank Institute Working Paper 176. The author thanks colleagues at the Federal Reserve Bank of Atlanta for many helpful discussions. He also thanks Scott Frame, Gillian García, David Mayes, Krirk Vanikkul and participants in a workshop at the University of North Dakota and at the Asian Development Bank Institute for helpful comments on an earlier draft. The views in this chapter are solely those of the author and do not necessarily reflect the view of the Federal Reserve Bank of Atlanta or the Federal Reserve System. Any remaining errors are the author's responsibility.
2. Rosengren (2009) similarly emphasized that macroprudential supervision needs to look across institutions.
3. A presentation by Miyoshi (2006) made this point in a more general setting. Miyoshi pointed out that the analytic framework for macroprudential regulation is underdeveloped, as are the assumptions used in stress tests. Given these weaknesses, Miyoshi's presentation showed that it can be difficult to get regulated institutions and the public to accept tighter regulation.
4. See Bliss and Kaufman (2006) for a comparison of the US corporate bankruptcy regime with the special resolutions regime applicable to commercial banks.
5. Stanton (1991: 182) previously proposed a version of reverse convertible securities for US government sponsored enterprises.
6. In a few cases, preferred shareholders have been persuaded to convert to common shares. In some other cases, preferred stock dividends have been suspended and they do not cumulate while suspended. However, the charter must be withdrawn before preferred stock can be written down. Moreover, if a distressed firm's condition should improve sufficiently to allow it to pay dividends, preferred dividends will continue to have priority over common dividends. This raises the possibility that common shareholders will

control the governance of the firm even though these shareholders have little prospect of receiving dividends in the foreseeable future.
7. The bank supervisors would also be authorized to appoint interim managers after the conversion and before the new board meets if doing so would, in the supervisor's judgment, help to preserve the value of the bank.

REFERENCES

Bliss, R.R. and G.G. Kaufman. 2006. US Corporate and Bank Insolvency Regimes: An Economic Comparison and Evaluation. Federal Reserve Bank of Chicago Working Paper 2006-01. Chicago, IL: Federal Reserve Bank of Chicago. http://ssrn.com/abstract=878355 (accessed 28 November 2009).

Cho, Y.J. 2009. Comments made in Session VIII: Wrap Up Session on First Two Days at Asian Development Bank Institute Conference on Global Financial Crisis: Financial Sector Reform and Regulation, ADBI, Tokyo, 21–22 July.

Culp, C.L. 2002. Contingent Capital: Integrating Corporate Financing And Risk Management Decisions. *Journal of Applied Corporate Finance* 15(Spring): 46–56. http://rmcsinc.com/articles/JACF151.pdf (accessed 28 November 2009).

Demyanyk, Y.S. and O. Van Hemert. 2008. Understanding the Subprime Mortgage Crisis. http://ssrn.com/abstract=1020396 (accessed 28 November 2009).

Flannery, M.J. 2005. No Pain, No Gain? Effecting Market Discipline via Reverse Convertible Debentures. In *Capital Adequacy Beyond Basel: Banking, Securities, and Insurance*, edited by H.S. Scott. Oxford: Oxford University Press. http://www.cba.ufl.edu/fire/docs/publishedpapers/Published_RCD_Chapter.pdf (accessed 28 November 2009).

Hüpkes, E.H.G. 2004. Too Big to Save – Towards a Functional Approach to Resolving Crises in Global Financial Institutions. Paper presented at Chicago Federal Reserve Bank Conference on Systemic Financial Crises: Resolving Large Bank Insolvencies, Chicago, IL, 30 September–1 October. http://www.chicagofed.org/news_and_conferences/conferences_and_events/files/systemic_hupkes.pdf (accessed 28 November 2009).

Kashyap, A.K., R.G. Rajan and J.C. Stein. 2008. Rethinking Capital Regulation. Paper presented at the Federal Reserve Bank of Kansas City Symposium on Maintaining Stability in a Changing Financial System, Jackson Hole, WY, 21–23 August. http://www.kc.frb.org/publicat/sympos/2008/KashyapRajanStein.08.08.08.pdf (accessed 28 November 2009).

Mayes, D.G. 2006. Financial Stability in a World of Cross-Border Banking: Nordic and Antipodean Solutions to the Problem of Responsibility Without Power. *Journal of Banking Regulation* 8: 20–39. https://secure.palgrave-journals.com/jbr/journal/v8/n1/abs/2350034a.html (accessed 28 November 2009).

Mayes, D.G., M.J. Nieto and L.D. Wall. 2008. Multiple Safety Net Regulators and Agency Problems in the EU: Is Prompt Corrective Action Partly the Solution? *Journal of Financial Stability* (September): 165–304.

Miyoshi, T. 2006. Financial Stability Analysis in Japan. Presentation notes for the Macroprudential Supervision Conference: Challenges for Financial Supervisors, sponsored by Korea Financial Supervisory Commission/Financial Supervisory Service and the International Monetary Fund, Seoul, 7–8 November.

http://www.imf.org/external/np/seminars/eng/2006/macropr/pdf/Miyoshi.pdf (accessed 28 November 2009).

Padoa-Schioppa, T. 2003. Central Banks and Financial Stability: Exploring a Land in Between. In *The Transformation of the European Financial System*, edited by V. Gaspar, P. Hartmann and O. Sleijpen. Frankfurt am Main: European Central Bank. http://www.ecb.int/pub/pdf/other/transformationeuropeanfinancialsystemen.pdf (accessed 28 November 2009).

Rajan, R. 2009. Cycle-proof Regulation. *Economist*, 8 April: 79. http://www.economist.com/businessfinance/displayStory.cfm?story_id=13446173 (accessed 28 November 2009).

Rosengren, E.S. 2009. Could a Systemic Regulator Have Seen the Current Crisis? Speech given at the 10th Seoul International Financial Forum, Seoul, 15 April. http://www.bos.frb.org/news/speeches/rosengren/2009/041509.htm (accessed 28 November 2009).

Ryback, W.A. 2006. Macro Prudential Policy: A New Name for Some Old Ways of Thinking? Presentation to the Korea Financial Supervisory Commission /Financial Supervisory Service and International Monetary Fund Macro Prudential Supervision Conference: Challenges for Financial Supervisors, Seoul, 7–8 November. http://imf.org/external/np/seminars/eng/2006/macropr/pdf/ryback.pdf (accessed 28 November 2009).

Squam Lake Working Group (SLWG). 2009. An Expedited Resolution Mechanism for Distressed Financial Firms: Regulatory Hybrid Securities. Squam Lake Working Group Paper. New York, NY: Council on Foreign Relations. http://www.cfr.org/content/publications/attachments/Squam_Lake_Working_Paper3.pdf (accessed 28 November 2009).

Stanton, T.H. 1991. *A State of Risk: Will Government-Sponsored Enterprises Be the Next Financial Crisis?* New York: HarperCollins.

Thoma, M. 2009. Rajan Roundtable: Seize the Moment. *Economist.com: Free Exchange*, 9 April. http://www.economist.com/blogs/freeexchange/2009/04/rajan_roundtable_1.cfm (accessed 28 November 2009).

Vanikkul, K. 2009. Comments on Larry Wall's Paper on Prudential Discipline for Financial Firms: Micro, Macro and Market Regimes. Comments delivered at ADBI Conference on Global Financial Crisis: Financial Sector Reform and Regulation, ADBI, Tokyo, 21–22 July.

4. Dynamic provisioning: some lessons from experience

Santiago Fernández de Lis and Alicia García-Herrero

4.1 INTRODUCTION

This chapter deals with lessons drawn from experiences of dynamic or countercyclical provisioning. Section 4.2 summarizes the reasons for the procyclicality of the financial system; section 4.3 deals with policies used to address this problem; section 4.4 describes the experiences of Spain, Colombia and Peru; section 4.5 draws some lessons from this comparison; and section 4.6 reviews the main conclusions.

4.2 WHY IS THE FINANCIAL SYSTEM SO PROCYCLICAL?

The global financial storm that hit the banking systems of major developed economies in 2007 and sent dangerous waves to the emerging world has shown clearly that the financial system exacerbates the cyclical movements of an economy. The procyclicality of the financial system is not new. It is caused by a number of different factors, which need to be understood before assessing why some financial systems are more procyclical than others, and how to best combat such procyclicality.

First of all, the financial system is prone to more lax assessments of risk in good times than in bad, being influenced by the economy's general environment.

Second, borrowers' net worth – as well as cash flow – is bound to be higher during upturns, facilitating their access to credit. This mechanism, identified by Kiyotaki and Moore (1997), has been branded the 'financial accelerator'. In the same vein, the value of collateral is bound to increase in good times and fall in bad times. Such asset price dynamics – and the related wealth effects – clearly increase borrowers' capacity to obtain collateralized lending during booms. However, during subsequent slowdowns, it becomes clear that the collateral backing the loans did not have the expected value.

Third, because banks depend on external funding to lend and funding is scarcer in bad times, their lending policies are necessarily procyclical. This procyclical tendency may be exacerbated by regulation, as will be explained at the end of this section.

Fourth, investors and thus financial institutions as intermediaries of savings have a strong incentive to behave in line with their peers – so-called herd behavior (Rajan 1994; Devenov and Welch 1996) – as their evaluation is in relative and not absolute terms which, at an aggregate level, fosters lending during booms and limits it during recessions. In fact, credit mistakes are generally judged more leniently if they are common to the whole industry.

Fifth, the classical principal–agent problem between bank shareholders and managers can also feed excessive volatility into loan growth rates. Managers, once they obtain a reasonable return on equity for their shareholders, may engage in other activities that depart from firm value maximization and focus more on managers' rewards. One of these strategies might be excessive credit growth in order to increase the social presence of the bank (and its managers) or the power of managers in a continuously enlarging organization (Williamson 1963).

Sixth, compensation policies are generally such that the principal–agent problem is not even necessary for managers of financial institutions to behave procyclically. Bonuses, linked to business growth in good times and to business retrenchment in bad times, are a powerful reason for financial institutions to become very procyclical.

Seventh, human capital cannot grow as fast as a financial institution does in good times. When the economy booms, loan officers need to grant loans faster and probably feel pressure to conduct less rigorous screening to meet demand. Furthermore, the more time that has passed since the last downturn, the less prepared are loan officers to realize that the economic environment can change very quickly. This is what Berger and Udell (2004) have called a lack of institutional memory.

Eighth, the increasing sophistication, harmonization and automation of risk management also add to procyclicality. Furthermore, network externalities increase risk assumption in good times and propagate financial distress during downturns. These risk externalities will tend to be amplified when aggregated across the network as a whole. In order to address this problem, financial institutions should not look at unconditional value at risk (VaR), but consider conditional VaR (Haldane 2009).

Ninth, competition in the banking system, especially in the commercial banking system, is such that cross-subsidization is used more and more to attract clients. An important feature of cross-subsidization is the offering of credit access to clients so that they pay commissions for other products. In good times, this can bring about a relaxation of credit standards for the sake of attracting new clients (Nys 2008; Lepetit et al. 2008).

Finally, financial regulation may be an additional source of procyclicality. In fact, traditional loan-loss provisions are tied to loan delinquency. That means that in good times financial institutions need to provision less, but when delinquencies begin to occur, they need to step up provisions immediately. This will obviously reduce their available capital and, thus, their lending capacity when it is most needed. Additionally, the traditional focus of risk-sensitive capital adequacy requirements is not dependent on the macroeconomic situation, but only on the types of assets on each bank's balance sheet. The way in which the capital adequacy ratio is defined, that is, as basically allowing for hybrid capital to be included, can also induce additional procyclicality. This is because hybrid capital, to the extent that it has a debt component, is subject to debt market swings. Moreover, as Caruana and Narain (2008) argue, how much Basel II exacerbates procyclicality very much depends on the mitigating measures the local regulator is willing to introduce under Pillar II, which includes regulatory responses and other aspects of financial stability besides capital adequacy.[1] This is related to the rules versus discretion debate that will be dealt with in section 4.3.1.

The increasingly homogeneous assessment of risk and common trading techniques may also exacerbate herd behavior. The same can be said about the introduction of fair value in accounting standards, which may create the illusion of very good solvency (based on high market prices during boom periods), resulting in an apparent sudden change in the solvency situation as soon as market prices change (Jiménez and Saurina 2006; Taylor and Goodhart 2006).

Finally, a vicious circle could even be created by procyclical regulation feeding the asset price bubble. This point has been formalized by Aiyagari and Gertler (1999) and Gruss and Sgherri (2009).

4.3 HOW TO REDUCE THE PROCYCLICALITY OF THE FINANCIAL SYSTEM

Procyclicality cannot be eliminated but only mitigated. This is true for the behavior of the financial system as a whole, but also for regulatory tools. After limiting expectations to what is achievable, it seems important to determine the most effective way to mitigate procyclicality. The first question is whether measures taken should be rule-based or discretionary. The second relates to which regulatory tool is better placed to mitigate procyclicality: provisions or capital. Both questions will be addressed in this section.

4.3.1 Rules versus Discretion[2]

Two key choices need to be made when designing the details of a countercyclical regime. The first is how the level of buffers should be determined; the second is how the impact should be presented. The level of buffers can be defined in either a discretionary or a formula-driven fashion.

Under a discretionary system, the bank regulator will need to judge the appropriate level of required capital ratios in light of an analysis of the macroeconomic cycle and of macroprudential concerns. A discretionary system would have the advantage of allowing a nuanced analysis of macroeconomic and macroprudential conditions to guide decisions; however, it would depend crucially on the quality and independence of the judgment made by the bank regulator.

Under a formula-driven system, the required level of capital would vary according to some predetermined metric, such as the growth of the balance sheet or estimates of lending over the cycle. It would provide a preset discipline not dependent on judgment and not subject to the influence of lobbying, but would rely heavily on the possibility of calibrating the business cycle *ex ante*, an issue that will be addressed below. A rules-based system is superior to a discretionary mechanism in situations where the policymaker's commitment lacks credibility.[3] In dealing with procyclicality, this may result from the expectation of widespread forbearance toward banking problems in the downturn. From this point of view, a rules-based system would be superior.

4.3.2 Capital versus Provisioning

While broad agreement exists on the procyclicality of the financial system, much less is known about how to reduce such procyclicality. According to one extreme view, booms and busts cannot be prevented. The opposite view is that they can be fully mitigated, while the truth is somewhere in between.

The key question is how to have an impact on the financial system without creating unwarranted distortions. It seems very difficult to persuade bank managers to follow more prudent credit policies during an economic upturn, especially in a highly competitive environment. Even conservative managers might find market pressure for higher profits very difficult to overcome.

One policy alone cannot possibly achieve the goal of mitigating procyclicality. In fact, financial regulation is only one of the many tools that policymakers can use toward this aim. Monetary policy is another obvious candidate, but is outside the scope of this chapter.

There is debate over which instrument (that is, provisions or capital) should be used to mitigate procyclicality. Provisions and capital have different objectives: the former aims at covering expected losses, while the latter's goal is to cover unexpected losses. Considering that excessive growth in credit is the best-known early indicator of a banking crisis (or of a default in the microsphere), one would tend to think that it would generate an expected loss that banks should try to cover once credit grows too fast. In other words, using provisioning as a tool to counteract procyclicality would look more natural.

On the other hand, provisions accumulated during a boom can be used to distribute higher profits in a bust, which is something the regulator may not be inclined to facilitate, whereas capital (or reserves) is not subject to this problem. One should therefore think of capital and provisioning measures as complementary.

While provisioning measures have been developed, measures to avoid procyclicality in banks' capital requirements are only embryonic. A widely discussed potential measure is to modify the current calculation of required capital by introducing a multiplying parameter based on macroprudential criteria (Brunnermeier et al. 2009).

The Financial Stability Board (FSB) is focusing on the quality of capital and, therefore, on the difference between core capital, Tier 1 capital and Tier 2 capital reserves. The FSB suggests that in the future less reliance will be placed on VaR measures and more on stress test techniques as determinants of capital adequacy. Finally, the FSB recommends that the monitoring and adjustment of the cyclicality of Basel III[4] should be a continuous task, but does not elaborate on a specific proposal.

There are other possible capital instruments that can be used to reduce procyclicality. One option is to introduce limits on leverage, an approach supported by the FSB and the Basel Committee on Banking Supervision, among other organizations. Another is to set a capital charge on off-balance-sheet credit, which is already being done in Spain. The Bank of Spain imposed an 8 percent capital charge against assets in structured investment vehicles, in keeping with the significant exposure that banks maintained vis-à-vis these vehicles. This charge effectively made these vehicles unattractive to Spanish banks, thus limiting the development of a 'shadow banking system' that was one of the sources of the subprime crisis in the United States.

Experience with provisioning measures is limited to Spain, where dynamic provisioning was introduced in 2000, Colombia (starting in 2007) and Peru (from 2008). The FSB has been supporting the introduction of dynamic provisioning in several ways, including by trying to overcome the opposition of accountants to such measures. The international consensus seems to be moving toward a generalized adoption of some form of dynamic provisioning. More specific proposals concerning provisions are to: (1) consider the allocation of general provisions in banks' regulatory capital; (2) reconsider Basel II thresholds for reserves (currently 1.25 percent in the standard approach and 0.6 percent in the internal ratings-based approach) that imply a disincentive for improved provisioning; and (3) enhance the transparency of provisions in Pillar 3 of the Basel II Accord, which focuses on disclosure and transparency.

It is important to ensure the compatibility and coherence of the various measures being discussed, especially as other related tools, such as leverage ratios, liquidity ratios, and limits to loan-to-value ratios on mortgages are also planned.

4.4 EXISTING EXPERIENCES

4.4.1 Spain

The introduction of dynamic provisioning in Spain should be seen in the context of the profound impact of euro adoption on the Spanish economy. Historically, the economy was characterized by a propensity to instability, which implied ample cyclical swings, difficulties in maintaining price stability, chronic balance-of-payments problems and periodic currency crises to restore competitiveness levels.

Spain joined the European Monetary Union from the start, which entailed the irrevocable fixing of parities on 1 January 1999. As a result, the Spanish economy benefited from a significant reduction of risk premia, in particular those related to inflation and currency risk. The real long-term interest rate (defined as the difference between nominal rates and contemporary inflation) moved from a level of 4–5 percent to around zero in the aftermath of monetary union.

The European Central Bank kept interest rates at around 4.0 percent in the late 1990s, a level which was consistent with average conditions in the eurozone, but which implied very lax monetary conditions for the Spanish economy. This expansionary impact was compounded by the depreciation of the euro vis-à-vis the United States dollar in these years. It is true that convergence criteria for euro adoption limited the extent of these initial discrepancies. But the asymmetric shock of the reduction of risk premia for peripheral countries led to a progressive widening of gross domestic product (GDP) growth differentials.

In the early 2000s, the Spanish authorities saw with increasing anxiety the combination of high credit growth, inflation differentials with the eurozone average, loss of competitiveness, and widening current account deficits. Monetary policy and the nominal exchange rate were no longer available as policy instruments. In this context, dynamic provisions (or statistical provisions, as they were then termed) were seen as an instrument with a double objective: (1) to contain credit growth by increasing the cost of granting new credit; and (2) to protect Spanish banking institutions from future losses as a consequence of the relaxation of lending standards typical of the boom phase. While the first objective was probably more important at the time the system was adopted, the results were much more satisfactory in terms of the second objective (Fernández de Lis and García-Herrero 2009).

Dynamic or statistical provisioning was therefore a macroprudential tool, in the sense that a prudential instrument (that is, provisions) was used to achieve a systemic or macroeconomic goal (that is, limiting credit growth). The second objective was mostly aimed at ensuring adequate protection for individual institutions (and could therefore be seen as a microprudential tool), but to the extent that excessive risk assumption was partly a result of herd behavior and collective myopia by credit institutions, it also had a macroprudential aim.

How was the system expected to work?

As can be seen in Figure 4.1, under a normal provisioning system, provisions are a function of contemporary non-performing loans (NPLs), although the link with NPLs may be smoothed by the possibility of using 'generic' provisions based on credit stock. In an upturn, when GDP grows above potential, credit growth also accelerates. Because business conditions are favorable, collateral prices are increasing and optimism is pervasive, debtors have, in general, no problem in servicing their debt. Low provisioning efforts fuel low risk aversion and credit growth, and thus economic growth. In a downturn, the opposite spiral operates.

The objective of dynamic provisioning is to smooth the provisioning effort over the cycle, as shown in Figure 4.2; how much to smooth the effort is an open question. While the idea is to avoid the procyclical effect of the normal system, a regulator would hardly aim at the opposite pattern of provisions (that is, to increase provisions in good times and decrease them in bad times). As risk is cyclical, this reality should be reflected in provisions. The ideal would be to obtain a flat provisioning effort along

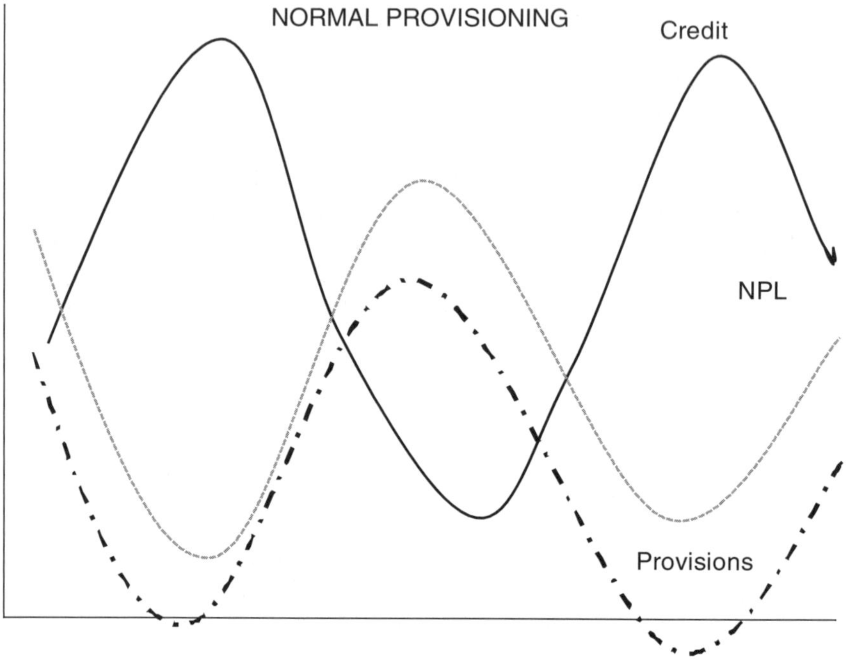

Figure 4.1 *Normal provisioning cycle*

the cycle in terms of the ratio of provisions to credit, as illustrated in Figure 4.2, which is more or less what was aimed at in Spain.

How did the system really work?

Credit growth stabilized at around 15 percent annually after the introduction of dynamic provisioning in 2000, and decreased slightly between 2001 and 2004. It is difficult to assess, however, to what extent this was related to the new provisioning system. Most probably, the impact of the burst of the dot-com bubble was more relevant in this period. After 2004, however – coinciding with a reform of the provisioning system – credit accelerated sharply, reaching rates of growth of over 25 percent in 2006. The impact of the global financial crisis since mid-2007 has led to a sharp contraction of both credit and GDP.

Initially, the system reform of 2000 was based on three types of provisions: specific and generic (both already existing), and statistical (introduced in 2000). Specific provisions depended on current bad loans, generic provisions made up 1 percent of the credit stock, and statistical provisions were designed to offset specific provisions, and depended on credit growth.

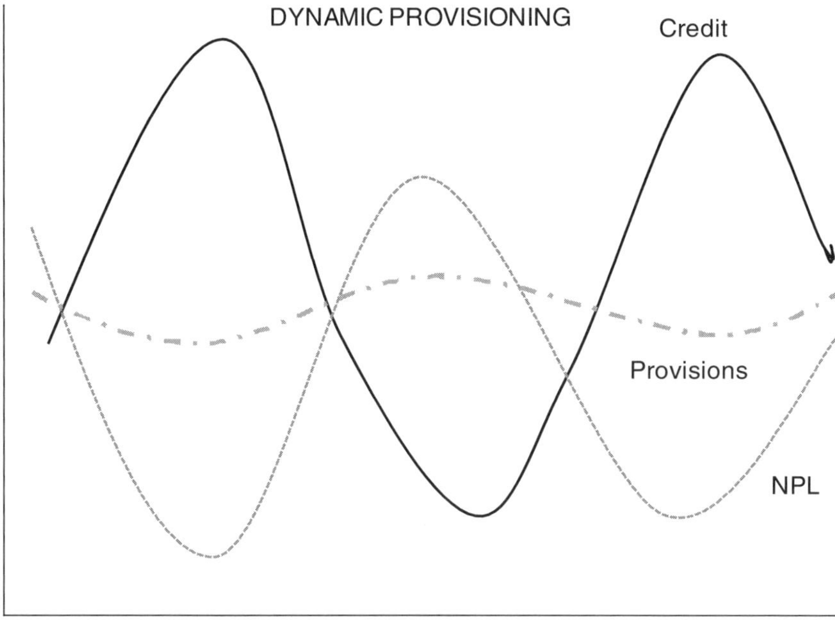

Figure 4.2 Dynamic provisioning cycle

This mechanism was criticized on several grounds: international accounting bodies argued that it implied profit smoothing along the cycle, masking the real situation of the banks. Spanish financial institutions complained about being subject to higher provisioning requirements than their competitors, which they considered an important competitive disadvantage in the single European market for financial services.

By 2004, there was a sense that these provisions were excessive. By that time, they had reached a level of more than 2.5 percent of credit (of which less than 0.5 percent was specific provisions, that is, related to bad loans), as can be seen in Figure 4.3. The coverage of provisions over bad loans reached nearly 500 percent in 2004.

The system was therefore reformed, integrating the generic and statistical provisions and establishing limits for the accumulated fund. According to the new formula:

$$\textit{Generic provisions} = a\,\Delta\,\textit{credit} + b\,\textit{credit} - \textit{specific provisions}$$

where $0 \leq a \leq 2.5\%$;
$0 \leq b \leq 1.64\%$;
and Δ stands for change.

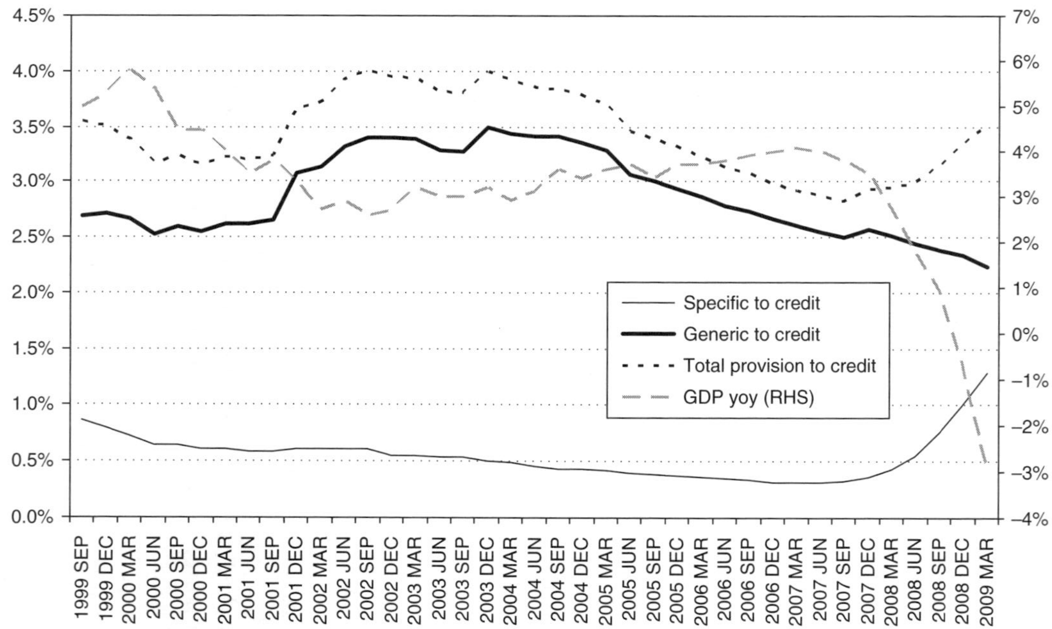

Notes:
Provisions have been corrected for the impact of the 2004 accounting relation.
yoy = year over year; RHS = right-hand side(axis).

Source: Banco de España.

Figure 4.3 Spain: provisioning to credit and GDP (%)

Table 4.1 Coefficients applied to dynamic provisioning

Type of risk	α (%)	β (%)
No apparent risk	0.00	0.00
Low risk	0.60	0.11
Low-medium risk	1.50	0.44
Medium risk	1.80	0.65
Medium-high risk	2.00	1.10
High risk	2.50	1.64

Source: Fernández de Lis et al. (2001).

The coefficients of the different types of assets were as shown in Table 4.1.

Limits for the Generic Fund, which was the result of accumulated provisions, were set between 0.33 percent and 1.25 percent of the alpha in 2004. Because several institutions were already above the upper limit when it was set, this implied the liberation of 14 billion euro from the Generic Fund. These 'liberated' provisions, however, were not distributed, but consolidated as reserves. In the subsequent quarters, as more institutions reached the Generic Fund's upper limit and credit accelerated over 25 percent annually, the ratio of provisions to credit went down, from 2.5 percent in 2004 to 2.2 percent in 2007.

To a certain extent, the reasoning behind the 2004 reform can be assessed, in retrospect, as a lack of faith in the system. It was innovative, with no precedent and no similar system in any other country, and was contested by the banks and by international accounting bodies. In the mid-2000s there were questions on whether the system could be explosive and whether there would be limits to the accumulation process. Had the magnitude of the shock that was incubating – and that would erupt in 2007 – been known, it is open to discussion whether the authorities would have changed the system, or set the limits so close to then-prevailing levels.

The events since 2007 have had a dramatic effect on the Spanish economy. GDP and credit dropped rapidly, NPLs started to rise swiftly, and specific provisions grew fivefold from the summer of 2007 to the spring of 2009. Generic provisions also decreased very quickly, but not sufficiently to compensate for the increase in specific provisions, so that total provisions to credit in early 2009 exceeded the maximum reached in 2004. This was also partly due to rapidly decreasing credit growth as the global crisis hit Spain. The limited use of generic provisions in the downturn can be explained by the prudence of financial institutions (that were aware that the worst was yet to come) and by the authorities' guidelines (aimed at limiting profit distribution when the impact of the shock was starting).[5]

Some preliminary lessons emerge from the Spanish case. First, dynamic provisions helped create a cushion in good times, but did not have a significant impact on credit growth or rises in house prices. When the size of a boom is big enough, the impact of an additional provision on credit supply is marginal. Second, the Spanish system – although being rule-based – allows for some discretion. Despite the fact that Spain has probably one of the most complete and reliable data sets of credit and NPLs based on a long-standing credit registry, the initial difficulty in calibrating the cycle *ex ante* led to doubts about the reliability of the estimates. This explains why the rules were changed in the middle of the game. Third, the treatment of off-balance-sheet entities also played an important role in the system. The issuance of covered bonds and securitization did not 'save' capital for the institutions. The joint effect of dynamic provisions and the treatment of off-balance-sheet entities explains how the Spanish banking system was able to confront the crisis in a better initial state than were others in Europe.

4.4.2 Colombia

In 2007, Colombia adopted a model of dynamic provisioning for commercial and consumer loans. These loans currently represent about 90 percent of the total outstanding loan portfolio. When the model was adopted, the banking regulator implemented reference models for commercial and consumption credit risk. Although each bank can use its own credit risk model, which must be approved by the regulator, at present all banks are using the reference model.

The reference model established three types of provisions that are tax deductible: individual, countercyclical and generic. Individual provisions reflect the characteristic risk of every borrower and every type of loan, and can only be used in the case of an NPL. Countercyclical provisions seek to cover changes in borrowers' credit risk due to changes in the economic cycle, and have the same characteristics as individual provisions. With the present regulation, it is not easy to distinguish between individual and countercyclical provisions as both are registered under the same balance account. Finally, generic provisions account for at least 1 percent of the total loan portfolio, and this type of provision can be used to meet countercyclical provision regulation requirements.

Once the model of countercyclical provisions was implemented, there was a dramatic fall in generic provisions. In fact, the system was criticized because the rise in individual provisions, though it had a countercyclical effect, was compensated in part by the reduction in generic provisions.

How was the system designed?

The regulator, using historical data, had to calculate two risk scenarios: A and B (where B was the riskier scenario). The outputs of this calculation (see below) were two default probability matrices that contained default probabilities for every type of credit and borrower.

Provisions = outstanding value of the loan × default probability × loss once defaulted

Every year the regulator had to decide which matrix to use to compute individual provisions. During years of high credit and economic growth, matrix A was used to determine the accumulation of individual provisions. Matrix B was used to calculate riskier scenario provisions, so that countercyclical provisions were the difference between the riskier scenario provisions and the individual provisions. During years of low growth, matrix A was used to calculate individual provisions and there would be no accumulation of countercyclical provisions.

The regulator could exercise discretion in determining when banks could use countercyclical provisions to compensate for the increase in individual provisions during an economic downturn. Once the regulator declared a change of state, all banks could use countercyclical provisions, regardless of the financial health of individual institutions.

This model created great uncertainty, and in 2009 led the Colombian regulator to announce a revision of the system in a direction that would make it more rules-based and more similar to the Spanish system. In September 2009, the Colombian banking supervisor issued a new regulation that considers just two types of provisions: general and individual. The individual provisions are now composed of two categories: procyclical and countercyclical provisions. The amount of each type of provision is automatically determined for each financial institution according to standard indicators, the financial cycle of each institution, and the model parameters. As a result, as of September 2010 countercyclical provisions accounted for 18 percent of loan provisions, equivalent to 1 percent of the outstanding loan portfolio.

4.4.3 Peru

In 2008, when Peru's GDP grew by 9.8 percent and credit by 36 percent, changes in generic provisions were introduced. These changes transformed part of the voluntary provisions banks had accumulated in the previous two years into permanent provisions.

Since December 2008, the generic rate has depended on the type of debtor and is not homogeneous. The rate is 0.7 percent in the case of 'normal' commercial and mortgage loans, and 1 percent in the case of 'normal' micro-firm and consumer loans. As a result of this change, generic rates now penalize more those (riskier) loans that have historically shown a higher rate of non-performance. Secondly, cyclical provisioning was introduced at the same time, primarily aiming at moderating credit growth rates and reducing the probability of eventual consumer over-indebtedness.

How was the system designed?

The Peruvian financial supervisor or regulator (Superintendencia de Banca, Seguros y AFP, SBS) set a rule based on GDP growth. In this way, cyclical provisioning is activated when the rate of growth of GDP exceeds a certain threshold (in boom periods), which is related to an estimation of potential output growth. Figure 4.4 illustrates the rule.

These cyclical provisions are part of generic provisions. When cyclical provisioning is activated, generic provision charges increase. Table 4.2 shows how these charges change.

Rates for additional generic provisions were based on data from the last episode of financial crisis in the late 1990s. They were, therefore, calibrated for stress situations. In times of economic slowdown, on the other hand, cyclical provisioning is deactivated and generic rates are reduced. Figure 4.5 summarizes the functioning of the rule in stress situations.

Although additional accumulated generic provisions cannot be directly allocated to profits, the possibility of using them to cover other required provisions reduces the provisioning effort banks need to make during a cycle's downturn. Thus, they indirectly benefit bank profits in bad times, smoothing them over the cycle.

Why is the rule based on GDP? Why not on credit (a banking system variable)? According to the SBS, in the case of Peru changes in GDP precede changes in credit. In this sense, credit growth is not as good a predictive indicator of future bank losses as GDP.

Another issue to consider is that a GDP-based rule is systemic. This means that it does not depend on any individual bank's behavior, but on the behavior of the economy (that is, the system) as a whole. For this reason, the effect could be asymmetric on banks: it could be the case that more prudent banks would have to increase generic provisions when the rule is activated because the more aggressive behavior of other banks leads to higher credit and GDP growth.[6]

Peruvian regulations state that as of January 2010, instead of classifying loans into four groups (by debtor type), financial institutions have to classify them into eight groups. This should increase the homogeneity of loans for each credit type, which will increase the accuracy of the assessments that can be made and, therefore, enhance risk management.

Cyclical provisioning[7] was activated in Peru in December 2008, at the same time the GDP-based rule was implemented. However, given the fast deceleration the Peruvian economy has experienced since the fourth quarter of 2008, it was deactivated according to rule B2 in the autumn of 2009.

4.5 COMPARISON BETWEEN SPAIN, PERU AND COLOMBIA

The first important difference between the three systems is how they are activated and deactivated (see Table 4.3 for a full comparison). The Spanish and Peruvian systems are both rules-based, whereas the Colombian system is discretionary (in the sense that the activation of the accumulation mechanism is decided by the banking supervisor). However, as Spain has demonstrated, discretion can be applied to rule-based systems.

Another important difference is the variable chosen to calculate the amount of provisioning required. The Spanish system is based on credit, whereas the Peruvian system is based on GDP. In Colombia (given the discretionary nature of its system), no explicit variable has been used thus far, although the authorities have confirmed that credit is taken into account. These differences have important implications.

First, as credit is a banking variable and is institution-specific, provisions under the Spanish system are tailored to each institution, whereas under the Peruvian system the activation or deactivation of the mechanism is common to the whole system. Choosing a common path for all banks may have different implications for institutions depending on their individual strategies, their geographical or client specializations, or their levels of efficiency and profitability. Some may be gaining market share, others may be shrinking, but a mechanism that is not institution-specific will tend to treat banks similarly (although the size, variation or riskiness of their portfolios will result in differences in provisions even with a system-based mechanism).

Second, the choice of GDP as an aggregate variable, as opposed to domestic demand, also poses questions: with a current account deficit, a domestic demand-based objective would, *ceteris paribus*, introduce more pressure than a GDP-based objective and would facilitate an automatic

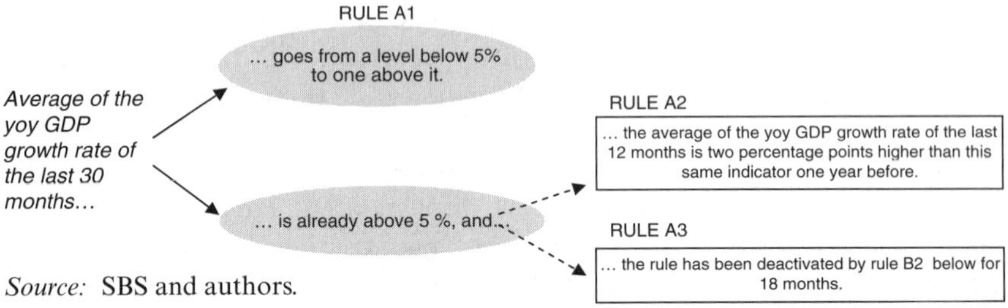

Source: SBS and authors.

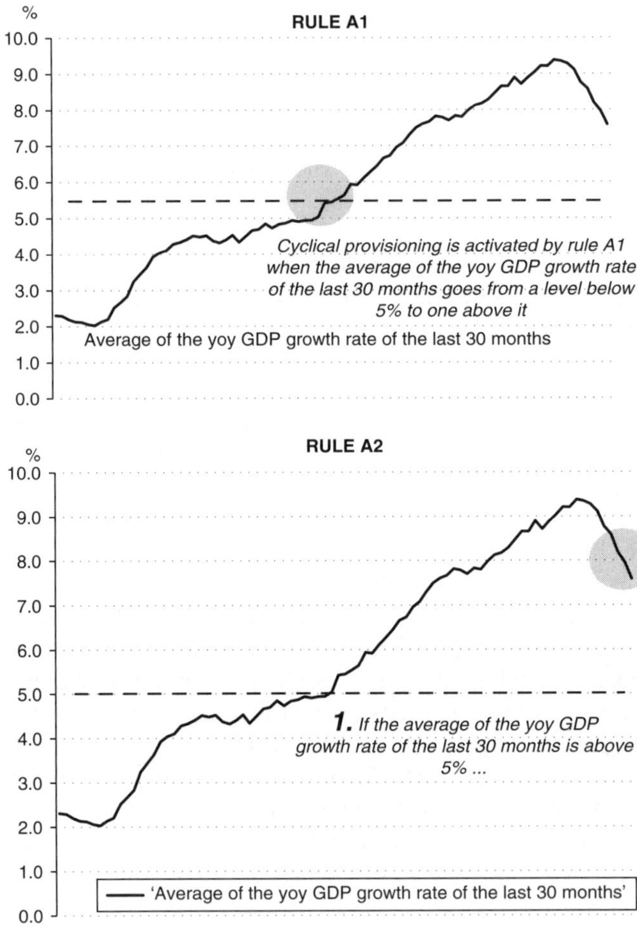

Source: Banco Central de Reserva del Perú.

Figure 4.4 Cyclical provisioning activation

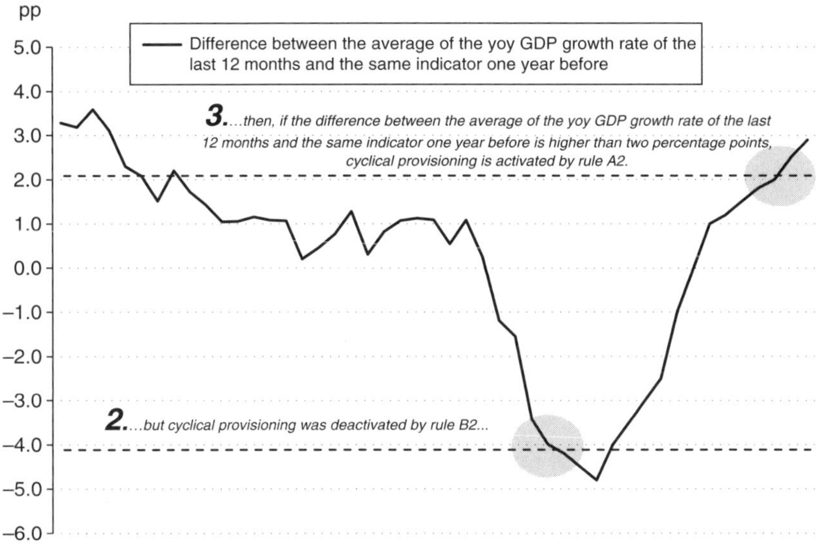

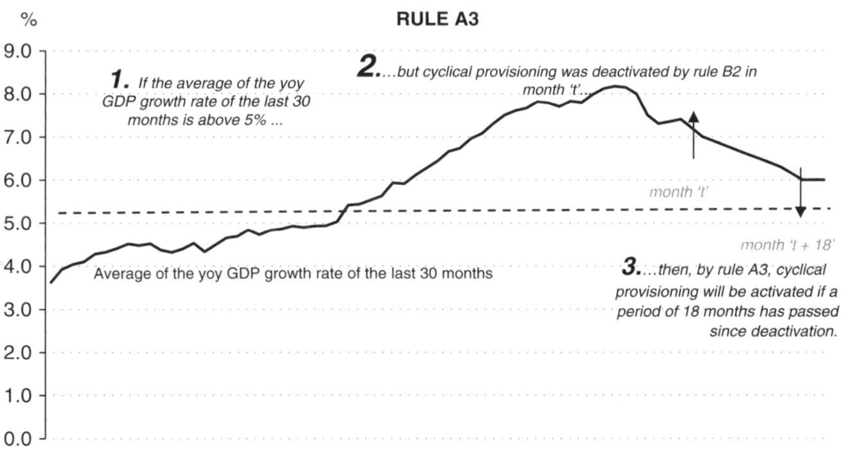

Source: SBS and authors.

correction mechanism for the deficit. The differences between using credit and GDP, however, would depend on the calibration and the choice of parameters in each case.

Finally, even if an aggregate variable were to be chosen, credit would seem more naturally linked to banking activity than GDP. However, for

Table 4.2 Provisioning rules

Type of debtor	Since December 2008 Generic rate (%)	
	When the rule is not activated	Additional when the rule is activated (cyclical)
Commercial	0.7	0.5
Micro-firms	1.0	0.5
Consumers	1.0	1.0
Mortgage	0.7	0.4

Source: Superintendencia de Banca, Seguros y AFP (SBS).

countries in the process of financial deepening, high credit growth may not be a signal of excess in the financial sector, but a result of a healthy financial inclusion process. The Peruvian system could thus be better suited to the needs of emerging market economies (EMEs).

Yet another important difference in the systems of Spain, Peru and Colombia lies in the sources of data used. Credit is a banking statistic and, therefore, is much easier for the central bank and/or supervisor to use than GDP, which is an estimate normally calculated by national statistics agencies.

One more relevant distinction is whether the provisioning mechanism is system-wide or institution-specific. The Spanish system is based on individual bank performance, whereas the Peruvian and the Colombian provisioning mechanisms are systemic (although the latter has announced that it will change to an institution-specific mechanism during the next reform). Under the Spanish system, some banks may be required to increase generic provisions while others reduce provisions. The Peruvian mechanism is activated for the system as a whole, although its impact on each institution depends on the riskiness of individual bank portfolios. This implies that an institution losing market share, having a more prudent lending policy or experiencing a negative shock in its area of activity will be forced to provision above the normal level, simply because GDP is growing above a certain threshold.

The implications of the above are interesting from a competition point of view. The Spanish system could penalize institutions that are gaining market share because they are more efficient. The Peruvian system penalizes institutions that are more prudent; it also treats small and large institutions differently. The bigger (that is, more systemic) a firm is, and the more diversified it is geographically, the less likely it is to face a rate of

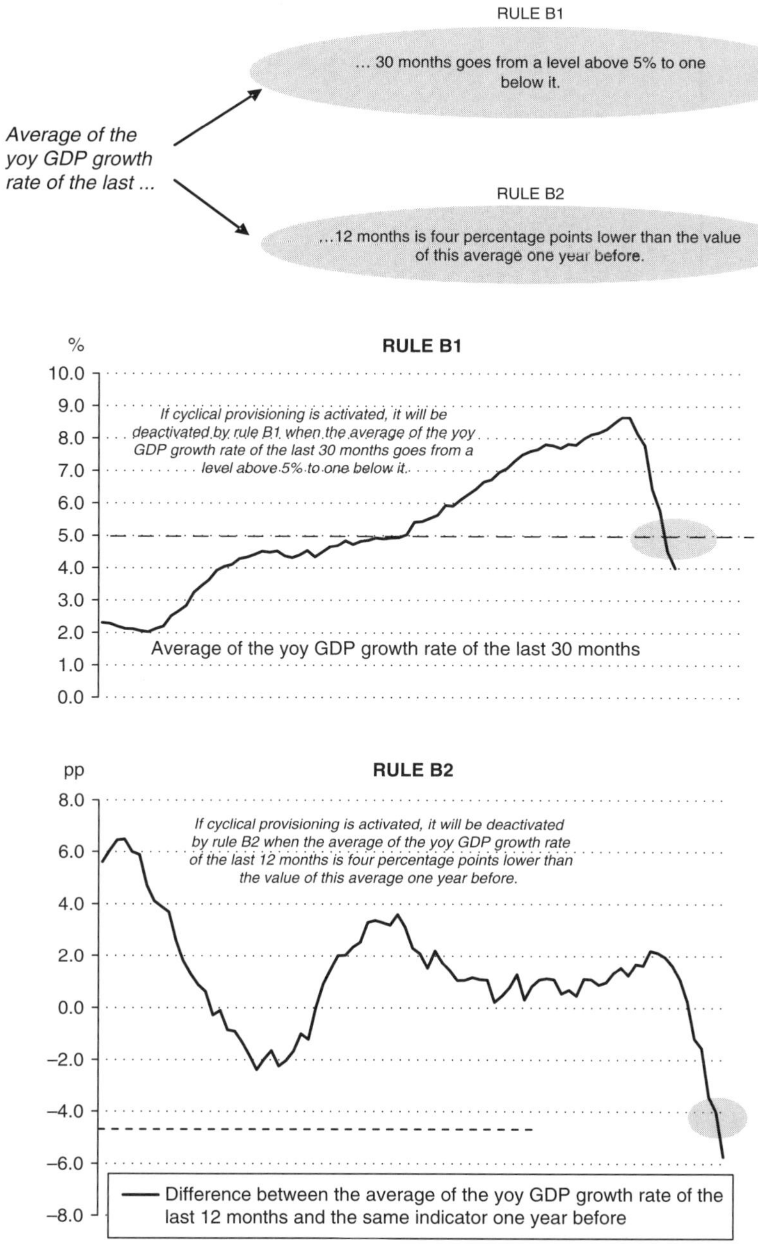

Source: SBS and authors.

Figure 4.5 Cyclical provisioning deactivation

Table 4.3 Dynamic provisioning in Spain, Peru and Colombia

	Spain	Peru	Colombia
Introduced	July 2000	November 2008 (discontinued Sep 2009)	June 2007 (commercial) June 2008 (consumption)
Based on	Rule: credit (stock and growth)	Rule: GDP	Discretion of supervisor. Credit will be taken into account (reform)
Discrete/continuous	Continuous	Discreet (on/off)	Discreet (on/off)
System vs. institutions	Institution-specific	System-based	System-based (planned change to institution-specific announced)
Thresholds	Fund limits: 10%–125%	Potential GDP (5%) as a minimum threshold. Change in GDP growth also plays a role	No
Symmetry	Yes, generic provisions can increase or decrease	Yes, procyclical provisions can increase or decrease	Use of provisions in a downturn at discretion of supervisor
Use: individual or general	General. Can smooth profits in a downturn	General. Can smooth profits in a downturn	Individual (planned change to generic in a downturn announced)
Amount	Depends on specific provisions, credit level, credit growth, and riskiness of portfolio	Depends on riskiness of portfolio	Depends on specific (individual) provisions and riskiness of portfolio
Tax deductible	Yes (1% limit)		Yes

expansion very different from the average, thus perhaps leading to a bias against smaller institutions.

Specific and generic provisions can net off. In the Spanish case, this compensation is, in principle, automatic (although there is some room for discretion). The goal is to reach a constant total provisioning effort over the cycle,[8] which could be criticized as being arbitrary, but any other objective would probably be even more arbitrary because, as explained in section 4.2, it is difficult to justify a countercyclical pattern. In the Peruvian case there is no benchmark. Banks are only required to provision more in a boom phase, without any real point of reference.

Finally, on the important issue of compatibility with international accounting standards (IAS), the Peruvian model seems even less compatible than the Spanish model. It is explicitly based on the expected loss model that, in IAS, is only used for off-balance-sheet items. The Spanish model, following its 2004 reform, has tried to achieve a higher degree of compatibility with IAS. However, IAS are expected to adopt (or at least admit) the expected loss model.[9]

One interesting proposal is that of Restoy and Roldan (2009), formulated similarly by Turner (2009), whereby a transparent distinction between regular profits and distributable profits in public financial statements should be made, which would imply that without undermining the discipline of accounting standards, the regulator could use a countercyclical tool along the cycle to smooth reserves. This proposal, however, relates to capital rather than to provisions. According to this type of proposal, accounting principles – including the provisioning model chosen by the bank – would govern, as at present, how the regular profit and loss account is prepared. Regulators would, however, set clear rules establishing which portion of income could actually be paid out as dividends. The difference between those two concepts of profit would therefore be a set of publicly reported compulsory reserves that would not interfere with the determination of the regular profit and loss account. That set could include a (through-the-cycle) reserve that would be earmarked against future losses and crafted along the lines of the Spanish dynamic provision.

4.6 CONCLUSIONS

There is ample evidence to suggest that the financial system amplifies economic cycles. The current crisis has illustrated that, even worse, this mechanism could be exacerbated by financial regulation. One key objective of the ongoing efforts toward the reform of the international financial architecture is to reduce such procyclicality, although a healthy starting point for such efforts is to assume that regulation cannot completely eliminate procyclicality.

The adoption of dynamic provisions typically pursues a double objective: (1) smoothing credit growth; and (2) allowing for the creation of reserves in good times that can serve as buffers in bad times. Experience so far suggests that when a boom reaches a certain size, the usefulness of provisions in achieving the first objective is very limited; the role of provisions from the viewpoint of achieving the second objective is much more promising.

A key challenge in designing a countercyclical mechanism is to decide whether it should be rules-based or discretionary. If the commitment of authorities lacks credibility, a rules-based mechanism would seem to be the best solution. But, this requires a very reliable *ex ante* calibration of the cycle, which is not realistic, especially taking into account the fact that the current crisis has highlighted that the usefulness of models depends, *inter alia*, on the length of the time series and quality of the data upon which they are based. It seems, therefore, more realistic to assume that any system will require ad hoc adjustments and a certain degree of discretion, as illustrated by the Spanish experience. This does not imply, however, that total discretion (as in the old Colombian system) is a superior option. One interesting comparison between the Spanish and Peruvian cases is the use of GDP versus credit as the key variable in determining the volume of provisions. In the case of EMEs, a GDP-based mechanism would accommodate financial deepening, whereas a credit-based mechanism would need to deal explicitly with this problem. GDP also has the advantage, at least in some countries, of being a leading indicator of credit. On the other hand, the drawback of using GDP is that it is neither a banking variable, nor is it a variable that provisions have a direct impact on.

One key difference between GDP and credit is that the former variable is systemic, whereas the latter is institution-specific. A systemic mechanism would be well placed to deal with systemic problems, but its implications in terms of competition and equal treatment would also need to be considered carefully. One could argue that if a regulator wants to use a systemic variable, overall credit could be used. But, it also follows that a countercyclical provisioning mechanism (based on overall credit growth) could be activated for the system as a whole as a result of one or a few institutions behaving more aggressively in their credit policies. If one agrees that this would not be acceptable, it follows that the choice of GDP cannot be based exclusively on its virtues as a systemic variable.

To what extent should dynamic provisioning systems be applied differently to industrial and emerging countries? One key requirement for such systems is the availability of good-quality data, ideally corresponding to more than one full economic cycle; this limits the possibilities in EMEs. Another requirement, especially important for EMEs, is that the system should allow for financial deepening (in other words, it should be able to differentiate, *ex ante*, between an excessive credit boom and a legitimate financial deepening process). From this point of view, GDP is superior to credit as a system variable.

The debate on whether to use provisions or capital and reserves to inject a countercyclical element into banks' behavior has received a lot of attention recently. The arguments in favor of provisions relate to their link to expected losses, whereas the arguments in favor of capital point to the fact that the latter is disconnected from profit distribution (as provisions, but not capital, can be used to distribute more dividends in a downturn). The jury is still out on this, but international consensus seems to favor the use of both mechanisms. This seems sensible given the strong forces toward procyclicality that need to be counteracted, insofar as the system does not become too complex.

Finally, any solution to the problem of procyclicality needs to maintain the equilibrium between making regulation more countercyclical and reinforcing the transparency of banks' accounting statements. It is important to keep in mind that the current crisis has been the result of procyclical financial system behavior and regulation, but also of the opaqueness of financial institutions, which implies that both aspects need to be addressed in forthcoming reforms. Reinforcing countercyclical mechanisms at the expense of transparency is not a solution.

NOTES

1. On the possible procyclicality of Basel II, see Saurina and Trucharte (2007) and Repullo and Suarez (2008).
2. See Turner (2009).
3. One way of dealing with this problem, which has been discussed in some countries, is to set up an independent body to determine the business cycle.
4. Basel III is a new global regulatory standard on bank capital adequacy and liquidity agreed by the members of the Basel Committee on Banking Supervision.
5. The tax treatment of generic provisions is important in this regard. Although institutions are free to provision above the minimum (and this can limit the use of the fund in the downturn), only 1 percent of credit (the level of the old generic provision) is tax deductible.
6. There is another regulation for consumer loans that makes generic provisions more institution-specific, forcing lenient banks to increase them if they lend to overindebted clients.
7. There is a terminology problem here, despite the fact that the three countries considered share the same language: in the Peruvian system, cyclical provisioning is referred to as 'procyclical' as new provisions are tied to changes in GDP. In Spain and Colombia (and in international discussions), cyclical provisioning is labelled 'countercyclical' as provisions contribute to smoothing the cycle.

8. See the simulations included in Fernández de Lis et al. (2001).
9. See International Financial Reporting Standards (2011).

REFERENCES

Aiyagari, S.R. and M. Gertler. 1999. Overreaction of Asset Prices in General Equilibrium. *Review of Economic Dynamics* 2(1): 3–35.

Berger, A. and G. Udell. 2004. The Institutional Memory Hypothesis and the Procyclicality of Bank Lending Behavior. *Journal of Financial Intermediation* 13: 458–495.

Brunnermeier, M., A. Crockett, C.A. Goodhart, A. Persaud and H.S. Shin. 2009. *The Fundamental Principles of Financial Regulation*. Geneva, Switzerland and London, UK: International Center for Monetary and Banking Studies and Centre for Economic Policy Research.

Caruana, J. and A. Narain. 2008. Banking on More Capital. *Finance and Development, International Monetary Fund* 45(2): 24–28.

Devenov, A. and I. Welch. 1996. Rational Herding in Financial Economics. *European Economic Review* 40(3–5): 603–615.

Fernández de Lis, S. and A. García-Herrero. 2009. The Spanish Approach: Dynamic Provisioning and Other Tools, in Central Banking: Towards a New Framework for Financial Stability. In *Towards a New Framework for Financial Stability*, edited by D. Mayes, R. Pringle and M. Taylor. London: Central Banking Publications.

Fernández de Lis, S., J. Martínez and J. Saurina. 2001. Credit Growth, Problem Loans, and Credit Risk Provisioning in Spain. In *Marrying the Macro- and Micro- Prudential Dimensions of Financial Stability: BIS Papers 1*. http://www.bis.org/publ/bppdf/bispap01.htm.

Gruss, B. and S. Sgherri. 2009. The Volatility Costs of Procyclical Lending Standards: An Assessment Using a DSG Model. International Monetary Fund (IMF) Working Paper 09/35. Washington, DC: IMF.

Haldane, A. 2009. Why Banks Failed the Stress Test. Speech given at the Marcus-Evans Conference on Stress-Testing, London, 9–10 February. http://www.bankofengland.co.uk/publications/speeches/2009/speech374.pdf.

International Financial Reporting Standards. 2011. Financial Instruments: Impairment. http://www.ifrs.org/NR/rdonlyres/2BD9895F-459F-43B8-8C4D-AFE8ACA0A9AD/0/SupplementarydocFinancialInstrumentsImpairmentJan 2011.pdf.

Jiménez, G. and J. Saurina. 2006. Credit Cycles, Credit Risk and Prudential Regulation. *International Journal for Central Banking* 2(2): 65–98.

Kiyotaki, N. and J. Moore. 1997. Credit Cycles. *Journal of Political Economy* 105(2): 211–248.

Lepetit, L., E. Nys, P. Rous and A. Tarazi. 2008. The Expansion of Services in European Banking: Implications for Loan Pricing and Interest Margins. *Journal of Banking and Finance* 32(11): 2325–2335.

Nys, E. 2008. Service Provision and Loans: Price and Risk Implications. *Revue d'Economie Politique* May. http://ssrn.com/abstract=1268802.

Rajan, R.G. 1994. Why Bank Credit Policies Fluctuate: A Theory and Some Evidence. *Quarterly Journal of Economics* 109(2): 399–441.

Repullo, R. and J. Suarez. 2008. The Procyclical Effect of Basel II. Centre For

Economic Policy Research Discussion Paper No. 6862. London: Centre For Economic Policy Research.
Restoy, F. and J.M. Roldan. 2009. Dynamic Provisioning and Accounting: Can a Consensus be Reached. *Banker*, August.
Saurina, J. and C. Trucharte. 2007. An Assessment of Basel II Procyclicality in Mortgage Portfolios. *Journal of Financial Services Research* 32(October): 81–101.
Taylor, A. and C. Goodhart. 2006. Procyclicality and Volatility in the Financial System: the Implementation of Basel II and IAS 39. In *Procyclicality and Volatility in the Financial System in Asia*, edited by S. Gerlach and P. Grunewald. London: Palgrave Macmillan.
Turner, A. 2009. *The Turner Review: A Regulatory Response to the Global Banking Crisis*. London: Financial Supervisory Agency.
Williamson, O.E. 1963. Managerial Behavior and Business Discretion. *American Economic Review* 53(5): 1032–1057.

5. Securitized products, financial regulation and systemic risk

Mariko Fujii

5.1 INTRODUCTION

It is widely believed that the practice of securitization was one of the causes of the 2007–2009 financial crisis.[1] Krugman (2007) summarizes the issue as follows:

> in the later stages of the great 2000–2005 housing boom, banks were making a lot of dubious loans . . . For a while, the risks of subprime loans were masked by the housing bubble itself . . . Yet the banks making the loans weren't stupid: they passed the buck to other people. Subprime mortgages and other risky loans were securitized.

However, it turns out that the financial institutions that held a large amount of subprime-related securitized products recorded tremendous losses. As discussed by Diamond and Rajan (2009), it is surprising that these institutions held on to so many mortgage-backed securities (MBSs) in their portfolios, given that the originators would have sensed the deterioration of the underlying quality of mortgages.

The financial statements of some banks revealed large holdings of these 'toxic' securitized products. According to Citigroup financial statements (Citigroup 2007, 2008), at the end of September 2007, the total amount of their subprime-related direct exposures in securities and banking, which comprised net collateralized debt obligation (CDO) 'super-senior' exposures and gross lending and structuring exposures, amounted to United States (US)$54.6 billion. This amount decreased to US$19.6 billion one year later; at the end of March 2009, there was still US$10.2 billion in these investments. Although Citigroup claimed that much of its holdings were in super-senior tranches, its performance was far below what was expected. UBS was another company that was heavily exposed to the risk of CDOs – which were mainly backed by subprime-related structured products – and recorded huge losses. According to the report of the Swiss Federal Banking Commission (2008), in 2007 and through the first half of 2008,

UBS (including Dillon Read Capital Management) suffered write-downs totaling approximately US$42.8 billion, of which US$21.7 billion was a result of investments in super-senior CDOs. The bank's investment in these super-senior CDOs increased in the first half of 2007 and amounted to US$50 billion before the onset of the subprime crisis.

The American International Group (AIG) was heavily exposed to underwriting credit default swaps (CDSs) on subprime-related CDOs. According to its published documents (AIG 2008), at the end of March 2008, AIG's exposure to the risk of super-senior CDSs amounted to US$469.5 billion on a notional amount basis.[2] The CDS contracts on multisector CDOs were transferred to a special purpose company called Maiden Lane III LLC, co-funded by the Federal Reserve Bank of New York, to restructure AIG's balance sheet.

Because the amounts of MBSs held seem too high to have been purely inventory, Diamond and Rajan (2009) suspect that investment in MBSs might have been part of a culture of excessive risk taking, possibly brought about by incentives for the top executives to compete with their rivals, flawed internal compensation and control systems, short-term debt financing, or a combination of these. Under an incentive scheme based on short-term risk-adjusted performance, writing insurance on infrequent events (and thereby taking on what is termed 'tail risk') and treating most of the insurance premium as income, instead of setting aside a significant fraction as a reserve for an eventual payout, is a very attractive option for asset managers. It is difficult to precisely estimate the tail risk, and, therefore, it may not be possible to fully control the situation. Further, the so-called Greenspan Put may have encouraged banks to take on the risk of illiquidity.

In the context of the Asian economy, the subprime-related direct exposures of Asian financial institutions were substantially lower than those in the US or Europe. According to Kato (2008), Asia's exposure (excluding Japan) was estimated to be in the range of US$20–30 billion as of spring 2008. He suggested that this limited exposure in Asia reflects 'profitable domestic activities' that limit the 'search for yield' elsewhere.

In this chapter, the cash flow patterns of hypothetical MBSs and CDOs will be simulated to show that these securitized products are particularly vulnerable to systematic risk and tend to show higher tail risk. These characteristics, in turn, are closely associated with joint failures and systemic risk. In order to make the financial system more stable, it is important to prevent the recurrence of the collapse of specific markets, as this may result in the collapse of other components of the financial system. Some of the financial regulations that should be applied to these problematic financial products and their relation to possible systemic risks will also be discussed in this chapter.

The remainder of the chapter is organized as follows. Section 5.2 provides a brief description of the development of the securitization and CDO markets. Section 5.3 uses simulation examples to illustrate the problematic aspects of the securitization market, focusing on CDOs backed by asset-backed securities (ABSs). Section 5.4 discusses the possibility of banning these problematic assets. As the real issue lies in the systemic nature of the securitized products, section 5.5 discusses this issue as it relates to macro-prudential regulations. Section 5.6 presents the concluding remarks.

5.2 SECURITIZATION AND GROWTH OF CDO MARKETS

Securitization offers easier access to mortgage assets for institutional investors. Direct holdings of home mortgage loans are difficult for these investors to procure because of the uncertain credit quality of the loans and problems with servicing them. The pooling of assets achieves diversification as long as the assets are not perfectly correlated. By packaging together mortgages from various regions, diversification would reduce the risks measured in terms of variance.

Furthermore, slicing the mortgage pool into different tranches according to credit quality makes them more acceptable to institutional investors; the riskiest claims against the mortgage pool could be sold to those who can tolerate high risk, while the safest, AAA-rated portions could be held by more risk-averse investors. Because of the high demand for AAA paper during the credit boom of the early 2000s, lower-quality securities, such as BBB tranches, that were issued against the initial package of mortgages were repackaged together with similar securities from other packages to create new AAA securities. These repackaged securities became CDOs. See, for example, International Monetary Fund (IMF) (2008a) for a fuller description of this process.

5.2.1 Securitization and CDO Structure

In the manner described above, structuring tranches with different levels of seniority reallocates risk across different securities. In the real world, as opposed to in a Modigliani–Miller world characterized by perfect markets, there are gains from tranching because of transaction costs, market incompleteness and asymmetric information. Tranching allows the intermediary to concentrate the default risk in one part of the capital structure, rendering a large share of the liabilities almost riskless; this, in turn, leads to mitigation of the so-called lemons problem. As shown by

DeMarzo (2005), a financial intermediary having private information on its asset values would want to sell the assets in a structured manner. According to his model, when the number of assets is large, the private information is general and the residual risks are specific, the intermediary can maximize its revenue from the sale of assets by pooling and tranching, as opposed to by simply pooling or selling the assets individually.

This practice of 'slicing' through repeated securitizations of the original pools, common prior to the 2007–2009 financial crisis, created very complicated structures of securities. The underlying difficulties in valuing these securities were not evident when the housing prices were rising and interest rates were low; these factors, in turn, kept the default rate unusually low. Once housing prices began to decline and the default rates began to rise as a result, concerns over the pricing, true value and risk of these securities became apparent.

CDOs contain many underlying assets, and modeling the pay-offs of these securities requires sophisticated cash flow models. Investors rely heavily on credit ratings in their valuation. Before the 2007–2009 crisis however, there was little public information on how these ratings were calculated and how ratings of CDO securities were related to the underlying collateral quality.[3]

5.2.2 Growth of CDO Markets and Ratings

CDOs are special-purpose vehicles that hold portfolios of assets and issue securities backed by the cash flows from those assets. The collateral assets bear credit risk and are legally sold to a special-purpose entity to ensure bankruptcy remoteness from the originator. The first CDOs were created in the 1980s, but the growth of the CDO markets did not accelerate until the early 2000s, and peaked in the first half of 2007. CDOs were regarded as 'one of the most important new financial innovations of the past decade' (Longstaff and Rajan 2008: 533). Hereafter, CDOs backed by ABS (such as subprime RMBS) are referred to as ABS CDOs; these are typically resecuritized products.

The defining feature of CDOs is their multitiered liability structure. CDOs typically issue multiple classes of financial claims with differing levels of seniority against a diversified pool of assets. As funds to make interest and principal payments are generated by the underlying collateral, proceeds are distributed to the CDO investors in a prespecified manner, that is, in order of seniority. When assets in the collateral pool miss payments or default, the subordinated tranches are the first ones to absorb the losses.

One important aspect of these structured financial product markets is the extent to which investor demand is driven by credit ratings.[4] According to IMF staff estimates (IMF 2008a), the AAA-rated senior tranche of a typical mezzanine structured-finance CDO comprised just over 75 percent of the structure before the subprime crisis. In order to create a large share of safe securities from a pool of very risky assets, various tools of credit enhancement were employed. These tools included overcollateralization and subordination, excess spread and active management of the pool.

5.3 TOXIC ASSETS: WHAT WENT WRONG WITH ABS CDOS?

Although there are no exact data available about the *ex post* loss rate of products at any moment in time, the IMF estimates suggest that, among the many structured and property-related assets, ABS CDOs exhibited the highest loss ratio during the crisis, amounting to more than 70 percent of their par value as of late 2008 in mark-to-market valuation (IMF 2008b). This was an average number for the outstanding total; the number for lower-rated tranches (for example those rated below BBB) would probably be much higher. Usually only the lower rated tranches of these CDOs are regarded as 'toxic'; however, because these products were so vulnerable to a change in the default rate in the underlying assets and other related conditions, even the most senior tranches were not really immune to systematic risks and should thus also be regarded as 'toxic'.

The typical rating process for structured products involves two stages. In the first stage, an expected loss distribution for the underlying collateral pool is estimated; in the second stage, cash flow simulations are used to determine whether a tranche can withstand the necessary level of defaults to earn a given rating. In the calculation of cash flows of residential mortgage-backed securities (RMBSs), many items indicating the quality of the underlying loans are incorporated. However, in estimating an expected loss distribution for ABS CDOs, the model basically depends on five key parameters: current ratings, maturity, location, industry and type of the underlying structured products (Securities and Exchange Commission, SEC, 2008). Using this information, important data such as default rate, recovery and asset correlation were worked out for this study. Some simplified assumptions were also made about default correlation, and the Monte Carlo simulation was used to generate the distribution of portfolio cash flow losses.

To illustrate the possible causes that led to the collapse of subprime-related RMBS CDOs, a simulation exercise of cash flows was conducted that shows the sensitivity of these flows to the various parameter values.

5.3.1 Analytical Framework and Simplified Assumptions: A Simulation Exercise

Simple models were constructed for RMBSs and CDOs, both comprising three tiers: senior, mezzanine and equity tranches. For simplicity, it was assumed that all tranches have a maturity period of five years. In the first stage, 1000 loans were collected to create an RMBS. Underlying mortgages were assumed to be homogeneous with prespecified default and recovery rates, that is, the amount received in the event of a default as a fraction of the face value, which equals (1 − loss given default (LGD)). Specifically, it was assumed that the annual default rate was 3 percent and the LGD was 50 percent; both were set to be constant over the period. A default correlation was given as a parameter, and in the base case scenario, 0.1 was assumed as the model value of asset correlation. In the second stage, ten mezzanine tranches of RMBSs were pooled to create a new ABS CDO, which was also sliced into three tiers.

To obtain the loss distribution of the cash flows of the loan pool and tranches, a standard one-factor Gaussian copula model was used.[5] In this specification, the loss distribution depends on the following parameters: default probability of underlying mortgages, asset correlation and LGD. It should be noted that this exercise only shows the loss in terms of cash flows; the interactions between loan defaults and interest rate movements are abstracted because of a simplifying assumption on cash flows.

Tranching in RMBSs was carried out so that the senior tranche had 1 percent of the expected chance of default and 10 percent of the principal was rated as equity. Thus, the remaining part was rated as the mezzanine tranche, which consisted of approximately 10 percent of the total amount of the principal in the case of the first-stage RMBSs, as approximately 80 percent of the principal was rated as a senior tranche according to the criteria described above. For the second-stage hypothetical CDO, 30 percent was rated as senior and 60 percent as mezzanine.

Given the above assumptions, Figure 5.1 illustrates the relationship between the loss distribution of the hypothetical loan pool and the correlation parameter of the underlying mortgages. If there is zero correlation, the expected rate of loss approaches the mean, which is approximately 7 percent in the five-year maturity in this model. However, if the pool assets have a higher positive correlation, the loss distributions tend to be skewed to the left with a heavier tail. It should be noted that in the CDO-like multitier structure, a rise in correlation implies more adverse effects on senior tranches rather than on subordinated tranches.

The overall risk to the financial system is based not only on the sum of the risks arising from within individual institutions, but also on the degree

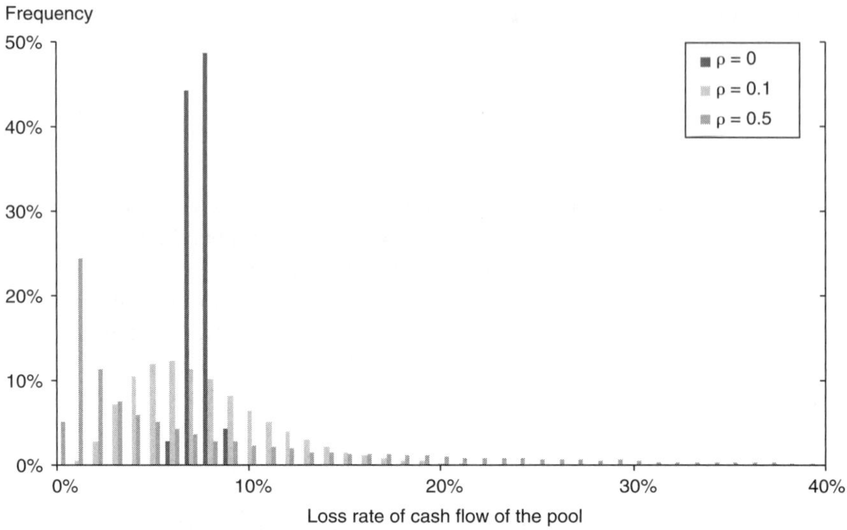

Note: Accumulated loss distributions are shown with different correlation parameter values (ρ) of 0, 0.1 and 0.5, respectively.

Source: Author's calculation.

Figure 5.1 Default correlation and the accumulated loss distribution of the pool

of correlation among the institutions' balance sheets; the higher the correlation, the higher one would expect the systemic risk to be.

5.3.2 Larger Tail Risk and Higher Sensitivity to Macro Risk in ABS CDOs

In this model, cash flows are subject to two types of risk: idiosyncratic risk and economy-wide systematic risk.[6] When the cash flows of these hypothetical RMBSs and resultant ABS CDOs were simulated, it was clearly shown that the tranches of the ABS CDOs are more vulnerable to systematic risk than those of RMBSs. There are two reasons for this. First, the quality of the underlying assets in CDOs is inferior to those in first-stage RMBSs. Note that second-stage CDOs comprise mezzanine tranches of RMBSs. Second, the size of each tranche matters; securitization is repeated and this causes the losses in that tranche to be highly sensitive to a default of any one of the underlying mortgages. Numerical results show these characteristics more clearly.

Table 5.1 shows the simulation results represented by several risk

Table 5.1 Simulation results of base cases

	Chance of default (%)	Expected loss rate (%)	Mode (loss rate) (%)	99% VaR (%)	99% ES (%)
Loan pool	100.0	7.1	6	17.8	19.5
RMBS senior	0.2	0.0	0	0.0	0.0
RMBS mezzanine	19.0	5.4	0	77.5	90.0
RMBS equity	100.0	65.2	100	100.0	100.0
CDO senior	1.3	0.7	0	20.3	63.3
CDO mezzanine	14.1	5.8	0	100.0	100.0
CDO equity	24.7	17.4	0	100.0	100.0

Note: Numbers are based on 10 000 Monte Carlo simulations.

Source: Author's calculation.

measures of each tranche of the hypothetical RMBSs and ABS CDOs. In the case of a CDO comprising mezzanine tranches of RMBSs, even a senior tranche has a higher tail risk – the risk of the event is infrequent but very damaging – as shown in the large values of 99 percent value at risk (VaR) and 99 percent expected shortfall (ES).

In the simple model employed in this chapter, the performance of the hypothetical RMBSs and CDOs is highly dependent on the quality of the underlying housing loans, specifically, the probability of default and the correlation among the loans. A higher probability of default markedly amplifies the tail risk, as shown in Table 5.2, in which the probability of default of the underlying loans was set to be 1.5 times higher than the base case, that is, 4.5 percent instead of 3 percent, annually. Similarly, Table 5.3 shows the simulation results of a higher correlation equal to 0.5, instead of 0.1 of the base case. It can be confirmed that the performance of senior tranches deteriorates greatly and there is a small positive impact on the equity tranche of RMBSs if the assumed correlation increases.

It is also possible to generate simulation results against various situations in economy-wide systematic risk, which is modeled as a latent macroeconomic variable. In the model, idiosyncratic risk is assumed to be independent given a particular value of a systematic risk. By changing the size of the systematic risk, the sensitivity of the cash flows of securitized products to the latent macroeconomic variable could be shown as a graph. The results suggest that each tranche of CDOs exhibits higher sensitivity to these changes than each tranche of RMBSs. Figures 5.2 and 5.3

Table 5.2 Sensitivity analysis of increased probability of underlying mortgages default

	Chance of default (%)	Expected loss rate (%)	Mode loss rate (%)	99% VaR (%)	99% ES (%)
Loan pool	0.0	+3.3	+2	+5.6	+6.2
RMBS senior	+3.1	+0.1	0	+4.2	+7.1
RMBS mezzanine	+28.1	+13.7	0	+22.5	+10.0
RMBS equity	0.0	+18.1	0	±0.0	+0.0
CDO senior	+7.7	+5.1	0	+79.7	+36.7
CDO mezzanine	+25.0	+15.6	0	0.0	0.0
CDO equity	+30.7	+27.3	0	0.0	0.0

Note: Default probability of the underlying mortgages is assumed to be 4.5% annually, which is 1.5 times higher than that of the base case. Numbers show changes from the base case in percentage points, based on 10 000 Monte Carlo simulations.

Source: Author's calculation.

Table 5.3 Sensitivity analysis of increased default correlation

	Chance of default (%)	Expected loss (%)	99% ES (%)
Loan pool	−5.2	+0.1	+23.7
RMBS senior	+10.4	+1.2	+28.9
RMBS mezzanine	+5.9	+11.5	+10.0
RMBS equity	−5.2	−20.0	0.0
CDO senior	+12.6	+11.4	+36.7
CDO mezzanine	+8.6	+12.2	0.0
CDO equity	+2.4	+6.8	0.0

Note: Default correlation is assumed to be 0.5, which is higher than the base case value of 0.1. Numbers show changes from the base case in percentage points, based on 10 000 Monte Carlo simulations.

Source: Author's calculation.

illustrate a contrast of these differences in the properties of the hypothetical RMBSs and ABS CDOs.

The charts clearly show that resecuritized products, such as the hypothetical ABS CDOs, have a higher sensitivity to macroeconomic risk factors (measured on the horizontal axis in the graph), and that this is also

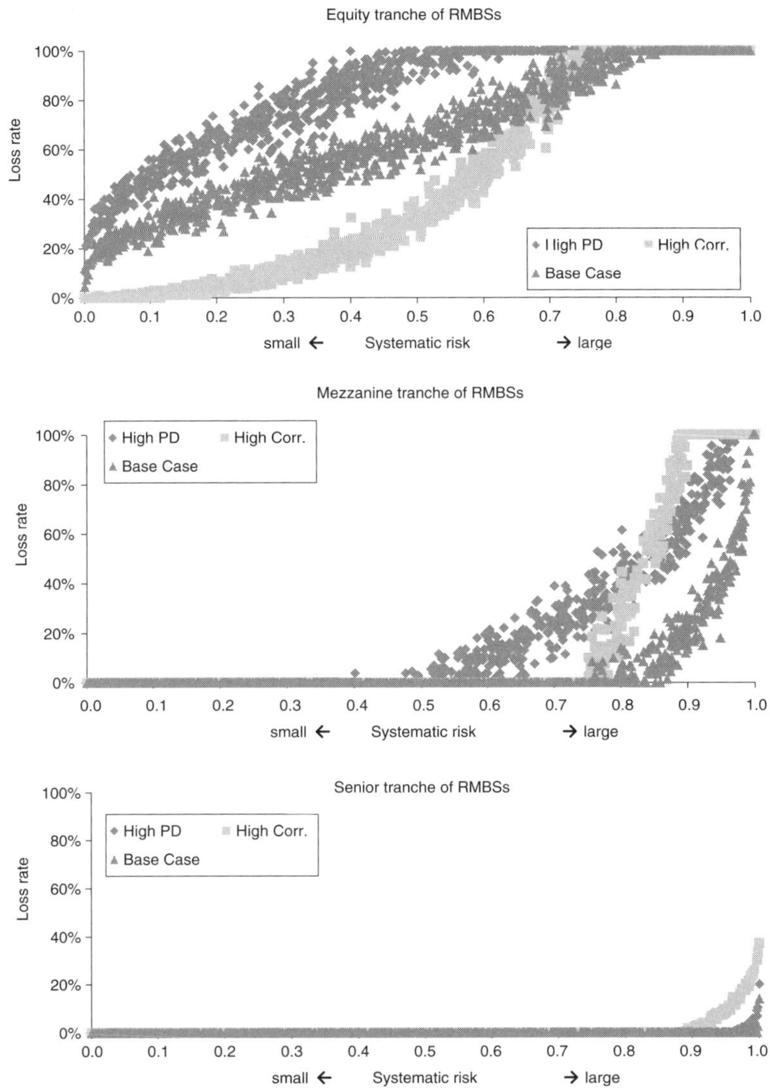

Note: Loss rates of RMBSs are shown for the cases of higher default probability of underlying mortgages (high PD), and higher default correlation (high corr.) than those of the base case. Numbers are based on 10 000 Monte Carlo simulations.

Source: Author's calculation.

Figure 5.2 Changes in systematic risk: case of RMBSs

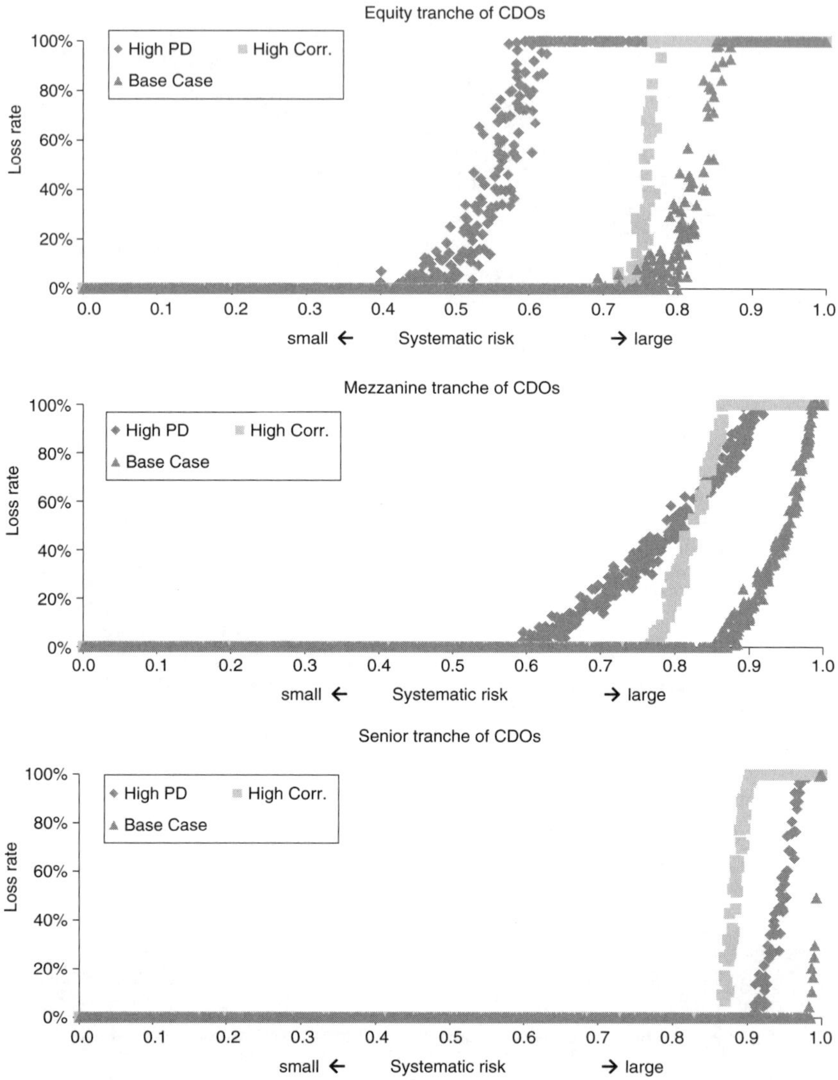

Note: Loss rates of ABS CDOs are shown for the cases of higher default probability of underlying mortgages (high PD), and higher default correlation (high corr.) than those of the base case. Numbers are based on 10 000 Monte Carlo simulations.

Source: Author's calculation.

Figure 5.3 Changes in systematic risk: case of ABS CDOs

true for their senior tranches. A high probability of default significantly reduces the level of the risk of macro factors at which the loss starts to increase sharply. Thus, once the subprime markets deteriorate and some other macroeconomic conditions affect them adversely, there should be a sharp rise in the losses in ABS CDOs. The simulation results suggest that this could lead to a collapse of the CDO market.

5.3.3 Collapse of CDO Markets

In the previous simulation examples, a latent variable representing systematic risk may correspond to the condition of the real estate markets or the level of interest rates that affect all mortgages simultaneously. In addition to this variable, a higher value of the default correlation among loans implies greater vulnerability of senior tranches, especially in ABS CDOs; there is a high probability of this characteristic of resecuritized products contributing to the collapse of the CDO market.

During the US credit boom of the early 2000s, several factors contributed to obfuscate the true risk of subprime-related CDOs. First, the housing boom and the Federal Reserve's interest rate policy lowered the default probability by providing opportunities to refinance with better terms, which also lowered the correlation among defaults. Second, the ratings of CDO tranches had been inflated on the basis of these data.

5.4 CDOS AND FINANCIAL REGULATIONS

The collapse of the CDO market was basically caused by the liability structure of resecuritization. In light of this, in February 2009, the Basel Committee on Banking Supervision at the Bank for International Settlements (BIS) decided to place a higher risk weight on these resecuritized products.[7]

However, resecuritization is only one of the factors that triggered the 2007–2009 financial crisis. The mechanism by which the collapse of one market spread rapidly to other markets and brought about a large-scale dislocation of financial markets, eventually leading to a systemic risk, should be discussed. Once the sources of systemic risk are identified, it is necessary to create institutional mechanisms that enhance safety.

The US Department of the Treasury released its report, Financial Regulatory Reform – A New Foundation: Rebuilding Financial Supervision and Regulation (US Treasury 2009), in June 2009. In its report, among other recommendations,[8] the US Treasury proposed strengthening the supervision and regulation of securitization markets through the following measures (US Department of the Treasury 2009: 13):

> (1) Federal banking agencies should promulgate regulations that require originators or sponsors to retain an economic interest in a material portion of the credit risk of securitized credit exposures.
> (2) Regulators should promulgate additional regulations to align the compensation of market participants with longer term performance of the underlying loans.
> (3) The SEC should continue its efforts to increase the transparency and standardization of securitization markets and be given clear authority to require robust reporting by issuers of asset backed securities (ABS).
> (4) The SEC should continue its efforts to strengthen the regulation of credit rating agencies, including measures to promote robust policies and procedures that manage and disclose conflicts of interest, differentiate between structured and other products, and otherwise strengthen the integrity of the ratings process.
> (5) Regulators should reduce their use of credit ratings in regulations and supervisory practices, wherever possible.

Item (3) appears to be most relevant to the discussion in this chapter.

5.4.1 Possibility of Product Regulation

Since the 1980s, financial innovations have been rapidly adopted and financial deregulation has advanced in the developed world. The implicit presumption was that these innovations improve welfare, with negligible downside risk exposure. The 'Great Moderation', namely, the fall in US business cycle volatility, further alleviated concerns about the downside risk associated with financial intermediation. This has turned out to be a misjudgment.

In hindsight, regulating specific risky products by either giving them a higher risk weight or placing them under more direct regulations seems to be possible; however, in reality it is not clear whether it is possible to regulate these products in advance because of their innovative nature.

Although the 2009 BIS annual report (BIS 2009) suggests the possibility of a registration and certification system for (newly introduced) financial products, the feasibility of such product regulation is highly doubtful. Past experiences with product regulation show that such regulation has proven to be not only ineffective because of the circumventing activities of financial institutions, but also inefficient (in that a significant amount of resources were used in checking and monitoring a variety of products).[9] Simply reversing the policy stances of the past 20 years could backfire as the needed adjustment may be overshot, creating other distortions.

The problem herewith is not confined to one particular type of financial product; it also concerns the problems arising from common exposure to a particular risk and high sensitivity to some changes in macroeconomic variables, such as interest rates and housing prices. Thus, in the next subsection, the issue will be discussed from the perspective of macroprudential regulations.

5.4.2 Securitized Products and Systemic Risk: Extensive Reporting Requirements

To address the nature of systemic risk, the aggregation of risk information is critical. CDOs are largely sold in private markets, and thus, detailed data are not publicly available. The undisclosed positions of the so-called toxic assets negatively affect the counterparty risk of financial institutions. In stressed situations, ambiguity with regard to the trading volume and relevant market information deteriorates liquidity. This fear was especially prevalent in over-the-counter trades in the early stages of the 2007–2009 financial crisis.

Against the background described above, an approach that financial regulators can adopt is to collect information about financial products, especially new and rapidly growing products, and release aggregate figures. Extensive required reporting of the marketable outstanding, size of issuance and positions should be considered. This could contribute to being cautious about the potential economy-wide risk that concerns regulators. As has already been proposed by some authorities, reporting requirements for the positions of large institutions would also be useful. The challenge lies in specifying the relevant measures of appropriate reporting items.

Aggregate data provide the basis of judgment for the soundness of a particular market. The Japanese Financial Services Agency has been releasing data on the total number of holdings of subprime-related assets by Japanese banks since November 2007. This must contribute to the elimination of an unfounded fear concerning Japanese banks associated with subprime-related losses. Although some major US banks began disclosing the positions of toxic assets in late 2007, it was unclear to what extent US banks altogether were exposed to these assets and whether the scale of capital was sufficient for these exposures.

In addition to the common exposure to particular risks and vulnerability to macroeconomic risks, the existence of complex and opaque instruments – for example, the various structured products, including securitized subprime mortgages that are difficult to value and sell – could create systemic risks, as has already been discussed.

First, the structured products present the obvious problem that evaluations of their riskiness are unlikely to be reliable. When a valuation is imprecise, it complicates not only risk management within individual institutions, but also the already difficult task of evaluating common exposures. A concentrated position or a series of counterparty relationships poses the systemic risk of joint failures if market participants and regulators fail to understand and accurately value these financial instruments.

The second systemic risk posed by such instruments is their capacity to exacerbate procyclicality. Typically, booms are characterized by financial innovations. When things are going well, firms and individuals feel confident to experiment. They create new, untested instruments that are difficult to understand and value. Investors tend to be highly optimistic about future economic conditions during a boom, without seriously considering the possible risks when markets deteriorate; further, sellers have little incentive to convince them otherwise. The result is that during a boom, flourishing financial innovation tends to create hidden, underpriced risks. However, as strains develop and the boom begins to wane, the previously unseen risks materialize, deepening the retrenchment that is already under way. Although financial innovation is a source of progress, it could become a source of procyclicality and systemic risk as well.

While the second issue is difficult to address using financial regulations, the first issue arising from the opaqueness of valuation may be improved by regulations on rating agencies and voluntary actions on the part of industry. For example, the data on CDS transactions became more extensively available after November 2008 through the Depository Trust and Clearing Corporation system, which could reduce the counterparty risk of these transactions.

5.4.3 Policy Implications for Asia

From the perspective of the benefits originally associated with securitization, it is important to develop the markets for securitization in emerging markets. With respect to securitization, the following lessons from the 2007–2009 financial crisis need to be learned. First, underlying assets should have appropriate credit quality with sufficient historical records of defaults, their relationship to macroeconomic variables and other relevant information. Second, complicated structures should be avoided as they lead to more opacity, vulnerability to macro shocks and, therefore, ambiguity in pricing. The original idea of securitization is simple: risk reduction through diversification. To the extent that large enough amounts of underlying assets are pooled, additional gain obtained from resecuritization must be limited.[10] Slicing pooled assets into too many tranches is also problematic; it makes the exact pricing of each tranche more difficult and more vulnerable to deterioration in the credit quality of the underlying assets.

To reap the benefits of securitization while minimizing risks, the Shadow Financial Regulatory Committees of Asia, Australia–New Zealand, Europe, Japan, Latin America and the US proposed that the system implemented in Denmark, which is a 'partially asset-backed' model, be followed. In the securitization system implemented in Denmark, leverage is effectively limited by capital requirements, as loans must remain on the banks' balance sheets. Covered bonds[11] offer a similar type of securitization and are popular in Europe. These bonds are characterized by essential features that are achieved under special-law-based frameworks or general-law-based frameworks with regard to the issuers' status and obligations.

In order to promote standardization and ensure transparency in securitization in emerging markets, it may be necessary to discuss the issue at a practical level. In Europe, the Directive on Undertakings for Collective Investments in Transferable Securities plays an essential role. In Asia, in order to introduce a standardized securitization framework, a mechanism to deepen the understanding of each market and discuss the future course of common factors in the basic legal framework for securitization is needed.

With regard to financial product regulations for retail investors, these investors can be safeguarded from the risk posed by a complex structure of securitization by applying more general principles of financial regulations, such as suitability and disclosure. According to a BIS report (2008b), the suitability principle is well recognized in regulatory requirements; however, there are differences in its application by sector, and probably greater differences by country, which partly stem from the fact that not all supervisors have consumer protection mandates. If an authority wishes to avoid the problems arising from overly complex products, the basic principles such as disclosure and suitability must at least aim to protect retail investors.

As discussed in the previous section, the financial debacles of 2007–2009 were more closely associated with 'sophisticated investors' and systemic risk. In this regard, the same prescriptions are applicable: timely disclosure of aggregated risk information should be prioritized.

5.5 NEED FOR MACROPRUDENTIAL REGULATIONS ON FINANCIAL INSTITUTIONS

The global nature of the 2007–2009 financial crisis highlighted the need for macroprudential regulations. Traditional prudential regulation concerns the factors that affect the stability of individual institutions, while the newly emphasized aspect of prudential regulation – macroprudential regulation – concerns the factors that affect the stability of the entire financial system.

One reason for implementing macroprudential regulations is that the presumption that regulators can safeguard the entire system by securing individual institutions is not necessarily true, as indicated by the 2007–2009 crisis. Another observation is that prior to the crisis, excessive risk taking may have raised leverage levels despite the fact that the risk-weighted capital ratios were maintained at the required regulatory level.

Financial problems that primarily stem from temporary liquidity issues could lead to solvency issues. The general understanding regarding 'insolvent' financial institutions is that the going-concern value of such institutions does not exceed the expected value of their liabilities. Under stressed market conditions, liquidity issues affect valuation and, sometimes, liquidity is highly related to the solvency of particular institutions. This is especially true if the concerned institution is highly leveraged.

This echoes the lessons learned from the 1998 experience of the hedge fund Long-Term Capital Management. When one institution holds a sufficiently large position, it can create common exposures that put the system at risk, and when transactions occur bilaterally, as they do in over-the-counter markets, the failure of one individual or institution can, through linkages across firms and markets, generate joint failures.[12]

Proposals to mitigate the risks arising from common exposures focus on the implementation of a systemic capital charge. Implementing such a scheme requires a measure of systemic risk and an understanding of the marginal contribution of each institution to the overall system. As discussed by Brunnermeier et al. (2009), the nature of the regulation applied to an individual financial institution crucially depends on how 'systemic' its activities are (with regard to its size and degree of leverage) and its interconnectedness with the rest of the system. One way to mitigate the possibility of systemic risk is for bigger or more interconnected players to hold more capital and have lower leverage; this is, in effect, taxing size to create a level playing field from a system-wide perspective. Again, the challenge lies in choosing the appropriate measures of effective size or interconnectedness.

All these concerns justify introducing some form of regulation for financial leverage, one example of which would be the non-risk-based measures suggested in the Group of Twenty statements issued in April 2009 (Group of Twenty 2009). In this regard, it should be emphasized that a change in leverage appears to be a more relevant indicator than the level of the leverage itself, as the latter differs significantly according to the business models of the different types of financial activities. A well-designed approach should be adopted with the goal of a dynamic change in leverage. Failed, merged or supported institutions, such as Bear Sterns, Lehman Brothers, Merrill Lynch, Citigroup and UBS, have shown significant increases in their gross leverage ratios from the early 2000s to 2007. Although this measure by itself is obviously not enough to monitor the soundness of the financial activities of each institution, it seems to provide some additional information about their risk profiles.

In a complicated financial system, it is unrealistic to expect that one specific measure, such as a risk-weighted capital ratio, could detect any risk of financial fragility. A mix of several measures focusing on the soundness of the system is needed to cover all types of financial institutions. Even the example of leverage described above suggests the usefulness of additional complementary measures in gauging the riskiness of institutions, although further research is required to choose the most appropriate and feasible measure for efficient implementation.

A macroprudential policy generally refers to the policy tools that are confined to financial regulations and that do not include monetary policy; specifically, tools used to control the capital adequacy ratio, growth of loan extensions and restrictions on an institution's portfolio. For a national economy, credit growth may be controlled against the historical averages, and/or relative to the gross domestic product. In this regard, the figures used to measure the aggregate leverage of domestic banks should be carefully monitored to detect signs of systemic risk.

For example, in Ireland, the leverage ratios of the aggregate major banking sector increased from 11.9 in 2000 to 21.6 in 2008 as the boom accelerated. The ratio of the major banks' total assets to nominal gross domestic product also rose from 1.8 times to 5.35 times between 2000 and 2008.[13] Because the current Irish financial crisis was basically brought about by a classical bust of its property bubble and not by a new innovative product such as CDOs, these leverage figures may be useful in examining the typical bubble–bust type of crisis. It is not clear whether this could be applied to the US case where the types of financial institutions are more diverse.

It is important to note that one of the most pressing tasks is the proper consolidation of the balance sheets of financial institutions. The 2007–2009 financial crisis clearly exposed the risks created by the shadow banking system that was spun off by regulated institutions. Therefore, the first order of business in improving capital management is to bring all of these entities, including structural investment vehicles and the like, within the regulatory framework to ensure that appropriate capital is held against all the obligations of financial institutions. This will provide a more accurate picture of an institution's exposures.

5.6 CONCLUDING REMARKS

A healthy financial system is a precondition for sustained recovery. Ensuring financial stability requires the redesigning of financial sector policies. For regulatory and supervisory policies, it is necessary to adopt a macroprudential perspective to mitigate systemic risks.

Systemic risks are inherent to financial systems: specifically, financial products, financial institutions and markets. Regulators must pay attention to various aspects of the financial system, and act to identify, measure and mitigate problems to guard against future crises. In this regard, reporting requirements should cover not only financial products but also institutions, funds and markets. Addressing risk in only one area will not ensure the safety of the others. Therefore, direct regulations, such as product regulation, may not be sufficient or effective. Extensive reporting requirements, especially from those systemically important institutions, should be urgently introduced with close consultation between the regulatory authorities and these financial institutions.

It is worth considering the introduction of complementary measures in addition to the BIS risk-based capital adequacy ratio. Leverage ratios of individual institutions and similar measures at a national level may serve to detect signs of a boom and, thus, of the accompanying systemic risk.

For Asian financial authorities, it is important to learn from the risk management and regulatory failures in the US and Europe. The introduction of Basel II recommendations in several Asian countries will enhance the financial resilience in Asia to some extent and, furthermore, tools corresponding to macroprudential concerns could be used to reinforce financial stability in the region.

NOTES

1. Nadauld and Sherlund (2009) provide some empirical evidence for this relationship.
2. This is the net figure held by AIG Financial Products.
3. See, for example, Securities and Exchange Commission (SEC) (2008). Bank for International Settlements (BIS) (2008a) also describes CDO markets from 2005 to 2007 in detail.
4. Benmelech and Dlugosz (2009) discussed the ratings of CDOs and related issues, focusing on collateralized loan obligations.
5. For more information on the use of the copula approach to describe default correla-

tion, see Li (2000). Details of the model used in this chapter are described in Fujii and Takemoto (2009).

6. In the one-factor Gaussian copula model, conditional independence is assumed.
7. CDO structures, particularly their AAA tranches, are partly driven by investor demand, which is closely related to rating-dependent regulation. The relatively common view held is that an extensive use of credit ratings in the regulation of financial institutions created a natural clientele for CDO securities, especially for highly rated securities. The reliance on the ratings in evaluating financial risks should be reviewed by both individual institutions and regulatory authorities.
8. The following were also proposed: 'All advisers to hedge funds (and other private pools of capital, including private equity funds and venture capital funds) whose assets under management exceed some modest threshold should be required to register with the SEC under the Investment Advisers Act. The advisers should be required to report information on the funds they manage that is sufficient to assess whether any fund poses a threat to financial stability' (US Department of the Treasury 2009: 12).
9. For example, in Japan, there were extensive and tight regulations on financial products and other detailed decisions made by commercial banks until the late 1990s; however, these regulations could not prevent the creation of a bubble.
10. See Fujii and Takemoto (2009).
11. Covered bonds are debt instruments secured by a cover pool of mortgage loans to which investors have a preferential claim in the event of default. Legal requirements specify the safe nature of covered bonds.
12. Procyclicality – which implies that over time, the dynamics of the financial system and of the real economy reinforce each other, thus increasing the amplitude of booms and busts and undermining stability in both the financial sector and the real economy – is another key issue in macroprudential policy.
13. Author's calculation based on the statistics in Central Bank and Financial Services Authority of Ireland (2009).

REFERENCES

American International Group, Inc. (AIG). 2008. Conference Call Credit Presentation. Financial Results for the Quarter Ended June 30, 2008. New York: AIG.

Bank for International Settlements (BIS). Basel Committee on Banking Supervision, Joint Forum. 2008a. *Credit Risk Transfer: Developments from 2005 to 2007.* Basel: BIS.

Bank for International Settlements (BIS). 2008b. Customer Suitability in the Retail Sale of Financial Products and Services. Basel: BIS.

Bank for International Settlements (BIS). 2009. *79th Annual Report.* Basel: BIS.

Benmelech, E. and J. Dlugosz. 2009. The Alchemy of CDO Credit Ratings. NBER Working Paper 14878. Cambridge, MA: NBER.

Brunnermeier, M., A. Crockett, C. Goodhart, A.D. Persaud and H. Shin. 2009. *The Fundamental Principles of Financial Regulation, Geneva Reports on the World Economy 11.* Geneva: International Center for Monetary and Banking Studies and Centre for Economic Policy Research.

Central Bank and Financial Services Authority of Ireland. 2009. *Quarterly Bulletin* 02(April).

Citigroup. 2007. Schedule of Sub-prime Related Direct Exposures in Securities and Banking, Third Quarter Summary. New York: Citigroup.

Citigroup. 2008. Schedule of Sub-prime Related Direct Exposures in Securities and Banking, Third Quarter Summary. New York: Citigroup
DeMarzo, P. 2005. The Pooling and Tranching of Securities: A Model of Informed Intermediation. *Review of Financial Studies* 18(1): 1–35.
Diamond, D. and R. Rajan. 2009. The Credit Crisis: Conjectures about Causes and Remedies. NBER Working Papers 14739. Cambridge, MA: NBER.
Fujii, M. and R. Takemoto. 2009. Securitization and Financial Crisis: Risk Characteristics and Assessment of ABS CDO (in Japanese, Shokenka to Kinnyukiki: ABS CDO no Risuku Tokusei to Sono Hyouka). *FSA Research Review* 5: 215–245.
Group of Twenty. 2009. Declaration on Delivering Resources Through the International Financial Institutions. London, 2 April. http://www.g20.org/Documents/Fin_Deps_IFI_Annex_Draft_02_04_09_-1615_Clean.pdf.
International Monetary Fund (IMF). 2008a. *Global Financial Stability Report, April*. Washington, DC: IMF.
International Monetary Fund (IMF). 2008b. *Global Financial Stability Report, October*. Washington, DC: IMF.
Kato, T. 2008. The Financial Crisis and Economic Outlook – Lessons for Securing the Benefits of Financial Deepening. Keynote address at the 43rd SEACEN Governors' Conference, Jakarta, 21 March.
Krugman, P. 2007. Just Say AAA. *New York Times*. 2 July.
Li, D.X. 2000. On Default Correlation: A Copula Function Approach. *Journal of Fixed Income* 9: 43–54.
Longstaff, F. and A. Rajan. 2008. An Empirical Analysis of the Pricing of Collateralized Debt Obligations. *Journal of Finance* 63(2): 529–563.
Nadauld, T. and S. Sherlund. 2009. The Role of the Securitization Process in the Expansion of Subprime Credit. Fisher College of Business Working Paper 2009-9. Columbus, OH: Ohio State University.
Securities and Exchange Commission (SEC). 2008. Summary Report of Issues Identified in the Commission Staff's Examinations of Select Credit Rating Agencies. July. http://www.sec.gov/news/studies/2008/craexamination070808.pdf.
Swiss Federal Banking Commission. 2008. Subprime Crisis: SFBC Investigation Into the Causes of the Write-downs of UBS AG. http://www.finma.ch/archiv/ebk/e/publik/medienmit/20081016/ubs-subprime-bericht-ebk-e.pdf.
US Department of the Treasury. 2009. *Financial Regulatory Reform – A New Foundation: Rebuilding Financial Supervision and Regulation*. Washington, DC: US Treasury.

6. Liberalization and regulation of capital flows: lessons for emerging market economies

Rakesh Mohan and Muneesh Kapur

6.1 INTRODUCTION

Since the early 1990s, there has been a large trend increase in the volume of private capital flows to and from emerging market economies (EMEs). This increase can be attributed to EMEs' growing degree of financial openness, the perception of continuing strong growth prospects, increasing productivity, growth in the overall profitability of firms, positive interest differentials in favor of these economies and, sometimes, the expectation of continuing currency appreciation. However, capital flows are not necessarily the outcome of domestic developments alone in recipient countries; they also reflect the role of push factors emanating from source countries. The stance of monetary policy and the state of financial markets in major advanced economies have led to the emergence of comparatively low interest rates and overall low returns in these economies, giving rise to the search for yields. These factors again came to the fore in 2010 following unprecedented quantitative easing by the central banks in major advanced economies and the likelihood of such policies being pursued for an extended period of time. With near zero interest rates in these countries likely to continue into 2011, EMEs are attracting large capital flows. The consequent rapid appreciation of exchange rates has generated concerns over potential 'currency wars', with a number of EMEs resorting to capital controls. Issues related to capital flows and their management have, therefore, re-emerged as a key concern for EMEs.

The traditional pattern of capital flows to EMEs has been the result of the need to finance current account deficits. However, during recent years, even as capital flows to EMEs have increased manyfold, current account balances, in aggregate, have actually moved from modest deficits to substantial surpluses. These surpluses have led to increasing foreign reserves in these countries. The external financing constraint that existed until the 1990s is now no longer an issue for most EMEs. Large capital flows emerged as a problem of plenty during 2003–2007 for major EMEs, creating significant new challenges for macroeconomic management and financial stability.

Boom periods in capital flows have been frequently followed by periods of reversal of these flows resulting from both push and pull factors (Committee on the Global Financial System, CGFS, 2009). Such large swings in capital flows in a short period typically give rise to serious challenges for macroeconomic management and often impose serious costs on the real economy. Capital flows that are well above their financing requirements are a relatively new phenomenon for EMEs. If such unrequited flows are not managed actively and appropriately, they can be associated with real exchange rate misalignment, credit and asset price booms, inflationary pressures, overheating and financial imbalances culminating in a financial crisis and capital outflows. Real appreciations, not depreciations, generally worry policymakers the most outside crisis periods (Obstfeld 2009; Grenville 2008). Since the 1980s, about 15 percent of the episodes of large capital inflows have ended in crisis (Schadler 2008). Thus, in order to insulate their economies from undue volatility, most EMEs actively manage their capital accounts to varying degrees, while also intervening in foreign exchange markets accompanied by sterilization. This policy response has been the norm among EMEs, despite much advice to the contrary.

Against this backdrop, this chapter undertakes a critical review of lessons for the capital account management of EMEs. Section 6.2 assesses the theoretical and empirical literature on the benefits of capital account liberalization on growth; section 6.3 discusses lessons for the sequencing of capital account liberalization; section 6.4 reviews country experiences in regard to the management of large capital flows; section 6.5 describes the impact of the global financial crisis on Asian emerging markets; and section 6.6 assesses the efficacy of capital controls. Concluding observations and key lessons are set out in section 6.7.

6.2 CAPITAL FLOWS TO EMES: THEORETICAL PERSPECTIVES AND EMPIRICAL EVIDENCE

6.2.1 Theoretical Debate

There has been a very active, contentious and continuous academic debate on the benefits of capital account liberalization in terms of economic performance. In principle, the free flow of capital across borders should lead to a more efficient allocation of resources between savers and investors across the world. Capital should flow from countries with abundant capital (and low returns) to capital-scarce countries (with higher risk-adjusted returns), and this, along with technical know-how, should increase growth in recipient countries. The availability of external capital should also help smooth consumption and investment in response to exogenous shocks. Thus, one should expect capital account liberalization to be associated with higher growth and lower volatility in consumption and investment.

Whereas there is widespread agreement among economists about the desirability of open trade in goods, there is much disagreement with respect to the virtues of financial openness. Even strong proponents of free trade, such as Bhagwati (1998), have expressed considerable doubts about the gains to be had from unfettered trade in assets. In his recent comprehensive review of capital account liberalization, Obstfeld (2009: 71) noted that: 'concrete evidence of gains from financial globalization – at least gains of the type traditionally claimed on the basis of simple economic theory – has proved hard to document in any definitive way'. Thus, although a good portion of mainstream economists continue to support a broad opening of the capital account, many – including Bhagwati (1998), Rodrik (1998), Cooper (1999), Stiglitz (2003), Obstfeld (2009) and Rodrik and Subramanian (2009) – have expressed reservations. Much of this thinking was induced by the Asian financial crisis of 1997–1998, and the global financial crisis will no doubt give rise to further questioning of the merits of financial globalization. What is also of interest is that a review of actual policies followed shows that full capital account opening has been viewed with caution by almost all Asian EMEs.

The theoretical benefits expected from financial globalization are predicated on the assumption that, with the opening of the capital account, resources will flow from developed, capital-abundant economies to less-developed, capital-scarce economies. Capital should then flow toward activities exhibiting higher returns and higher productivity. As EMEs move toward the global production possibilities frontier, they should show higher productivity, higher profitability and higher growth. The recent experience of Asian economies has been the opposite: their saving rates have exceeded their investment rates, so resources have been flowing in the 'reverse' direction. In such situations, traditional gains expected from a full opening of the capital account in terms of greater investment and growth are clearly absent. In the presence of relatively high investment rates, it is difficult to argue that such benefits would have accrued if the exchange rate had adjusted enough to create a current account deficit, leading to absorption of capital flows, from which all the expected benefits would then follow. The evidence relating to the increase in two-way flows does, however, suggest that there could be some microeconomic gains to market participants through improved access to global capital markets, as long as the authorities can manage the macroeconomic effects of such excess flows.

6.2.2 Empirical Evidence

Empirical evidence does not seem to support the theoretical propositions of the expected benefits of opening the capital account (CGFS 2009). Prasad et al. (2007) found a positive correlation between current account balances and growth among non-industrial countries – a reduced reliance on foreign capital is associated with higher growth. This result could be attributed to the fact that even successful developing countries have a limited absorptive capacity for foreign resources, either because their financial markets are underdeveloped or because their economies are prone to overvaluation resulting from rapid capital inflows. In a similar vein, Rodrik and Subramanian (2009) argue that developing economies are more likely to be constrained by investment opportunities than by the availability of savings. In such circumstances, foreign finance can often aggravate existing investment constraints by appreciating the real exchange rate and reducing profitability and investment opportunities in the traded goods sector, resulting in adverse long-run growth consequences. Given the existence of relatively high levels of investment and growth in Asian economies, even this argument is difficult to sustain.

In view of the failure to find empirical evidence of the beneficial effects of capital account liberalization on growth, some have argued that the benefits of financial globalization may be indirect. 'Collateral' benefits of financial opening could be in the form of better financial sector development, institutions, governance and macroeconomic stability, which then help growth prospects. Such indirect effects are likely to be far more important than any direct impact via capital accumulation or portfolio diversification (Kose et al. 2009). According to Kose et al. (2009), the indirect benefits of financial opening could collectively show in productivity growth. However, it is difficult to understand how there could be positive effects on productivity growth without corresponding positive effects on overall growth.

The indirect benefits are not straightforward, however; they are dependent upon certain 'threshold' levels of financial and institutional development. The thresholds are lower for foreign direct investment (FDI) and portfolio equity liabilities than for debt liabilities (Kose et al. 2009a). There is an important issue of causality here: is it the opening up of the capital account that leads to indirect benefits, or is it the gradual development of domestic financial markets that allows the benefits of subsequent opening of the capital account to be reaped? A coordinated and calibrated approach to movement in financial market and sector development, combined with a gradual opening up of the capital account, might be expected to lead to higher growth in an environment of macroeconomic and financial stability. As such, unless the strengthening of local financial institutions and improvements in macroeconomic policies are in place, the liberalization of capital flows can entail dangers.

Henry (2007) argues that the empirical methodology of most existing studies is flawed because these studies look for permanent effects of capital account liberalization on growth, whereas the neo-classical growth model posits only a temporary impact on the growth rate. Once such a distinction is recognized, opening the capital account within a given country is found to generate economically large and statistically significant effects, not only on economic growth, but also on the cost of capital and investment. The beneficial impact, however, is discernible only from the liberalization of equity flows. The free movement of debt flows is not found to be associated with any positive impact on growth. Instead, the liberalization of debt flows – particularly short-term, foreign-currency-denominated debt flows – may cause problems. On the other hand, empirical evidence indicates that countries derive substantial benefits from opening their equity markets to foreign investors (Henry 2007). FDI and portfolio liabilities boost productivity growth, whereas debt liabilities have a negative impact (Kose et al. 2009b). However, as Kose et al. (2009c) argue, the significant positive impact of equity market liberalization on growth could be masking the impact of other supportive reforms because equity market liberalization typically takes place only when governments are sure that supportive conditions are in place.

Large volatility in sudden and substantial exchange rate movements constitutes an important channel through which capital flows can potentially have an adverse impact on the domestic economy. The impact of exchange rate changes on the real sector is significantly different for currency of invoicing countries than for other countries. For reserve currency countries, which specialize in technology-intensive products, the degree of exchange rate pass-through is low, enabling exporters and importers to ignore temporary shocks and set stable product prices despite large currency fluctuations. Moreover, mature and well-developed financial markets in these countries help to absorb the risk associated with exchange rate fluctuations with negligible spillover to real activity. On the other hand, for the majority of developing countries that specialize in labor-intensive and low and intermediate-technology products, profit margins in the intensely competitive markets for these products are very thin and vulnerable to the pricing power of large retail chains. Consequently, exchange rate volatility has significant employment, output and distributional consequences (Mohan 2004; Aghion et al. 2009).

In the context of substantially large capital flows to EMEs from 2003 to 2007, it is generally argued that deep financial markets would be helpful for channeling such capital flows efficiently. The merit of such an argument is subject to doubt in light of recent experience. If capital flows reach levels as high as 10 percent of GDP or more per annum, as they did for some countries during 2007, it is arguable whether even a highly advanced financial system could have intermediated such capital flows efficiently and in a stable manner. For such a large volume of capital flows to be fully absorbed, an equivalent current account deficit, a large real appreciation or any combination thereof would be the immediate consequence. These outcomes would in turn be manifested in asset price and credit booms and financial imbalances. All these options are clearly unsustainable and can lead to future fragility, as revealed by the developments in some Asian economies during the Asian financial crisis of 1997–1998 and in Eastern European nations and Baltic States in the recent global financial crisis.

On balance, an assessment of the available empirical literature suggests that full capital account liberalization does not in itself lead to higher growth in EMEs. Instead, it can impart avoidable volatility and have an adverse impact on EME growth prospects. A majority of historical crises have been preceded by financial liberalization. Since 1800, if not before, surges in capital inflows have often preceded external debt crises at the country, regional and global levels (Reinhart and Rogoff 2008). Available evidence is strongly in favor of a calibrated and well-sequenced approach to the opening of the capital account and its active management by authorities, along with complementary reforms in other sectors and the taking into account of country-specific features (Mohan 2007a; CGFS 2009; Obstfeld 2009; Grenville 2008).

6.3 CAPITAL ACCOUNT LIBERALIZATION: SEQUENCING

There is a broad consensus about the appropriate sequencing of the opening of the capital account among economists and practitioners (Obstfeld 2009; Kim and Yang 2008; Yu 2008; among others). FDI flows should be the first to be liberalized because they are among the most stable flows and also provide enhanced management and technical know-how. Next to be liberalized should be portfolio equity inflows.

Greater caution is needed in the liberalization of debt flows. Most studies have found that debt flows have an adverse impact on growth, especially in economies with underdeveloped financial markets. However, even if the domestic financial markets in EMEs were well developed, it is not apparent that a fully free regime in regard to debt flows would be stabilizing. Given the relatively higher growth rates, as well as higher inflation rates in EMEs, interest rate differentials favor EMEs. Such growth- and inflation-induced interest rate differentials are likely to continue. During periods of low interest rates and yields in advanced economies – the source countries for capital flows – a freer regime could potentially lead to large volumes of capital inflows to EMEs, which could reverse as monetary policy becomes normalized in advanced economies. This can impart large volatility to capital flows and induce macroeconomic and financial instability. As Grenville (2008) noted, capital inflows reflect an ongoing structural disequilibrium: foreign capital will be attracted by the higher returns and the prospect of currency appreciation. In such an environment, the exchange rate will be poorly anchored by fundamentals, thereby threatening the stability of the financial system. With the intensification of capital inflows and the consequent exchange rate appreciation, even greater inflows will take place in the short term, putting more upward pressure on the real exchange rate. With this overshooting of the exchange rate, the trade and current account deficits will eventually begin to rise, leading to a subsequent fall in international confidence and a consequent sudden reversal of capital flows. Thus, as long as interest rate differentials favor EMEs on a structural and sustained basis, a more cautious approach to liberalization of debt flows, especially short term, is warranted. In particular, investments by foreigners in government securities should be subject to some ceilings to avoid excessive arbitrage-led flows.

Regarding debt flows, *ceteris paribus*, the policy preference could be in favor of local-currency-denominated liabilities relative to foreign-currency-denominated liabilities. In terms of the various categories of resident entities, there may be merit in more stringent prudential restrictions on the access of financial intermediaries, especially banks, to external finance relative to corporates. Whereas the failure of a non-financial corporate entity does not have any systemic implications, bank failures do result in substantial systemic consequences. The adverse implications for financial stability of the boom-and-bust pattern associated with capital inflows are created and exacerbated by the banking system. In boom periods, excess liquidity generated by capital inflows, if not sterilized effectively by the central bank, can lead to a relaxation of lending standards, and generate credit and investment booms and financial imbalances. Thus, a liberal regime in regard to banks' access to foreign capital can be destabilizing and lead to huge fiscal costs. A related issue is foreign ownership of domestic banks. A larger presence of foreign banks can increase the vulnerability of the domestic economy to foreign shocks. Significant liquidity and capital shocks to the parent foreign bank can force it to scale down its operations in the domestic economy, even as the fundamentals of the domestic economy remain robust.

Regarding the liberalization of outflows, restrictions can be relaxed for corporate entities, institutional investors and individuals – in that order. The difficulty is that during periods of rising capital inflows resulting from the perception of higher financial returns in EMEs, including arbitrage flows, the liberalization of outflows can actually result in even greater net inflows. Domestic residents tend not to take advantage of the diversification opportunity offered in the light of higher expected returns domestically. Speculative inflows are strengthened by the increased confidence in repatriating these flows. Thus, it is important to liberalize outflows carefully, in terms of both timing and the categories of outflows.

6.4 MANAGING LARGE CAPITAL INFLOWS

Most EMEs, including Asian EMEs, have used a judicious menu of options in trying to modulate the volume of net capital inflows, manage currency volatility, intervene in the market and sterilize interventions, while simultaneously going ahead with structural reforms. Increasing the flexibility of the exchange rate as the only tool to manage capital inflows is likely to be ineffective, even though it is desirable in and of itself. Major Asian EMEs have continued with the gradual and calibrated liberalization of capital outflows, while retaining restrictions on some categories of inflows, along with greater exchange rate flexibility.

In December 2006, Thailand imposed unremunerated reserve requirements on fixed income flows – the only country in the Asian region to do so. These requirements were withdrawn in March 2008 as foreign capital flows moderated. Unremunerated reserve requirements on portfolio equity flows were also imposed in December 2006, but were immediately withdrawn as a consequence of the immediate and extremely adverse market reaction. In India, access norms to external commercial borrowing were tightened in August 2007 in the wake of heavy inflows, but were relaxed in 2008 following the onset of the global financial crisis. Interest rate ceilings on non-resident deposits with the banking system were reduced during 2006–2007 to moderate inflows and were raised again in 2008, when inflows had reversed. In April 2007, foreign banks in the Republic of Korea (hereafter Korea) were advised not to respond to strong arbitrage incentives to swap United States dollars for Korean won. Limits on lending in foreign currency to Korean firms were also reimposed. The non-taxable amount that foreign bank branches can borrow from their parent companies was reduced from six times capital to three times capital (the 'thin capitalization rule'), starting in January 2008. The use of foreign exchange loans by banks was limited to real demand (that is, for financing imports and real investment), beginning in August 2007. McCauley (2008) found that these restrictions on capital flows were effective in the case of Korea, the People's Republic of China (PRC) and Thailand.

India and the PRC raised cash reserve ratios (CRRs) from 2004 to mid-2008 to moderate the expansionary impact of large capital inflows on domestic monetary and credit aggregates and prevent overheating (Mohan 2008a). The increases in these ratios were rolled back in late 2008 and early 2009 as capital flows reversed. The domestic banking systems of these two countries were thus largely insulated from both the large influx and the subsequent reversal of capital flows. CRRs provided these central banks with a liquidity 'cushion' that could be released when the banks faced greater funding difficulties in October and November 2008. Banks could be given back their own liquidity, and there was thus no need for any dilution of collateral to be accepted by the central banks to inject liquidity into the system. In Indonesia, Malaysia and the Philippines, reserve requirements were cut in the aftermath of the global financial crisis and capital flow reversals to provide the banking system with adequate liquidity. Central banks in the PRC and Korea also issued their own bills to sterilize capital inflows, while India introduced (in 2004) an innovation in the form of the Market Stabilisation Scheme for sterilization.

To absorb enduring surplus liquidity, a policy choice exists between the central bank issuing its own securities and the government issuing additional securities purely for sterilization purposes. A large number of countries, such as Chile, the PRC, Colombia, Indonesia, Korea, Malaysia, Peru, the Philippines, Russia, Sri Lanka, Thailand and Taipei,China, have issued central bank securities. However, central banks in some of these countries have faced deterioration in their balance sheets. As such, there is merit in issuing sterilization bonds on a government account. Moreover, in cases where an already well-established government debt market exists, the issuance of new central bank bills or bonds of overlapping maturity could cause considerable confusion and possible market segmentation. Such confusion could obfuscate the yield curve, reduce the liquidity of the instruments and make monetary operations that much more difficult.

In India, the Market Stabilisation Scheme has considerably strengthened the Reserve Bank of India's ability to conduct capital account and monetary management operations (Mohan 2008b). Apart from using monetary policy instruments such as policy rates and the CRR, in 2005–2007 India also tightened prudential norms (for example risk weights and provisioning norms) for certain sectors such as real estate and stock markets, in which relatively high credit growth was being witnessed. The prudential norms were rolled back in late 2008 in the face of the global financial crisis.

Such an approach to financial regulation helps to throw sand in the wheels of sectors witnessing high growth, possibly fueled by the availability of abundant liquidity arising from excess capital flows, and helps to foster financial stability. The integrated approach combining monetary and prudential instruments used in India was facilitated by the fact that both monetary policy and financial regulation responsibilities are entrusted to a single agency: the Reserve Bank of India (Mohan 2007b, 2009). It is also important to strengthen financial regulation to avoid regulatory arbitrage. Thus, in India, the regulatory regime with regard to non-banking financial institutions has been gradually tightened since 2004 so that weaknesses do not emerge in sectors that are poorly regulated. This use of prudential measures suggests that the management of capital inflows can also be done through such an approach, in addition to the more conventional use of sterilization instruments. In the case of India in 2007–2008, almost all possible instruments were used in the face of exceptional excess capital inflows, amounting to almost 10 percent of gross domestic product (GDP), which can now be seen as an outlier in the world.

The issue of capital controls has taken center stage in the aftermath of the global financial crisis. Capital flows to EMEs plummeted in 2008 and the first quarter of 2009 due to massive deleveraging by financial market participants in advanced economies and extreme risk aversion. Since the second quarter of 2009, capital flows to EMEs have resumed, gathering momentum in 2010. This reflects both pull and push factors, including near zero interest rates in the United States and other major advanced economies, ultra accommodative policy in these advanced economies (and promises to pursue this type of policy for an extended period), search for yield, and the growing recognition that EMEs have weathered the crisis well and the fundamentals in these economies remain robust. In view of the large volume of capital inflows and their adverse impact on exchange rates, countries have again started imposing controls on capital flows to ensure domestic stability. The most notable of these was the imposition by Brazil of a Tobin-like financial transaction tax of 2 percent on all capital inflows (except FDI flows) in October 2009.[1] The tax rate was increased in two stages to 6 percent in October 2010. In November 2009, Taipei,China barred foreign investors from parking their money in time deposits after bringing funds into the country. Foreign investors are not allowed to extend the deposit maturity beyond three months. In

June 2010, Korea undertook macroprudential measures to curb excessive volatility of capital flows through ceilings on foreign exchange derivatives, positions of banks, regulations on foreign currency bank loans and prudential regulations for improving the foreign exchange soundness of financial institutions. In October 2010, Thailand reintroduced a withholding tax of 15 percent on interest and capital gains by foreign investors on Thai bonds. In addition, measures were undertaken to liberalize capital outflows.

Lord Adair Turner, chairman of the Financial Services Authority in the United Kingdom, has spoken in favor of Tobin-type taxes. Former British prime minister Gordon Brown argued for a global financial levy – such as a tax on transactions or an insurance fee – to build up a resolution fund as a buffer against future bailouts. Although these proposals have not been mooted from the perspective of capital controls, they are akin to putting sand in the wheels of global finance.

6.5 GLOBAL FINANCIAL CRISIS AND ITS IMPACT ON ASIAN EMES

All the economies in the Asian region witnessed a significant slowdown in late 2008 and 2009 because of the global financial crisis. The downturn in growth that occurred in the wake of the global financial crisis can largely be attributed to external causes. This is in contrast with the Asian financial crisis of 1997–1998, when internal weaknesses – large current account deficits, exchange rate misalignments, external sector vulnerability, and weaknesses in corporate and financial sector balance sheets – led to the currency and banking crisis, culminating in severe output losses and an overall crisis of confidence. In response to the lessons of the Asian crisis, the external and financial sectors of the major Asian EMEs have seen significant strengthening. Policies encompassing enhanced exchange rate flexibility and current account surpluses, in conjunction with a cautious approach to full capital account opening and an accumulation of foreign exchange reserves, have characterized the overall macro and monetary management of these economies in the period prior to the current crisis. Large foreign exchange reserves have acted as effective buffers in the face of reversals in capital flows.

This time, the domestic financial sectors of Asian EMEs did not exacerbate the crisis in these economies, unlike those of advanced economies. In general, the banking sectors of Asian economies have been strengthened considerably: capital adequacy ratios are above the international norm and non-performing loans have witnessed a significant decline from their

Table 6.1 Liquidity ratios in banks in Asian EMEs (end 2008) (%)

Country	Loans to domestic deposits	Loans to total liabilities	Foreign liabilities to domestic deposits
China, People's Rep. of	0.69	0.68	0.01
Hong Kong, China	0.50	0.28	0.78
India	0.82	0.79	0.07
Indonesia	0.80	0.75	0.07
Korea, Rep. of	1.36	1.05	0.30
Malaysia	0.96	0.86	0.11
Philippines	0.78	0.69	0.14
Singapore	0.85	0.51	0.66
Taipei,China	0.77	0.71	0.08
Thailand	0.98	0.94	0.04
Viet Nam	0.98	0.91	0.07

Sources: Asian Development Bank (2009); Reserve Bank of India (2009).

post-Asian crisis levels. Direct exposures of Asian EMEs to subprime assets were negligible. Corporate balance sheets are also reported to have been robust. These features provided a certain degree of resilience to these economies. Nonetheless, as the governments of major advanced economies and emerging economies in other regions proceeded to enhance their coverage of deposit insurance and guarantees of other bank liabilities in the face of faltering public confidence in the banking systems, many governments in the region, with the exception of India and the PRC, were also forced to extend similar sorts of guarantees and insurance.

Another factor that minimized the adverse impact of the global financial turmoil on Asian EMEs is that banks in the region rely more on domestic funding to finance their domestic loans than on international sources of funding. The ratio of loans to domestic deposits is typically less than one in most of Asia (Table 6.1). A ratio of less than one indicates that domestic deposits are sufficient to fund the banking system's loans and, therefore, that problems in global financial markets will not have any direct impact on domestic lending. A ratio above one suggests a reliance on foreign sources of funding. In such cases, a global credit crunch could cause liquidity problems for banks. The only major Asian country in which the loan-to-deposit ratio is high enough to cause some concern is Korea, which indeed experienced some financial instability, especially evident in the foreign exchange markets. A further factor indicating Korea's greater vulnerability during the crisis was its exceptionally open capital account (Asian Development Bank 2009).

6.6 CAPITAL CONTROLS AND EFFICACY

Despite the widespread and relatively successful practice of active capital account management by many EMEs, particularly those in Asia, some economists continue to question its efficacy. It is argued that capital controls are ineffective, except over a short time horizon, and that capital controls are often leaky with potential capital flows even showing up as current account flows or as permissible capital flows. For instance, an International Monetary Fund (IMF) working paper (Cardarelli et al. 2009) observed that episodes of large capital inflows are often associated with real exchange rate appreciation, deteriorating current account balances and a significant drop in subsequent growth. It concluded that resisting nominal exchange rate appreciation through sterilization is likely to be ineffective when the influx of capital flows is persistent, and tightening capital controls has not, in general, been associated with better outcomes. Instead, the paper suggests that keeping expenditure growth steady is helpful for limiting currency appreciation and fostering better growth.

These findings deserve some comment. First, it is not clear what is meant by 'persistent' flows. It is not possible in real time to determine with certainty whether capital inflows are permanent or temporary. With hindsight, it is possible to conclude that the unprecedented surge in capital inflows to EMEs during 2003–2007, especially in 2007, was not permanent, although at the time it was considered by many commentators to be so. Many policymakers, on the other hand, appear to have treated the capital flows boom as temporary, uncertain and subject to reversal by intervening in the markets.

Second, the case for fiscal restraint is based on the assumption that it will contain aggregate demand and hence reduce interest rates. Therefore, fiscal restraint may be useful if capital inflows are made up entirely of debt flows looking for interest rate arbitrage. Even then, however, fiscal prudence may turn out to be ineffective if private demand replaces government demand in the economy such that aggregate demand is unchanged. If the surge in capital inflows reflects push factors (for example low interest rates and yields in advanced economies), it is not clear whether fiscal restraint would be of much help. Fiscal policy decision making is subject to long decision lags, while capital flows are highly volatile. By the time fiscal contraction is implemented, capital inflow surges may have given way to outflows, and the policy response may be destabilizing (Kim and Yang 2008).

Third, the IMF paper discussed the hazards of preventing nominal appreciation, but in practice, major EMEs have permitted growing flexibility in the nominal exchange rate. The relevance of the IMF paper's observations is, therefore, questionable given the present circumstances in Asian countries.

Finally, most studies are handicapped by the use of binary or similar indices to capture capital controls. Furthermore, information on such measures is available on an annual basis, whereas policy actions are taken more continuously and also undergo intrayear fluctuations. Existing measures of cross-country differences are crude and misleading in many cases, often leading to incorrect conclusions. Available measures of capital controls on inflows, therefore, may not successfully capture the nuances of policy measures and their level of efficacy.

In regard to firm-based micro studies reaching the conclusion that capital controls hurt corporates, this should be true by definition: such controls, if effective, would indeed raise the cost of financing for affected firms. The key issue, however, is not the micro impact, but the macro impact. Capital controls tend to moderate the influx of foreign capital so that domestic macroeconomic and financial stability can be maintained. Thus, while individual firms may be hurt by controls, the economy may reap benefits at the aggregate level, which are rather harder to capture. As Rodrik and Subramanian (2009: 126–127) point out, studies based on individual firms:

> cannot address the counterfactual question of what would have happened to aggregate investment in the absence of the controls, especially once the induced real exchange rate changes are factored in. It is entirely possible for aggregate investment to be higher in the equilibrium with restricted capital mobility (and therefore a more competitive real exchange rate) than in the equilibrium with full capital mobility, even though some firms are in effect facing higher costs of finance in the latter equilibrium.

It is also often argued that financial market development can enable firms to minimize the adverse impact of volatility in exchange rates through hedging. Whereas this may indeed benefit individual firms, the macroeconomy can still suffer because hedging transfers the risk to other domestic players only if it is mostly done in domestic financial markets (Grenville 2008).

The quasi-fiscal and other costs of sterilization are likely to be outweighed by benefits from the maintenance of domestic macroeconomic and financial stability. With hindsight, the large build-up of foreign exchange reserves by the major EMEs since 1998 (and especially since 2003) appears to have been a useful first line of defense in the current episode of reversal of capital flows.

A prolonged period of large-scale intervention, as the sole policy response to managing a large and growing volume of capital inflows, can create expectations of future exchange rate appreciation and runs the risk of creating distortions in the local financial system. There are, however, good grounds for believing that such dangers can be reduced when foreign exchange intervention is combined with allowing currency flexibility over a medium-term perspective in conjunction with continuous development and strengthening of the domestic financial sector.

The IMF, which hitherto was not in favor of capital controls, now seems to see some role for them: 'Recognizing that capital inflows can be very large and partly transitory, depending on circumstances, macro-prudential policies aimed at limiting the emergence of new asset price bubbles, some buildup of reserves, and some capital controls on inflows can be part of the appropriate response' (IMF 2010: 5).

To sum up, modulating the volume of capital inflows, through active capital account management, can at least reduce the amplitudes of the various economic variables in both the upswing and downswing of the capital flows cycle, while also contributing to domestic stability. Authorities need to respond symmetrically and keep their options open when managing the volatility in capital flows and any subsequent consequences to the domestic economy. If capital flows are found to be persistent and unidirectional over a long time period, policies will have to respond to such a development. If such persistent flows are not deemed to be disruptive, there is little need for intervention. In principle, the objective of capital account management is to manage the departures from fundamentals that such flows may entail. Flows are 'persistent' or 'permanent' only if they are responding to economic fundamentals. The fact that capital account management can be leaky has to be recognized. When excess flows exist, they are the result of perceived potential gains to be reaped from such flows. It is then axiomatic that both residents and non-residents will attempt to circumvent any attempts to curb the flow, including through current account transactions.

6.7 CONCLUDING OBSERVATIONS

A good deal of discussion on the management of capital accounts and foreign exchange intervention has been influenced by the concept of the open economy trilemma, that is, that no country can simultaneously enjoy free capital mobility, operate a fixed exchange rate, and practice independent monetary policy directed at managing domestic objectives. Most Asian countries have actually managed to overcome this open economy trilemma successfully since the crisis of the 1990s. Although they have operated managed exchange rates, they have also allowed increased flexibility (that is, their exchange rates no longer exhibit rigidity). Similarly, although many Asian countries have actively managed their capital accounts, they have been neither totally open nor totally closed at any time. This middle ground of managed but flexible exchange rates and managed but mostly open capital accounts has enabled Asian EMEs to operate independent monetary policies despite high volatility in external capital flows during the post-Asian crisis period. By and large, Asian countries have been able to set their own policy interest rates even in the presence of persistent interest rate differentials with advanced countries. The practice of adequate sterilization has been successful in preventing the unwarranted growth of base money and other monetary aggregates in the face of rising foreign exchange reserves. Hence, they have also been successful in containing inflation.

Capital account management can be made more effective by the appropriate use of prudential regulation, given that it is financial sector weaknesses that ultimately cause financial crises. Some countries have, therefore, used prudential regulatory measures to limit the intermediation of foreign inflows through domestic banks and financial institutions (Reddy 2009). Restrictions on the use of capital flows in speculative activities, such as real estate, can also be helpful. Thus, capital account management and prudent regulation of the financial sector go hand in hand, and countries following such an approach can minimize the adverse impact of exogenous shocks.

The flow of capital between nations, in principle, brings benefits to both capital-importing and capital-exporting countries. But the historical evidence, reinforced by the current global financial crisis, shows that it can also create new exposures and bring new risks. The failure to analyze and understand such risks, excessive haste in liberalizing the capital account, and inadequate prudential buffers to cope with the greater volatility in more market-based forms of capital allocation have at one time or another compromised financial or monetary stability in many EMEs. On the other hand, rigidities in capital account management can also lead to difficulties in macroeconomic and monetary management. Although theory has much to say on the conditions desirable for an end state equilibrium, it has little guidance to offer on the sequencing of capital account liberalization.

Overall, as the CGFS (2009) concludes, it is a combination of sound macroeconomic policies, prudent debt management, exchange rate flexibility, effective management of the capital account, accumulation of appropriate levels of reserves as self insurance, purposive use of prudential regulation, and development of resilient domestic financial markets that provide the optimal response to the large and volatile capital flows to

EMEs. Individual countries have used different combinations of measures from time to time. If the pressure of excess flows is very high, as it was in India in 2007, it becomes necessary to use almost all the possible measures available. Thus, how these elements can be best combined will depend on the country and on the context: there is no 'one size fits all' solution.

Such a discretionary approach does put great premium on the skill of policymakers in finance ministries and central banks. It also runs the risk of markets perceiving central bank actions as uncomfortably unpredictable. If the actions of the authorities result in the virtuous circle of high growth, low inflation, and financial stability (as has been the case in many Asian countries in recent years), however, such an approach has much to commend it.

NOTE

1. Brazil had earlier imposed a tax of 0.38 percent on fixed income flows, which was raised to 1.5 percent in March 2008. The tax was removed in October 2008 as the global financial crisis intensified. In the latest move (in October 2009), the tax net was widened to include portfolio equity inflows.

REFERENCES

Aghion, P., P. Bacchetta, R. Ranciere and K. Rogoff. 2009. Exchange Rate Volatility and Productivity Growth: The Role of Financial Development. *Journal of Monetary Economics* 56: 494–513.

Asian Development Bank. 2009. *Asian Development Outlook 2009*. Manila: ADB.

Bhagwati, J. 1998. The Capital Myth: The Difference between Trade in Widgets and Dollars. *Foreign Affairs* 77(May–June): 7–12.

Cardarelli, R., S. Elekdag and M.A. Kose. 2009. Capital Inflows: Macroeconomic Implications and Policy Responses. IMF Working Paper WP/09/40. Washington, DC: IMF.

Committee on the Global Financial System (CGFS). 2009. Capital Flows and Emerging Market Economies. CGFS Papers No. 33. Basel: Bank for International Settlements.

Cooper, R.N. 1999. Should Capital Controls be Banished? *Brookings Papers on Economic Activity* 1: 89–141.

Grenville, S. 2008. Central Banks and Capital Flows. ADBI Discussion Paper 87. Tokyo: ADBI.

Henry, P.B. 2007. Capital Account Liberalization: Theory, Evidence and Speculation. *Journal of Economic Literature* 45(December): 887–935.

International Monetary Fund (IMF). 2010. World Economic Outlook Update, January. Washington, DC: IMF.

Kim, S. and D.Y. Yang. 2008. Managing Capital Flows: The Case of the Republic of Korea. ADBI Discussion Paper 88. Tokyo: ADBI.

Kose, M.A., E.S. Prasad and A.D. Taylor. 2009a. Thresholds in the Process of International Financial Integration. National Bureau of Economic Research Working Paper 14916. Cambridge, MA: National Bureau of Economic Research.

Kose, M.A., E.S. Prasad and M.E. Terrones. 2009b. Does Openness to International Financial Flows Raise Productivity Growth? *Journal of International Money and Finance* 28(4): 554–580.

Kose, M.A., E.S. Prasad, K. Rogoff and S.J. Wei. 2009c. Financial Globalization: A Reappraisal. *International Monetary Fund Staff Papers* 56(1): 8–62.

McCauley, R.N. 2008. Managing Recent Hot Money Inflows in Asia. ADBI Discussion Paper 99. Tokyo: ADBI.

Mohan, R. 2004. Challenges to Monetary Policy in a Globalising Context. *Reserve Bank of India Bulletin* January: 81–102. And in *Monetary Policy in a Globalised World: A Practitioner's View*, by R. Mohan. New Delhi: Oxford University Press.

Mohan, R. 2007a. Capital Account Liberalisation and Conduct of Monetary Policy: The Indian Experience. *Reserve Bank of India Bulletin* July: 1129–1154.

Mohan, R. 2007b. India's Financial Sector Reforms: Fostering Growth While Containing Risk. *Reserve Bank of India Bulletin* December: 2199–2226.

Mohan, R. 2008a. Capital Flows to India. *Reserve Bank of India Bulletin* December: 2047–2079.

Mohan, R. 2008b. The Role of Fiscal and Monetary Policies in Sustaining Growth with Stability in India. *Asian Economic Policy Review* 3: 209–236.

Mohan, R. 2009. Emerging Contours of Financial Regulation: Challenges and Dynamics. *Reserve Bank of India Bulletin* June: 949–65.

Obstfeld, M. 2009. International Finance and Growth in Developing Countries: What Have We Learned? *International Monetary Fund Staff Papers* 56(1): 63–111.

Prasad, E.S., R.G. Rajan and A. Subramanian. 2007. Foreign Capital and Economic Growth. *Brookings Papers on Economic Activity* 1: 153–230.

Reddy, Y.V. 2009. India and the Global Financial Crisis: Managing Money and Finance. New Delhi: Orient BlackSwan.

Reinhart, C.M. and K.S. Rogoff. 2008. This Time is Different: A Panoramic View of Eight Centuries of Financial Crises. National Bureau of Economic Research Working Paper 13882. Cambridge, MA: National Bureau of Economic Research.

Reserve Bank of India. 2009. *Handbook of Statistics on the Indian Economy 2008–09*. Mumbai: Reserve Bank of India.

Rodrik, D. 1998. Who Needs Capital-Account Convertibility? In *Should the IMF Pursue Capital Account Convertibility?*, edited by S. Fisher, R. Cooper, R. Dornbusch, P. Garber, C. Massad, J. Polack, D. Rodrik and S. Tarapore. Princeton Essays in International Finance 207. Princeton, NJ: Princeton University.

Rodrik, D. and A. Subramanian. 2009. Why Did Financial Globalization Disappoint? *International Monetary Fund Staff Papers* 56(1): 112–138.

Schadler, S. 2008. Managing Large Capital Inflows: Taking Stock of International Experiences. ADBI Discussion Paper 97. Tokyo: ADBI.

Stiglitz, J.E. 2003. *Globalization and its Discontents*. New York: Norton.

Yu, Y. 2008. Managing Capital Flows: The Case of the People's Republic of China. ADBI Discussion Paper 96. Tokyo: ADBI.

PART II

Regional Financial Monitoring and Coordination

7. The financial crisis: a wake-up call for strengthening regional monitoring of financial markets and regional coordination of financial sector policies?

Adalbert Winkler[1]

7.1 INTRODUCTION

This chapter analyzes the recent experience with regional monitoring and coordination of financial regulation as a way of improving overall regulatory performance, increasing the attractiveness of regional financial markets and mitigating the risk of crisis. The focus is on the integration of financial markets and the associated strengthening of regional monitoring and coordination in Asia and Europe, as it has been argued that the current crisis reveals the need for deeper financial integration in both regions.[2]

The chapter is structured as follows. Sections 7.2 and 7.3 review developments in financial integration and regulation in Europe and Asia up to the 2007 financial crisis.[3] The implications of the crisis for financial integration and regulation are the focus of section 7.4. Section 7.5 offers some tentative conclusions for policy.

The main conclusions are that financial integration is not only, and not even primarily, a function of regulatory and supervisory convergence. Rather, it is a function of progress in overall economic integration, that is, in the integration of goods, services and labor markets, as well as monetary integration. The lack of economic and monetary integration represents an important barrier to increasing the attractiveness of Asian financial markets to investors, both within and from outside the region. Thus, the crisis is a wake-up call for further progress on monetary integration in Asia along the lines of the reformed Chiang Mai Initiative. In Europe, where economic, monetary and financial integration are much more advanced, the crisis reveals the need to establish a sustainable regulatory and supervisory structure that properly defines and reflects the responsibilities of regional and national authorities in crisis management, including its fiscal dimension.

7.2 REGIONAL FINANCIAL INTEGRATION AND REGULATION: THE PRE-2007 CRISIS EUROPEAN EXPERIENCE

7.2.1 Drivers of European Integration: From Trade via Money to Finance

Trade and money have been the main forces driving European economic integration. By 1968, the European Union (EU) was already operating as a customs union. Monetary union became an issue of European integration in the late 1960s, when the deficiencies of the Bretton Woods System threatened exchange rate stability in Europe. By contrast, finance played only a minor role in the first 30 years of the integration process. Indeed, several EU member states continued to apply capital account restrictions until the early 1990s. This changed with the single European market project, which included – as one of the four freedoms – the complete liberalization of capital movements across EU countries.

The free movement of capital exposed Europe to the 'inconsistent quartet' problem, which holds that countries cannot simultaneously pursue autonomous monetary policy, free trade, fixed exchange rates and open capital accounts (Padoa-Schioppa 1995).[4] The introduction of the common currency solved this problem by abolishing the monetary policy autonomy of eurozone countries. It also provided a further boost for efforts toward financial integration. In March 2000, the Lisbon European Council endorsed the Financial Services Action Plan, which consisted of 42 measures to achieve a single wholesale financial market and to establish an open and secure retail market by strengthening the rules on prudential supervision (Richards 2003). The introduction of the euro caused a decline in currency mismatches in the financial sectors of eurozone countries, as the currency of denomination of foreign claims and liabilities among eurozone countries became the domestic one by definition. Moreover, the share of foreign liabilities denominated in domestic currency as a percentage of total foreign liabilities recorded a substantial increase. This was most pronounced in those eurozone countries with legacy currencies that had been barely used in international transactions before 1999.

Overall, financial integration among eurozone countries advanced rapidly before the financial crisis (ECB 2009). In particular, wholesale money markets became much more integrated. Cross-country holdings of long-term debt among eurozone countries increased as well, while corporate and sovereign bond spreads narrowed substantially. There is also evidence that country-based diversification strategies with regard to equities lost importance compared to sector-based strategies, indicating integration and a reduction in home bias. Moreover, cross-border holdings of shares within the eurozone increased. By contrast, cross-border lending on the retail level remained at low levels, albeit doubling between 1999 and 2007. Cross-country dispersion of bank interest rates to the non-financial private sector showed no tendency of decline either, which may reflect cross-country differences in credit risk, taxation, regulation, supervision and consumer protection.

European financial integration has been characterized by strong and persistent cross-country divergences in the development of total foreign assets and liabilities as a share of gross domestic product (GDP). While all countries have seen substantial increases, Luxembourg and Ireland show by far the most, reflecting their status as international financial centers and their comparatively small GDPs. Luxembourg and Ireland have also recorded the most rapid increase in financial development, measured by capital market size.[5] Since the early 1990s, this indicator of financial depth has doubled in Greece, Spain, Italy and the Netherlands, while the United Kingdom and Sweden came close to reaching this mark. By contrast, financial development was more subdued in Germany, France, Finland and Belgium.

7.2.2 Institutional Financial Integration between the New EU Member States (as well as EU Candidate and Potential Candidate Countries) and the EU-15[6]

Financial integration between the EU-15 and the new member states (and EU candidate and potential candidate countries) has been advancing rapidly, albeit in a different form than among the EU-15 countries. Integration, measured by standard quantity and price-based indicators, is still low, and in some areas is significantly lower than within the EU-15 (Baltzer et al. 2008). At the same time, institutional integration has reached an unprecedented level due to the massive entry of EU-15 banks into Central and Eastern European (CEE) and Southeastern European (SEE) countries.[7] By the end of 2007, EU-15 banks had become major players in several CEE and SEE countries (European Central Bank, ECB, 2006). In turn, the banking sectors of the respective EU-15 countries have become heavily exposed to these CEE and SEE countries in their total foreign activities (Árvai et al. 2009).

EU-15 banks entered the region after a series of banking and currency

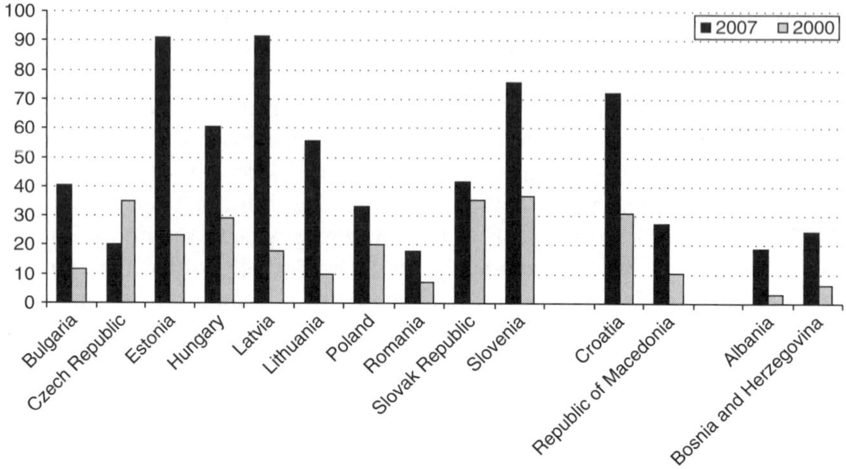

Sources: European Bank for Reconstruction and Development Structural Change Indicators database, http://www.ebrd.com/downloads/research/economics/macrodata/sci.xls (accessed 17 June 2009), author's own calculations.

Figure 7.1 Private sector credit (as % of GDP) in CEE and SEE countries, 2000 versus 2007

crises hit CEE and SEE countries in the 1990s. By opening their banking sectors to foreign players, these countries aimed to put domestic financial development on a more stable and sound institutional footing (Mehl et al. 2006). However, it also fostered financial integration with the EU-15 by facilitating and expanding cross-border flows. Moreover, via the close relationship between subsidiaries and their respective parent banks, CEE and SEE countries seemed to have secured access to international liquidity in times of crisis, including indirect access to the relevant international lender of last resort (LOLR), the ECB (Winkler 2009). From a financial stability perspective this is a crucial feature of European financial integration, as financial development in CEE and SEE countries has been characterized by substantial currency mismatches due to a high share of euro-denominated loans and deposits in domestic banking sectors (ECB 2007b).

Institutional financial integration has been highly conducive to financial deepening in CEE and SEE countries, as well as financial integration with European and global financial markets. Standard indicators, like the private sector credit to GDP ratio (Figure 7.1), saw substantial growth over the period 2000–2007. Cross-country asset holdings (the sum of foreign assets and liabilities, as a percentage of GDP) by CEE and SEE countries also rose substantially during this period. Moreover, countries have continued to open their financial systems *de jure*, following the requirements laid down in the *acquis communautaire*.[8]

7.2.3 Rising Current Account Imbalances in Europe

Persistent and steadily rising current account imbalances within Europe have been another characteristic of European financial integration over the last decade. Often overlooked due to the focus on global imbalances, strong capital flows to CEE and SEE countries fostered financial deepening that supported investment and consumption. The domestic demand-led growth process was reflected in increasingly negative current account balances. By contrast, the Benelux countries, Finland and – since 2001 – Austria and Germany have been recording persistent and rising current account surpluses. Thus, European financial integration has been associated with capital flowing from rich to poor countries (Abiad et al. 2007; Herrmann and Winkler 2008; Fabrizio et al. 2009).

7.2.4 Regional Coordination and Monitoring

With European financial integration advancing rapidly, the need for strengthening coordination, cooperation and regional monitoring was increasingly recognized. The so-called Lamfalussy process (Lamfalussy 2001) – that is, establishing special procedures and committees to ensure an EU-wide coordination of national policies and institutions in the field of financial sector regulation and supervision – is the main instrument for securing a level playing field as well as financial stability. It reflects the traditional principles of market building within the EU and aims at squaring (1) the principles of subsidiarity, harmonization and mutual recognition with (2) the political will to leave financial regulation and supervision in the hands of national authorities and (3) the rising degree of European financial integration.

Most assessments of the Lamfalussy process come to the conclusion that progress has been slow. Complexity has made decision making a difficult task (Hardy 2009; de Larosière 2009; Vives 2009). However, the main challenge to achieving the stated goal of regulatory and supervisory convergence seems to be substance. There is no agreed and shared benchmark to guide regulatory and supervisory convergence (Trichet 2007). This constitutes a major difference from monetary integration, which reflects a consensus on the proper goals and conduct of monetary policy that was established by the early 1990s.

Regional monitoring, coordination and decision making on financial regulation are also affected by fiscal issues. In crises, governments may have to intervene to stabilize the financial system by putting the taxpayers' money at risk, in the form of either guarantees or equity (de Larosière 2009; Brunnermeier et al. 2009). This fiscal dimension of financial regulation and supervision is not covered at the EU level, implying that decisions taken by majority vote are unlikely to be implemented in all countries. It also makes unattractive the alternative to the Lamfalussy process (raised in the report itself) – namely, the option of establishing a European supervisory agency with regulatory powers for a unified European financial market – as long as there is no EU fiscal policy, or at least a significant expansion of EU resources (Brunnermeier et al. 2009).

The difficulties in achieving regulatory and supervisory convergence are further aggravated by two asymmetries in European financial integration. The first asymmetry is caused by EU countries operating international financial centers whose global competitive advantage stems, in part, from differences in taxation, regulation and supervision, enabling regulatory arbitrage (de Larosière 2009). For these center countries – that is, Ireland, Luxembourg and the United Kingdom – harmonization of regulation, supervision and taxation may undermine their competitiveness.

The second asymmetry is a result of the integration process between the EU-15 and the new EU member states. Subsidiaries of EU-wide operating banking groups have attained the status of systemically relevant institutions in their respective host countries. By contrast, their parent banks may not have the same status vis-à-vis their respective home-country supervisory agencies. Moreover, the individual subsidiaries may provide only a small contribution to the consolidated balance sheet of the group supervised by the home country. In such cases, consolidated supervision in the home country may not properly respond to potential financial stability risks in the host countries (European Shadow Financial Regulatory Committee 2004). Given the possible fiscal and monetary policy implications for host countries if such risks were to materialize, host-country supervisors have been claiming a stronger role in the supervision of parent banks' subsidiaries via a series of bilateral memoranda of understanding with home-country supervisors. A more integrated supervisory approach was made contingent on the existence of an integrated budget, deposit insurance and – for non-eurozone members facing the risk of international illiquidity due to currency mismatches – emergency liquidity assistance on the full spectrum of instruments developed for national financial systems to deal with crisis situations (Bednarski and Starnowski 2007).

7.3 REGIONAL FINANCIAL INTEGRATION AND REGULATION: THE PRE-2007 CRISIS ASIAN EXPERIENCE

7.3.1 The Asian Financial Crisis of 1997–1998 as a Driver of Official Efforts to Foster Financial Integration

Economic integration in Asia has been largely market-driven. It has neither the institutional underpinnings characteristic of European integration, nor the explicit political goal of establishing an economic community or union. Since the late 1990s, however, there have been official efforts to foster financial integration. The main impetus for this undertaking has been the financial crisis of 1997–1998 (Plummer 2006). First, the crisis was caused by a shortage of international liquidity following the sudden stop of capital flows, with Asian banking systems being substantially engaged in maturity transformation based on the United States (US) dollar (Chang and Velasco 2000). Second, the crisis reflected structural and institutional weaknesses of largely bank-based financial systems (Llewellyn 2002).

The Chiang Mai Initiative, enacted by the Association of Southeast Asian Nations (ASEAN)+3 countries[9] in 2000, has been the most prominent multilateral response to the currency mismatch problem of international financial integration (Mayes 2008). Given that the European approach – that is, monetary union and the introduction of an internationally accepted regional currency – was out of reach, the ASEAN+3 countries opted in favor of a network of bilateral swap and repurchase arrangements, under which they would provide each other with international liquidity assistance in times of need. While no Asian country is in a position to create US dollars (the main international currency used in the region) and thus cannot perform the role of an international LOLR, the network allows for the reallocation of existing US dollar assets held by authorities in the region according to need. However, by choosing a bilateral format, the original initiative lacked efficiency and coherence. Moreover, no regional surveillance mechanisms were installed. Thus, countries that would be in a position to provide liquidity had no means of regularly assessing the solvency of countries with a potential liquidity need in times of crisis. Finally, the arrangements were regarded as too small to provide a cushion in the case of severe turmoil.

The main response to the 1997–1998 crisis was of a unilateral nature, in the form of a massive build-up of foreign exchange reserves (Choi et al. 2007). With abundant foreign exchange reserves, countries hoped to counter sudden stops and capital flow reversals on their own by providing international (that is, US dollar) liquidity to domestic financial institutions and markets when needed (Obstfeld et al. 2008).

The Asian Bond Markets Initiative represents a multilateral response to the argument that the 1997–1998 financial crisis was caused by structural weaknesses in the financial sector, in particular the dominance of weak banks with poor governance. Those banks had been channeling funds to international financial centers, from where they were rechanneled to the region, causing the maturity and currency mismatch problems that triggered the crisis (Yoshida 2009). Thus, the initiative aims to foster the development of capital markets in the region, most importantly the development of regional bond markets trading securities denominated in local currency.

7.3.2 Financial Development and Integration in Post-Crisis Asia

Financial development in Asia has been stable over the last decade. Private sector credit issued by deposit money banks – as a share of GDP – was stagnant or even declined in several countries. Only Viet Nam and Cambodia followed the example of emerging Europe in showing strong growth in private sector credit. Bond market capitalization has remained, on average, at about the same level seen in 1999, while the stock exchanges of some countries have been recording substantial gains in market capitalization.

Quantity-based indicators of financial integration reveal that intra-regional cross-border holdings of financial assets – that is, portfolio investment and bank lending – have been growing slowly and remain at a low level (Cowen and Salgado 2006). Institutional integration via the entry of foreign banks has been limited. While the share of foreign-owned banks in total banking sector assets has been increasing in several Asian economies, almost nowhere have foreign-owned banks gained a similar dominance as in emerging Europe. Finally, progress in the convergence of regulation and supervision has been slow and limited.

7.3.3 Hurdles to Financial Integration in Asia

The lack of financial integration in Asia has been intensively documented and analyzed (García-Herrero et al. 2008). The low level of Asian financial integration compared to that in Europe can be traced to three observations:

- From a sequencing perspective, financial integration is difficult to achieve without progress in integration in other areas. In Europe, the swift integration of new member states (and candidate and potential candidate countries) has been driven to a large extent by the expectation that these countries would become part of a single market encompassing not only finance, but also goods, services and labor, based on a unified regulatory framework in the form of the *acquis communautaire.*

- From a market-building perspective (Padoa-Schioppa 2004), financial integration and the associated coordination of financial sector policies is one of the most difficult undertakings of economic integration. It lacks a benchmark model, is technically challenging and full of details and has substantial fiscal implications in times of crisis.
- From a financial stability perspective, financial integration without monetary integration has strong implications, due to the risks arising from maturity and currency mismatches, as demonstrated by the Asian crisis of 1997–1998. In Europe, these risks have declined substantially with the introduction of the euro and the establishment of the ECB as a full-fledged LOLR for the eurozone. While the Chiang Mai Initiative and the accumulation of foreign exchange reserves have been measures designed to address these vulnerabilities, they remain imperfect substitutes in dealing with stability challenges arising from maturity mismatches denominated in foreign currency.

Facing these constraints, in strong contrast to emerging Europe, most emerging Asian countries have developed a generally skeptical attitude toward capital account liberalization. Moreover, most countries in emerging Asia have been running current account surpluses, another feature that differs sharply from emerging Europe (Herrmann and Winkler 2008). The difference in current account patterns before and after 1997 is most pronounced in the countries hit by the Asian crisis. These countries, which had been running deficits before the crisis, with very few exceptions experienced persistent surpluses in the years after the turmoil.

7.4 REGIONAL FINANCIAL INTEGRATION, COORDINATION AND MONITORING: EXPERIENCES WITH THE FIRST GLOBAL FINANCIAL CRISIS OF THE CENTURY

7.4.1 The Impact of the Crisis on the Design of Financial Regulation and Supervision

The financial crisis has triggered a debate on the very nature and functioning of financial institutions and markets (Financial Services Authority 2009). The complete markets analogy, the assumption of rationally behaving agents, and the strong regulatory and supervisory focus on exogenous credit risk have been replaced by the fallacy of composition of safe institutions and liquid markets, self-amplifying dynamics and a renewed emphasis on endogenous liquidity risk (Brunnermeier et al. 2009). This change in view has reshaped the debate on fundamental principles of financial regulation and supervision, putting macroprudential regulation and supervision at the center of efforts to mitigate the risks of financial crises emerging from maturity and (in the case of international markets) currency mismatches.

The regulatory policy response has been comprehensive. It has been summarized by the Group of Twenty as a strategy in which 'all systemically important financial institutions, markets, and instruments should be subject to an appropriate degree of regulation and oversight' (Group of Twenty 2009: 3). The term 'systemically important' relates not only to the size of the institution and its solvency, but also to its potential for being 'part of a herd' (Brunnermeier et al. 2009) and liquidity concerns that might arise due to the level of maturity transformation performed by an increasingly integrated financial system, domestically as well as internationally.

Against this background, specific investor group types, such as hedge funds, are bound to be regulated because, by the very nature of their business models, they increase the degree of maturity transformation in the financial system and thus create systemic risk (Financial Services Authority 2009; Frank et al. 2008). This risk could only be tolerated if the core of the system, the banks, was to be strictly separated from such investor types. As this has been deemed infeasible (or inefficient and distortive),[10] all investor types that raise systemic risk by organizing maturity transformation have to be regulated nationally, regionally and internationally. For the same reason, a harmonization of regulations and finance-related taxes is needed to promote more stable and transparent capital flows. Finally, a major precondition for any meaningful assessment of global or regional stability risks requires information on cross-border links and exposures. Such information was not available before the crisis. This remains the case, possibly reflecting the reluctance of the governments of financial center countries to provide such data for fear of undermining the competitive advantage of their respective centers (Issing and Krahnen 2009).

7.4.2 The Impact of the Crisis on Regional Financial Integration: Europe

The financial crisis is global and, thus, its implications are global. However, the crisis has had a profound impact on regional financial integration in

Europe and in Asia, revealing strengths and weaknesses in the integration strategies pursued in both regions.

In Europe, the crisis confirmed the advantages of having access to a regional and international LOLR (Eichengreen 2008). It is difficult to imagine – assuming the same pattern and size of cross-country capital flows, credit growth and current account imbalances as have been observed in Europe from 1999 to 2007 – that the countries making up the eurozone would have remained a zone of relative stability without the euro. The swift reaction by the ECB to the money market collapse on 9 August 2007 has been a strong testimony to its willingness and ability to perform its LOLR function decisively and expeditiously.

Even with the euro, however, financial integration in the eurozone has been negatively affected. Several indicators of financial integration, in particular in money and bond markets (the markets that have seen the most rapid progress in integration over the last years), have shown signs of disintegration over the crisis period (ECB 2009). At least partly, this reflects the fact that the run for liquidity benefited German treasury bills over government debt titles of other eurozone countries. However, rising spreads have also been in line with traditional macroeconomic vulnerability indicators (such as current account deficits) and financial vulnerability indicators (such as the exposure of the respective banking sectors to the international financial system).

The financial crisis has also revealed the possible fiscal implications of uneven financial integration for non-financial-center countries. Two types of risk can be distinguished:

- The risk that non-financial-center countries would have to support financial-center countries in order to prevent default, which would undermine the credibility of the integration process in general, and monetary integration in particular.
- The risk that non-financial-center countries would have to organize and fund rescue operations for financial institutions that, at least in part, face insolvency due to engagements in financial centers motivated by the favorable regulatory, supervisory or tax regimes prevailing in the respective centers.

The financial crisis has severely tested the financial integration of the eurozone, EU-15 and the non-eurozone new member states (as well as candidate and potential candidates for EU membership). Non-eurozone CEE and SEE countries experienced an Asian-style sudden stop of capital flows when wholesale funding markets in mature economies dried up completely after the Lehman Brothers' collapse. Thus, the global financial crisis undermined the validity of two key assumptions that the financial stability of institutional integration between banking sectors in the EU-15 and the new member states (as well as candidate and potential candidate countries) had been built on (De Haas and Lelyveld 2008): (1) that parent banks are stable; and (2) that financial crisis scenarios are triggered by events in emerging (and not mature) Europe.

The experience of non-eurozone CEE and SEE countries in the current crisis provides several lessons on the links between financial integration, stability and regulation:

- Even in an almost ideal environment, with the EU being a single market in all dimensions and member states being subject to a high degree of harmonization in terms of financial regulation and supervision, financial integration does not provide a guarantee of financial stability.
- The access of parent banks to the ECB's LOLR facilities and rescue packages prepared by home-country governments have been key in preventing a full-blown Asian-style financial crisis in the region.
- Institutional integration, compared to integration via markets, facilitates crisis management. Parent banks, local governments and international financial institutions have joined forces to stabilize banking sectors in CEE and SEE countries in the absence of an international LOLR.

Finally, the financial crisis has had a strong impact on the pattern of net capital flows within Europe. Current account imbalances have been shrinking substantially as capital flows have been curtailed to the Southern European countries of Spain, Greece and Portugal, as well as to the new EU member states (and candidate and potential candidate countries), marking the end of a growth model that has relied on capital flow-based and credit growth-driven domestic demand (Fabrizio et al. 2009). The decline in spending in the deficit countries has led to a reduction of export revenues in the surplus countries, leading to an overall contraction of current account surpluses and deficits recorded by European countries in the past decade.

A report issued by the High-Level Group on Financial Supervision (de Larosière 2009) has responded to several challenges to European financial regulation and supervision by calling for further regulatory convergence in Europe. Moreover, it identified weaknesses in supervisory practices on a cross-border basis and the need for more 'effective means of challenging the decisions of the home regulator' (de Larosière 2009: 40). Finally, it proposed a European system of supervision and crisis management with regard to macro- and microprudential supervision.

7.4.3 The Impact of the Crisis on Regional Financial Integration: Asia

In Asia, the financial crisis was a déjà vu experience to that of 1997–1998, as countries again faced a sudden stop of capital flows, leading to a rise in interest rates and spreads as well as to exchange rate depreciation. This has led to enhanced efforts to ensure financial stability by following the agenda adopted ten years ago: a common protection against sudden stops and calls for an international LOLR. In May 2009, the Chiang Mai Initiative was transformed from a bilateral network into a multilateral foreign-exchange reserve pool (ASEAN+3 2009), putting an end to the inefficiencies inherent in the previous bilateral approach. Moreover, by establishing an independent regional surveillance unit, countries prepared the ground for independent LOLR activities based on a structured dialogue on macroeconomic and financial stability challenges facing the region. The European example suggests (Padoa-Schioppa 2003) that such a dialogue will be preceded by an information and data collection exercise, allowing countries to engage in a discussion on common benchmarks on which assessments of economic developments in individual countries can be based. It remains to be seen whether and when an agreement on those benchmarks will be reached given the lack of institutional foundations that characterizes Asian integration.

In addition, Asian policymakers, in particular from the People's Republic of China, have called for the creation of a truly international reserve currency. The most prominent proposal argues for an international monetary system that would replace the US dollar with the International Monetary Fund's (IMF) Special Drawing Right as the main international reserve currency (Zhou 2009). The proposal reflects the need for a sound monetary basis for financial integration, which in the Asian case has been much more global than regional. It is also an implicit acknowledgment that the largely unilateral approach of self-protection via the build-up of foreign exchange reserves and a cautious opening to capital flows is only a second-best strategy for dealing with the vulnerabilities resulting from financial integration. This remains the case even though the approach has allowed most countries in the region to fight the crisis successfully with monetary and fiscal policy measures that could not be used credibly in 1997 and without resorting to liquidity assistance from the US Federal Reserve or the IMF.

The theoretical foundations for the creation of a supranational currency are sound (Eichengreen 2009). However, the political and practical impediments seem to be even higher than in the case of regional monetary and financial integration along the lines set out by the reformed Chiang Mai Initiative. The European case suggests that even in an environment characterized by an extraordinary degree of economic and political integration, the introduction of a common currency – and the creation of a new international reserve currency would constitute a similar step – depends on the convergence of views on the conduct of monetary policy; that is, the principles according to which such a currency should be managed. Such a consensus is unlikely to be achieved on a global level in the near future.

Against this background, the pursuit of a regional approach might be more promising. Proposals have been made, for example, to establish an Asian financial stability dialogue (Kuroda 2008) among finance ministers, central bank governors, regulators, supervisors and private sector representatives. Such a dialogue would benefit from working closely with the independent surveillance unit set up by the reformed Chiang Mai Initiative and from discussing issues related to the regional monitoring and coordination of financial regulation together with the monetary aspects of integration.[11] Moreover, discussions on a regional level could provide a platform from which to enter, with more weight, discussions on a global level, for example with the Financial Stability Board and the IMF.

7.5 CONCLUSIONS

Against the background of the global financial crisis, this chapter has analyzed recent experience with respect to regional monitoring and coordination of financial regulation as a way to improve overall regulatory performance and increase the attractiveness of regional financial markets. Its main conclusions are the following.

Firstly, financial integration is not only, and not even primarily, a function of regulatory and supervisory convergence. Rather, it is a function of progress in overall economic integration, that is, in the integration of goods, services and labor markets, as well as monetary integration. The lack of economic and monetary integration represents an important barrier to increasing the attractiveness of Asian financial markets to investors, both within and from outside the region. By contrast, the speed and form of financial integration between the EU-15 and the new EU member states (and the other European countries with EU accession ambitions) have been strongly influenced by the business perspectives provided by the single market and a unified regulatory framework.

Secondly, the euro has fostered financial integration in the eurozone and has been safeguarding financial stability by significantly reducing currency mismatches in the eurozone financial system. Moreover, the ECB has been providing unlimited LOLR services to the integrated area. At the same time, the European experience suggests that financial integration as such does not offer a guarantee of financial stability. This holds in particular when financial integration takes place among countries that do not share a common currency and thus lack an international LOLR. Despite a high degree of *de jure* and de facto financial integration, several non-eurozone EU member states (as well as the European countries with an accession perspective) have been subject to a sudden stop of capital flows. As a result, international support by the IMF and other international financial institutions has been needed as a crisis management tool. At the same time, the peculiar institutional set-up, whereby EU-15 parent banks enjoy access to the relevant international LOLR and support in form of rescue packages by the respective home country governments, has contributed to the avoidance of an Asian 1997-style financial meltdown in non-eurozone CEE and SEE countries.

Thirdly, the European experience demonstrates the challenges to achieving progress in regulatory and supervisory convergence. Progress is hampered by:

- the lack of an agreed upon benchmark model;
- the many details and technical difficulties of regulation and supervision;
- cross-country asymmetries due to the financial center status of some member states, as well as significant differences in terms of the systemic relevance of banking groups' subsidiaries in home- and host-country markets; and
- the national responsibility of crisis management, in particular its fiscal dimension.

Fourthly, in Asia, the current crisis has led to renewed efforts to deal with the monetary side of financial integration via the multilateralization of the Chiang Mai Initiative, as well as new calls for the creation of a global supranational reserve currency. The self-protective measures taken after the 1997–1998 crisis – the reserve build-up and the cautious attitude toward financial liberalization – have strengthened the abilities of Asian countries to fight the global crisis with traditional monetary and fiscal policy instruments. However, these very same measures have hindered both the development of financial systems domestically and financial integration regionally.[12] Moreover, they have made countries even more dependent on export-led growth than they were before the 1997–1998 crisis.

Overall, the crisis has served as a reminder of the preconditions that have to be met for smooth and stable financial integration. It has been a wake-up call for strengthening regional monitoring of financial markets and regional coordination of financial sector policies. This wake-up call has many facets. It underlines the interdependencies with other integration efforts, notably monetary integration, as well as the difficulties in and implications of achieving progress in regulatory and supervisory convergence. This holds for Asia, but also for Europe, which has already gone a long way toward achieving overall economic integration and fostering regulatory and supervisory convergence.

On regulation and supervision, the crisis points to a corner solution (Brunnermeier et al. 2009). The first 'corner' is to standardize comprehensively all relevant aspects of national and regional financial integration.[13] The second 'corner' – which is also compatible with a strengthening of coordination and cooperation – is to keep regulation and supervision clearly in the domestic domain because the fiscal (and monetary) implications of a crisis have to be dealt with at the national level. The crisis provides much food for thought on monetary integration in Asia and a strong call to Europe to decide on a sustainable regulatory and supervisory structure.

NOTES

1. This chapter is a shorter version of a paper presented at the Asian Development Bank Institute (ADBI) conference Global Financial Crisis: Financial Sector Reform and Regulation, held in Tokyo on 21–23 July 2009, and published as ADBI working paper 199 in February 2010. It reflects the state of knowledge at the time of writing, that is, it has not been revised on substance to account for any developments in Europe or Asia occurring after early 2010. The author thanks Barbara Drexler, Michael Olsen and the participants of the ADBI conference, in particular Ali M. El-Agraa and David Mayes, for helpful comments and suggestions. He also thanks Ioana Dumitrescu for excellent research assistance.
2. See, for example, Paust (2008) and Kuroda (2008) for Asia, as well as European Central Bank (ECB) (2007a), de Larosière (2009), and Vives (2009) for Europe.
3. In doing this, the approach follows that of most of the literature on Asian financial integration in using the process of European financial integration as a benchmark for comparison. See, for example, Plummer (2006), Mayes (2008) and Pasadilla (2008).
4. In the international debate, this insight led to the 'bipolar view' or 'corner solutions view' on exchange rate regimes, suggesting that countries cannot open up their capital accounts while keeping the exchange rate stable and pursuing an autonomous monetary policy (Fischer 2001).
5. Capital market size is defined as the sum of stock market capitalization, bank credit to the private sector, and debt securities issued by the private sector to GDP.
6. The new EU member states include Bulgaria, Cyprus, the Czech Republic, Estonia, Hungary, Latvia, Lithuania, Malta, Poland, Romania, Slovakia and Slovenia. At the time of writing this chapter in early 2010, candidate and potential candidate countries

were Croatia, the Former Yugoslav Republic of Macedonia, Turkey, Albania, Bosnia and Herzegovina, Montenegro and Serbia. The EU-15 is composed of Austria, Belgium, Denmark, Finland, France, Germany, Greece, Ireland, Italy, Luxembourg, the Netherlands, Portugal, Spain, Sweden and the United Kingdom. The CEE and SEE countries are the new EU member states as well as candidate and potential candidate countries, except Cyprus and Malta.

7. In contrast, in the original eurozone member states and the EU-15, banking continues to be dominated by large national players conducting substantial cross-border activities, rather than by truly pan-European banks with a significant cross-border presence (ECB 2007a).
8. The term *acquis communautaire* refers to the total body of EU laws.
9. Brunei Darussalam, Cambodia, Indonesia, Lao People's Democratic Republic, Malaysia, Myanmar, the Philippines, Singapore, Thailand, Viet Nam, the People's Republic of China, Japan and the Republic of Korea.
10. See, however, Eichengreen (2009) and De Grauwe (2009).
11. Park (2009) proposed including a college of the region's supervisory authorities as an integral component of the Chiang Mai Initiative.
12. The dilemma that better developed and integrated regional financial markets may reduce financial vulnerabilities, but that the process of achieving such a level of development of integration involves a higher risk of financial instability, has been noted by Eichengreen and Park (2003).
13. Bruni (2008) refers to an incompatible trio of financial stability, financial integration and decentralized regulation and supervision: to maintain the first two components of the trio, the third has to be given up. A similar concept has been put forward by Schoenmaker (2009).

REFERENCES

Abiad, A., D. Leigh and A. Mody. 2007. International Finance and Income Convergence: Europe is Different. International Monetary Fund Working Paper 64. Washington, DC: International Monetary Fund.

Árvai, Z., K. Driessen and I. Ötker-Robe. 2009. Regional Financial Interlinkages and Financial Contagion Within Europe. International Monetary Fund Working Paper 09/06. Washington, DC: International Monetary Fund.

Association of Southeast Asian Nations (ASEAN)+3. 2009. Joint Media Statement of the 12th ASEAN+3 Finance Ministers' Meeting. Bali, Indonesia, 3 May.

Baltzer, M., L. Cappiello, R.A. De Santis and S. Manganelli. 2008. Measuring Financial Integration in New EU Member States. European Central Bank Occasional Paper 81. Frankfurt: European Central Bank.

Bednarski, P. and D. Starnowski. 2007. Home and Host Supervisors' Relations – A Host Supervisor's Perspective. In *Rapid Credit Growth in Central and Eastern Europe—Endless Boom or Early Warning*, edited by C. Enoch and İ. Ötker-Robe. Basingstoke: Palgrave Macmillan.

Bruni, F. 2008. The Governance of EU's Financial Regulation: Challenges from the Current Financial Turmoil. Presentation at Chatham House, London, 25 January.

Brunnermeier, M., A. Crockett, C. Goodhart, C. Persaud and H. Shin. 2009. The Fundamental Principles of Financial Regulation. 11th Geneva Report on the World Economy. Preliminary conference draft. London: Center for

Economic Policy Research. http://www.princeton.edu/~markus/research/papers/Geneva11.pdf.
Chang, R. and A. Velasco. 2000. Exchange-Rate Policy for Developing Countries. *American Economic Review* 90(2): 71–75.
Choi, W.G., S. Sharma and M. Strömqvist. 2007. Capital Flows, Financial Integration, and International Reserve Holdings: The Recent Experience of Emerging Markets and Advanced Economies. International Monetary Fund Working Paper 07/151. Washington, DC: International Monetary Fund.
Cowen, D. and R. Salgado. 2006. Globalization of Production and Financial Integration in Asia. In *Financial Integration in Asia: Recent Developments and Next Steps*, edited by D. Cower, R. Salgado, H. Shah, L. Teo and A. Zanello. International Monetary Fund Working Paper 06/196. Washington, DC: International Monetary Fund.
De Grauwe, P. 2009. Lessons from the Banking Crisis: A Return to Narrow Banking. CESifo DICE Report 2/2009. Munich, Germany: CESifo.
De Haas, R. and I. van Lelyveld. 2008. Internal Capital Markets and Lending by Multinational Bank Subsidiaries. European Bank for Reconstruction and Development Working Paper 105. London: European Bank for Reconstruction and Development.
Eichengreen, B. 2008. The Crisis of the Euro. Mimeo. http://www.econ.berkeley.edu/~eichengr/crisis_euro_projsyn.pdf (accessed 21 January 2010).
Eichengreen, B. 2009. Out of the Box Thoughts about the International Financial Architecture. International Monetary Fund Working Paper 09/116. Washington, DC: International Monetary Fund.
Eichengreen, B. and Y.C. Park. 2003. Why Has There Been Less Financial Integration in Asia Than in Europe? Political Economy of International Finance Series. Berkeley, CA: Institute of European Studies.
European Central Bank (ECB). 2006. Financial Development in Central, Eastern and South-Eastern Europe. Monthly bulletin, November. Frankfurt: European Central Bank.
European Central Bank (ECB). 2007a. Review of the Lamfalussy Framework – Eurosystem Contribution. https://www.ecb.europa.eu/pub/pdf/other/lamfalussy-review2007en.pdf (accessed 21 January 2010).
European Central Bank (ECB). 2007b. *Review of the International Role of the Euro*. Frankfurt: European Central Bank. http://www.ecb.int/pub/pdf/other/reviewoftheinternationalroleoftheeuro2007en.pdf.
European Central Bank (ECB). 2009. *Financial Integration in Europe*. Frankfurt: European Central Bank. http://www.ecb.eu/pub/pdf/other/financialintegrationineurope200904en.pdf.
European Shadow Financial Regulatory Committee. 2004. Challenges to Financial Regulators in the Accession Countries Statement 18. Budapest, May.
Fabrizio, S., D. Leigh and A. Mody. 2009. The Second Transition: Eastern Europe in Perspective. International Monetary Fund Working Paper 09/43. Washington, DC: International Monetary Fund.
Financial Services Authority. 2009. *The Turner Review: A Regulatory Response to the Global Banking Crisis*. London: Financial Services Authority.
Fischer, S. 2001. On the Need for an International Lender of Last Resort. *Journal of Economic Perspectives* 13(4): 85–104.
Frank, N., B. Gonzalez-Hermosillo and H. Hesse. 2008. Transmission of Liquidity

Shocks: Evidence from the 2007 Subprime Crisis. International Monetary Fund Working Paper 08/200. Washington, DC: International Monetary Fund.

García-Herrero, A., D. Yang and P. Wooldridge. 2008. Why is there So Little Regional Financial Integration in Asia? In *Regional Financial Integration in Asia: Present and Future*. Bank for International Settlements Paper 42. Basel: Bank for International Settlements.

Group of Twenty. 2009. Communiqué. Issued at the close of the G20 London Summit, London, 2 April. http://www.europa-eu-un.org/articles/en/article_8622_en.htm.

Hardy, D.C. 2009. A European Mandate for Financial Sector Supervisors in the EU. International Monetary Fund Working Paper 09/5. Washington, DC: International Monetary Fund.

Herrmann, S. and A. Winkler. 2008. Real Convergence, Financial Markets, and the Current Account – Emerging Europe versus Emerging Asia. European Central Bank Occasional Paper 88. Frankfurt, Germany: European Central Bank.

Issing, O. and J. Krahnen. 2009. Why the Regulators Must Have a Global 'Risk Map.' *Financial Times*, 19 February.

Kuroda, H. 2008. Asia's Contribution to Global Development and Stability. Speech at the Asian Development Bank Institute Annual Conference, Tokyo, 5 December.

Lamfalussy, A. 2001. Final Report of the Committee of Wise Men on the Regulation of European Securities Markets. http://ec.europa.eu/internal_market/securities/docs/lamfalussy/wisemen/final-report-wise-men_en.pdf (accessed 21 January 2010).

de Larosière, J. 2009. The High-Level Group on Financial Supervision in the EU. Report. Brussels: European Commission. http://ec.europa.eu/internal_market/finances/docs/de_larosiere_report_en.pdf.

Llewellyn, D.T. 2002. An Analysis of the Causes of Recent Banking Crises. *European Journal of Finance* 8(2): 152–175.

Mayes, D. 2008. Financial Integration in Asia. Bank of Finland Online 9. Helsinki: Bank of Finland. http://www.suomenpankki.fi/fi/julkaisut/selvitykset_ja_rapor tit/bof_online/Documents/BoF_Online_09_2008.pdf.

Mehl, A., C. Vespro and A. Winkler. 2006. Financial Sector Development in South-Eastern Europe: Quality Matters. In *Financial Development, Integration, and Stability: Evidence from Central, Eastern and South-Eastern Europe*, edited by K. Liebscher, J. Christl, P. Mosslechner and D. Ritzberger-Grünwald. Cheltenham, UK and Northampton, MA, USA: Edward Elgar Publishing.

Obstfeld, M., J.C. Shambaugh and A.M. Taylor. 2008. Financial Stability, the Trilemma and International Reserves. Center for Economic Policy Research Discussion Paper 6693. London: Center for Economic Policy Research.

Padoa-Schioppa, T. 1995. The Genesis of EMU: A Retrospective View. Robert Schuman Lecture given at the Sixth Session of the Academy of European Law, European University Institute, Florence, Italy, 29 June.

Padoa-Schioppa, T. 2003. Regional Cooperation: The Experience of Asia and Europe. Speech delivered at the Bank of Korea, Seoul, 1 July. http://www.ecb.int/press/key/date/2003/html/sp030701.en.html (accessed 21 January 2010).

Padoa-Schioppa, T. 2004. The European Union and the Russian Federation: Challenges of Market Building. Speech delivered at Russia in Global Affairs,

Moscow, 28 September. http://www.ecb.int/press/key/date/2004/html/sp040928_1.en.html (accessed 21 January 2010).
Park, Y.C. 2009. Reform of the Global Monetary System: Perspectives of East Asia's Emerging Economies. Paper presented at the World Bank Annual Bank Conference on Development Economics, Seoul, 22–24 June.
Pasadilla, G.O. 2008. Financial Services Integration in East Asia: Lessons from the European Union. Asia-Pacific Research and Training Network on Trade Working Paper Series 53. Bangkok: Asia-Pacific Research and Training Network on Trade.
Paust, S. 2008. Enhancing Regional Cooperation – The Role of ADB. Presentation given at the Conference of Deepening Financial Sector Reforms and Regional Cooperation in South Asia, Delhi, India, 6–7 November.
Plummer, M.G. 2006. The ASEAN Economic Community and the European Experience. Asian Development Bank Working Paper Series on Regional Economic Integration 1. Manila: Asian Development Bank Office of Regional Economic Integration.
Richards, P. 2003. The EU Financial Services Action Plan: A Guide. *Bank of England Quarterly Bulletin* Autumn: 352–365.
Schoenmaker, D. 2009. The Trilemma of Financial Stability. Working Paper Series. Finance Department VU University Amsterdam. http://ssrn.com/abstract=1340395 (accessed 21 January 2010).
Trichet, J.C. 2007. Towards the Review of the Lamfalussy Approach: Market Developments, Supervisory Challenges and Institutional Arrangements. Keynote speech at the First CEBS Conference, London, 9 May. http://www.ecb.int/press/key/date/2007/html/sp070509.en.html (accessed 21 January 2010).
Vives, X. 2009. Europe's Regulatory Chaos. Vox web site, 1 April. http://vox.cepr.org/index.php?q=node/3388 (accessed 21 January 2010).
Winkler, A. 2009. Southeastern Europe: Financial Deepening, Foreign Banks and Sudden Stops in Capital Flows. *Focus on European Economic Integration* Q1(09): 84–97.
Yoshida, M. 2009. Capital Flows in Asia and Recent Developments in Regional Financial Integration. Presentation at the International Conference on Strengthening Payment Systems in Asia, organized by the Asian Development Bank Institute, Keio University (GCOE), and Japan's Financial Services Authority (FRTC), Tokyo, 10 February.
Zhou, X. 2009. Reform the International Monetary System. 23 March. http://www.pbc.gov.cn/english//detail.asp?col=6500&ID=178 (accessed 21 January 2010)

8. Regional monitoring of capital flows and coordination of financial regulation: stakes and options for Asia

Michael G. Plummer

8.1 INTRODUCTION

The 2007–2009 global financial crisis may have had its origins in the United States (US), but its knock-on effects have pounded Asian economies no less than the US; negative growth rates in a number of Asian economies have been even more pronounced. Such an economic shock has not been seen in Asia since the economic crisis of 1997–1998. And for several economies in the region, the global financial crisis at some point took an even higher toll than did the previous crisis.

From an Asian perspective, the main difference between the two crises in terms of policy is arguably that the crisis of 1997–1998 was mostly home-grown, while the global financial crisis was imported. Most Asian economies were conservative in terms of their macroeconomic management prior to the global financial crisis, with relatively low inflation, budget deficits under control, stable exchange rates, high current account surpluses and the build-up of a large cushion of foreign-exchange reserves. Asian economies did not invest heavily in 'toxic' assets and other high-risk financial activities. While the 'savings glut' hypothesis would assign some blame to Asian economies in terms of the perpetuation of global economic imbalances (Bernanke 2005), ultimately the main responsibility for the crisis lies in the US and other developed economies where the global financial crisis broke.

The media places most of the blame for the crisis on unsustainable high-risk assets, such as subprime mortgages, credit-default swaps and mortgage-backed securities, overzealous financial deregulation, and a lack of consistent and effective oversight of the international financial system, as well as unethical financial actors. Economists would add to these macroeconomic factors, such as overly expansionary monetary policies, exchange rate misalignments and unsustainable global current account imbalances.

The purpose of this chapter is to ascertain how crises might be mitigated in the future through better regulation, supervision, institution building and regional cooperation. Section 8.2 is an overview of the regulation of capital flows and their implications for the economy in the context of rapidly changing international financial markets. Section 8.3 addresses issues surrounding the development of new regulatory regimes. In particular, many of the shortcomings of pre-crisis international and domestic regulatory and supervisory institutional structures are highlighted and critiqued. Section 8.4 considers this analysis in the context of Asia. It first makes the case for why improving financial markets in Asian economies is so crucial to future development, and surveys approaches to regional financial cooperation in recent years. Section 8.5 considers fresh approaches to financial cooperation. It begins with a discussion of when regional cooperation – as opposed to global cooperation – makes economic sense, and considers the potential for an Asian financial stability dialogue (AFSD) and how it might interact with the new Financial Stability Board (FSB) and other institutions. It also makes the case for closer financial integration in the region with a focus on deepening asset markets in developing Asian economies, and argues that this objective should be an important component of the AFSD. Finally, section 8.6 summarizes key recommendations regarding the improvement of monitoring and regulation in the global and regional economies.

This chapter mainly takes a microeconomic approach to the issue. But while it will be suggested that better regulation and monitoring can be developed in order to mitigate the effects and reduce the frequency of future crises, it should be understood that crises cannot be avoided altogether without stifling innovation. Plus, there will always be fraudsters. The task of policymakers, therefore, must lie in improving transparency, regulation and monitoring in such a way as to nip incipient excesses in the bud, identify bubbles (and do something about them), minimize 'moral hazard' problems inherent in finance, and detect scams as early as possible so as to reduce their potential effects on the real economy. Many of these issues will be addressed, but not the need to improve aggregate demand management in general and monetary policy in particular.

8.2 REGULATION OF CAPITAL FLOWS

Issues pertaining to the regulation of capital flows in the international system have been controversial, especially since the 1997–1998 Asian financial crisis. Up to that point, liberalization of the capital account was thought to be consistent with the free-market logic that was dominant in the 1990s. Open capital markets would allow investment to flow to countries where the return was highest, and therefore where it would be the most productive, just as open markets for goods and services allowed for greater efficiency based on comparative advantage. This logic would suggest that developing countries would have the most to gain from open capital flows as they tended to be capital-scarce and would receive the most investment, leading to gains in output, efficiency and productivity.

The problem with this approach is that it ignores the externalities associated with international capital flows. These externalities render finance different from international trade, as argued by Bhagwati (2004). International capital flows are a function of many different variables, not merely rates of return. And footloose (short-term) capital inflows can rapidly transform into capital outflows which, under certain conditions, could leave the financial system in ruins. Such a reversal was evident in the case of the Asian financial crisis of 1997–1998. The liberalization of domestic financial institutions beginning in the late 1980s freed up banks and non-bank financial institutions to expand their activities locally and internationally. The large current account deficits that accumulated over this period were increasingly financed by short-term capital inflows (rather than long-term flows, such as foreign direct investment), particularly short-term bank loans. The resulting 'double mismatch' (that is, maturity and currency mismatches) rendered the region vulnerable to external shocks and contagion; see Kim et al. (2001).

Thus, capital flows carry with them the potential for financial systemic risk – that is, a negative externality. Such an externality does not exist in the context of foreign direct investment or trade. In fact, some have characterized the complications as being akin to economic problems associated with pollution (that is, 'financial pollution'). In the general theory of second best, this would suggest a theoretical role for government in regulating capital flows.[1]

Kawai and Takagi (2008) identify three types of risks in the event that large capital inflows are not managed properly. First, poorly managed large inflows can increase macroeconomic risk as they lead to a boom in domestic credit and real exchange rate appreciation. Second, they can produce potential financial instability through the double mismatch phenomenon, as well as leading to asset bubbles. And third, there is a potential for capital-flow reversal (or the financial pollution effect). Kawai and Lamberte (2008) suggest that dealing with these problems is not easy, but they note that regional approaches to managing capital flows have considerable potential, in particular through greater regional exchange rate coordination, financial market surveillance and integration, and regulatory and supervisory capacity building, perhaps under the auspices of an AFSD. The AFSD was proposed by Asian Development Bank (ADB) president Haruhiko Kuroda in September 2008; it would include finance ministry and central bank officials, financial regulators and supervisors, and market participants, and could develop an early warning system to ameliorate surveillance of the region's financial markets. The AFSD is discussed at length in section 8.5.

The Asian experience of 1997–1998 reaffirmed that the capital-flow cycle so apparent in the crises of Latin American countries could actually be generalized. This has led to greater skepticism and reluctance to embrace open capital markets. Indeed, even Singapore, which has one of the most advanced financial systems in the world, put its foot down when the US insisted on its never using capital controls in negotiations leading to the Singapore–US Free Trade Agreement (Naya and Plummer 2005). In fact, there has been little imposition of capital controls in Asia between 1 September 1999, when the vast majority of Malaysian capital controls expired (one year after their imposition), and the advent of the 2007–2009 global financial crisis.[2] No doubt this is due to the fact that, since the 1997–1998 Asian crisis, the region has generated significant current account surpluses and, hence, the region's economies have become a significant net creditor to the global system. But it is no longer taboo to consider using controls if and when it may be necessary in the future, a reality that has been reflected in recent statements by Korean, Thai and other country officials.

Tables 8.1 and 8.2 compare the degree of openness of developing East Asian economies relative to other developed and developing regions, based on a new database developed by the International Monetary Fund (IMF) (Abiad et al. 2008). This database includes financial reforms in 91 countries over the period 1973–2005. The results are interesting: while developed countries obviously score top marks, East Asian economies are rather middle of the road in terms of their financial liberalization programs. For example, relative to Latin American countries, they score lower marks for every financial reform component except the securities market (Table 8.2). However, East Asian regimes are more stable in terms of backtracking: they had less frequent large reversals in financial-sector-related policies than did Latin America and Africa, receiving a score that is one-half the full sample average (Table 8.1). They also displayed greater reforms in this area than did any other region (including the advanced economies) save the transitional economies, which created an entirely new financial system over this period.

Empirically, as theory would suggest, the economic desirability of

Table 8.1 Distribution of financial sector policy change, selected country groups (%)

	Full sample	Advanced economies	Developing Asia	Latin America and Caribbean	Sub-Saharan Africa	Transition economies	Middle East and North Africa
Large reversal	0.50	0.14	0.25	1.65	0.45	0.00	0.00
Reversal	4.42	1.70	5.64	7.72	3.57	5.16	3.57
Status quo	65.16	73.15	63.73	59.19	70.09	45.24	69.64
Reform	24.65	20.60	27.21	24.26	21.88	39.29	22.77
Large reform	5.27	4.40	3.18	7.17	4.02	10.32	4.02
Total	100.00	100.00	100.00	100.00	100.00	100.00	100.00

Source: Abiad et al. (2008).

Table 8.2 Distribution of financial liberalization by components, average 2005

	Full sample	Advanced economies	Developing Asia	Latin America and Caribbean	Sub-Saharan Africa	Transition economies	Middle East and North Africa
Credit controls	2.374	2.784	2.154	2.191	2.304	2.292	2.286
Interest rate controls	2.725	3.000	2.615	2.765	2.429	2.611	2.857
Entry barriers	2.725	3.000	2.385	2.706	2.714	2.778	2.429
Bank regulations	1.978	2.636	1.538	1.706	1.500	2.167	1.857
Privatization	2.000	2.409	1.231	2.000	2.357	2.111	1.143
Capital account	2.363	3.000	2.154	2.412	1.500	2.556	1.857
Securities market	2.253	3.000	2.385	1.941	1.571	2.111	2.143

Note: All components vary between 0 and 3, with 3 indicating maximal openness.

Source: Abiad et al. (2008).

capital controls has been a source of controversy. Edison et al. (2002) offer a comprehensive survey of the literature on the economic effects of capital account liberalization, as well as undertaking their own empirical investigation. They come up with several salient conclusions: (1) while developed countries have largely liberalized their capital accounts and there has been a movement in this direction for some developing countries, the majority of developing countries continue to retain significant capital controls; (2) the empirical literature addressing the issue of capital account liberalization and economic performance is agnostic – that is, there is mixed evidence that capital account liberalization promotes long-term economic growth; (3) however, their own regression results suggest a positive relationship for East Asian economies and developed countries. Klein (2005) concludes that the ultimate effect of capital account liberalization on economic growth is a positive function of institutional development.

The Klein (2005) results are intuitive. But 'institutional development' is certainly an elusive term. The US and the United Kingdom arguably had in place what were deemed the most developed financial institutions in the world, yet the global financial crisis began with them. If developing financial institutions means moving to the frontier defined by the developed countries, it must be shown that the 'best practices' are truly best. Clearly this was not the case in certain aspects of the Anglo-American approach. This chapter will endeavor to identify means to ensure the creation of a new set of best practices within the framework of a more effective regulatory and monitoring system.

8.3 CREATING MORE STABLE REGULATORY REGIMES AND IMPROVING SUPERVISION

IMF (2009) notes that there are four key areas where the existing international financial architecture failed in the current crisis:

1. Surveillance of global economic developments and policies did not give sufficiently pointed warnings about the risks building up in the international financial system.
2. Coordination of macroeconomic policies across governments did not produce the international leadership needed for a concerted response to the global risks identified.
3. Regulation and supervision of internationally active financial institutions did not provide a sufficiently robust framework to allow problems to be resolved smoothly.

4. Arrangements for international public liquidity and loans to support adjustment did not fill gaps adequately as the crisis spread, reflecting shortcomings in design and size.

These shortcomings in the international system tend to be relatively uncontroversial. Topic (4) is briefly discussed in section 8.5. Topic (2) is a macroeconomic question that is beyond the scope of this study, so it is discussed here only in the context of surveillance.[3] Instead, in this section, Topics (1) and (3) are focused on as good points of departure in the planning of how to create a more stable international regulatory system while outlining the major shortcomings of the existing system.

8.3.1 Key Issues in Creating a more Efficient Regulatory and Surveillance Framework

Many financial-institution-related variables require reform in order to create a more stable and robust global financial system. Of course, as finance is the business of risk, there can be no ironclad way of imposing certainty without stifling innovation and efficiency. Still, some of the most salient areas that beg for reform are the following.

The global financial crisis revealed a need to improve information dissemination and transparency, particularly regarding exposures assumed by large and complex (bank and non-bank) financial institutions, complex structured products, the revamping of indicators of financial stability analysis to focus on improved early-warning mechanisms, and improved transparency in over-the-counter derivatives markets, in particular credit-default swaps (Johnston et al. 2009).

In a global economy, it is essential to develop common rules in order to prevent the most risky activities moving to areas where there is the least regulation – regulatory arbitrage. While there has been a good deal of effort to harmonize bank prudential requirements and supervisory practices across countries, the threshold for intervention differs considerably across countries.

Related to this, international rules on host-country versus home-country responsibilities in times of crisis need to be enhanced, as the dearth in rules in this area has become increasingly problematic as international financial services become more integrated.

While there were many warnings that the financial systems in the US, European Union (EU) and elsewhere were exhibiting problems well before the crisis hit, the speed and severity of the collapse beginning in 2008 were unanticipated. Clearly the system requires improved surveillance and early warning systems. What is needed is not only an objective framework, but also an effective way to determine the burden of adjustment (in the recent crisis, the latter issue was more of a problem than the former). It may be easier to address the burden of adjustment in the context of subregional and regional cooperation than at the global level, however.

In terms of macroeconomic surveillance, more attention needs to be focused on exchange rates. A considerable amount of attention has been paid to global imbalances and exchange-rate misalignments generally, though there is no reliable model that indicates when a situation is at the breakpoint. But there are also exchange rate issues that are recognized but generally ignored. For example, the 'carry trade' phenomenon has been cited as a major force in moving exchange rates, especially the value of the Japanese yen, but also of the US dollar (for example vis-à-vis the euro). A lack of data on carry-trade transactions is probably to blame for this; still, if exchange rates adjust rapidly during times of crisis, they should be part of the metric.

In order to avoid the procyclical nature of financial crises, financial authorities need to adopt effective prudential regulations and encourage larger liquidity buffers. Value-at-risk models are structured such that a firm will take on more risk during benign periods but will retrench during a crisis. Hence, they lead to procyclical investment strategies. Credit-risk management has the same effect. This problem is another reason why risk-management models need to be improved – for example by applying smoothing techniques to credit-risk capital allocations (Andritzky et al. 2009).

'Too big to fail': the moral hazard problem is inherent in international finance. Hence, it is something that needs to be watched closely, particularly with regard to banks. During the Asian financial crisis of 1997–1998, just a few key banks dominated the financial markets of the crisis-affected economies, which led to excessive risk taking.

8.4 FACTORS NECESSARY TO IMPROVE CAPITAL MARKETS IN ASIA

8.4.1 The Need for more Developed Financial Markets in the Region

As finance is the oil that makes the real economy run, improving financial markets in the region is essential. Market growth may be considered from three perspectives: the supply, demand and institutional aspects of financial markets. First, Asian countries have generally had high savings rates, at least compared to other developing countries. Given the region's growth prospects, demographics, institutional characteristics and savings behavior, it is likely that this supply of savings will continue to be high over the medium to long term.

So where have these savings been going? Before the 1997–1998 Asian crisis, a large share was invested in speculative markets such as real estate ventures. A considerable amount also went overseas, especially to the US, but also to Europe, only to come back to Asia in the form of short-term bank lending. The lack of financial instruments and capital market information reduced the options offered to savers in Asia, be they households or institutions such as pension funds. The highly developed financial markets outside the region, which were deemed low risk and characterized by economies of scale, made it all too easy to avoid the hard choices and institutional reform needed to rectify this.

Second, in recent decades Asia has been the most dynamic region in the world, with a very strong demand for credit. Infrastructure demand in particular is expected to grow significantly in the future. Moreover, as most Asian economies now have fiscal deficits, they are being forced to find cheap and innovative ways of raising funds, or at least there is a much higher incentive to do so. This strong demand for investible funds will no doubt persist over the medium to long term. Further, Asian economies have been nervous about such a high reliance on intermediation outside the region, a nervousness that was all too justified in light of the global financial crisis.

How has the region been able to finance its investments? To date it has mostly been through bank lending. Outside the financial centers of Japan and the Asian newly industrialized economies, equity markets tend to be thin, highly volatile and illiquid; fixed income markets are even less developed, particularly corporate debt markets in the developing Asian economies. While a strong reliance on bank lending is not necessarily an impediment to longer-term economic development – the continental European financial model, for example, is heavily based on bank intermediation – it strongly limits the options available to firms and places a greater strain on the banking system. It also creates a disproportionate reliance on the banking system for the health of the economy (which can, among other things, cause moral hazard problems, as was evident during the Asian crisis).

This lack of diversity in investment vehicles in many Asian economies has been burdensome for the larger companies and public sector entities facing limited sources of funds at home; either they work through the local banking system or they try to tap international markets, listing directly or via the bond markets. This strengthens the liquidity and efficiency of developed-country markets, but to the disadvantage of local development. Moreover, small companies, and especially start-up companies, can be left out of the system completely, as banks tend to rely on larger, more established clients and venture capital markets are generally absent. The lack of a reliable yield curve in many developing Asian economies has been a perennial problem for corporate issues.

Thus, the huge supply of savings and strong investment demand in Asia was (and is) directly or indirectly intermediated outside the region, or if it took place inside the region, it was done mostly through the local banking system. The shortcomings of such a situation are obvious; most importantly, it makes the system entirely dependent on the banking system and creates high exposure to the actions of market participants of, and the economic performance in, countries outside of the region. It also develops a tendency toward double mismatches. The global financial crisis has affected Asia through not only the real side-effects of decreases in export demand, but also the financial channels, including the wealth effect, trade finance and the drying up of international liquidity.

The processes for addressing the immediate problems of the banking system due to the Asian crisis have been generally successful – for example, in increasing foreign partnerships in the sector, new business lines and other forms of asset diversification, greater transparency, and improved supervisory and regulatory systems (Adams 2008). Policymakers in the region have also turned their attention to market diversification and deepening issues, but with less success. Nevertheless, most countries have enacted or have plans for reforms designed to deepen equity markets, and to create deeper and more liquid bond markets (this is discussed more fully in section 8.5).

The need to finance emerging government deficits in the region, robust demand for infrastructure projects, and ambitious business plans of many private-sector companies make the development of asset markets a natural priority, though a major challenge. According to numerous recent studies, including those conducted by the ADB Institute in Tokyo, the ADB in Manila and the Asia-Pacific Economic Cooperation, much remains to be done in strengthening local markets. To summarize briefly some of the findings from these reports, market impediments include: a lack of reliable yield curves and liquidity in the markets; a lack of local institutional investors that are active in the market; underdeveloped clearing and settlement systems; weak protection of intellectual property; and insufficient protection and fiduciary responsibilities. (See Chapters 11 and 12 of this volume for a more detailed discussion of these issues.) As is argued in this chapter, the global financial crisis will require new financial and regulatory frameworks. In this sense, the development of local and subregional financial markets reform should be undertaken in the context of the emerging best-practices framework, which hopefully will be superior to the previous one.

While developing asset markets in Asian developing economies is mainly a challenge for national governments, there is a strong case to be made for concerted development and regional integration of these markets.

8.4.2 Financial Cooperation to Date[4]

While formal trade agreements in Asia are more numerous and advanced than financial arrangements, it is notable that real-sector and financial cooperation are developing simultaneously in Asia. The normal sequencing elsewhere has trade cooperation deepening well before financial cooperation. In part, this reflects the timing of Asian regionalism: Asian regionalism took off after the Asian crisis, and given the financial nature of that crisis, cooperation in this area was only natural. However, it also reflects the recognition of the importance of financial cooperation in bolstering real-sector competition and economic growth.

One major development in regional cooperation after the Asian crisis was the establishment of currency swap arrangements among East Asian countries (basically bilateral swaps between Japan and individual countries at first), known as the Chiang Mai Initiative. These swaps have grown in terms of nominal values and the agreement was upgraded in May 2009 to become the Chiang Mai Initiative Multilateralization (CMIM) agreement, in which the swap arrangements have been multilateralized and the total value has risen to US$120 billion in the form of an 'Asia Fund' facility. The CMIM is designed to help countries with short-term liquidity problems. Of the US$120 billion in contributions, US$96 billion come from the Northeast Asian 'three'[5] and US$24 billion from the Association of Southeast Asian Nations (ASEAN)[6] countries, with drawing rights based on quotas. Countries are able to access 20 percent of their quota without a standing IMF agreement.

In order to support the CMIM, the ASEAN+3[7] financial authorities (including those of Hong Kong, China) have decided to create an ASEAN+3 Macroeconomic Research Office (AMRO), which will be an independent surveillance office located in Singapore. It will be tasked to: (1) monitor, assess and report on the macroeconomic situation and financial soundness of participating economies; (2) anticipate macroeconomic and financial vulnerabilities and provide assistance in developing policy recommendations to mitigate risks; and (3) ensure compliance of swap requesting parties with the lending covenants under the CMIM agreement (ASEAN 2009).

Another important regional body is the Executives' Meeting of the East Asia Pacific Central Banks, a forum of regional central banks. There are a number of other cooperative groups in the region, including the ASEAN+3 Finance Ministers Meeting (ASEAN+3 FMM) and the Asia-Pacific Economic Cooperation Finance Ministers Meeting process. Established in the wake of the Asian crisis, the ASEAN+3 FMM focuses on financial sector cooperation, surveillance (including monitoring of capital flows) and policy dialogue. The Economic Review and Policy Dialogue was created in April 1999, mainly to strengthen cooperation in the area of regional surveillance and foster dialogue on global, regional and national economic developments. In May 2005, the ASEAN+3 finance ministers integrated and enhanced the Economic Review and Policy Dialogue with the Chiang Mai Initiative framework.

In short, at the Asia and Pacific and Asian levels, there are several forums dedicated to dialogue, exchange of information and technical interaction. However, concrete initiatives in the form of applied financial cooperation initiatives are less impressive, with the exception of the CMIM.

The ASEAN Economic Community (AEC) was formally launched in January 2007 and is slated for completion (for the ASEAN-6[8]) by 2015. The AEC Blueprint (ASEAN 2007),[9] which delineates the areas to be included in the AEC program, has four principal areas of focus: the creation of a single market and production base; a more competitive economic region; equitable economic development; and enhanced integration in the global economy. Measures related to capital markets are included under the 'single market and production base' and promise a freer flow of capital. In fact, most concrete measures really refer to concerted efforts to develop national capital markets, rather than a regionally integrated market. While the blueprint does include the harmonization of standards, some aspects of mutual recognition (for example with respect to professionals working in the area), and measures to broaden the base of ASEAN debt issuance, the approach is a cautious one, with references to the need to maintain stability and adequate safeguards, and promote liberalization carefully.

8.5 IMPROVING APPROACHES TO COOPERATION AND COORDINATION: OPTIONS FOR ASIA

8.5.1 Optimal Levels of Cooperation: Global, Regional or National?[10]

In considering new approaches to financial cooperation, the level at which cooperation should take place should be considered first. Europe long grappled with this problem on the way to launching its Single Market Programme. A key idea that emerged was 'subsidiarity', namely that policy should be adopted at the most decentralized level possible. Subsidiarity suggests that trade and competition policy need to be formulated at the EU level, because these activities involve more than one nation, but business-related policies and taxation can take place at the national level provided that they do not disadvantage non-resident member-state participants. Global economic cooperation might embrace the same concept: cooperation at the global (regional, national) level should address policy externalities that are global (regional, national).

Subsidiarity also argues for regional solutions where the externalities are primarily regional. In practice, policies may have a disproportionate impact on one region, suggesting a corresponding policy role. This becomes even more compelling if political influences are factored in: a policy that may be feasible at the regional level may be difficult or impossible at the global level due to indifference or opposition by non-regional actors.

Examples are not difficult to find. The EU would gain more from free flows of labor from throughout the world, rather than from just among member states, but such a solution would be politically impossible. Still, the EU is better off with free flows of labor at the regional level than none at all. Similarly, the World Trade Organization members would benefit most from global free trade, a system that they have been pursuing for many decades. Yet regional trading agreements, such as free trade areas and other forms of deep integration, can be productive as well, and have been blossoming throughout the world because global cooperation is often unobtainable. Second-best approaches to cooperation may make sense if they are superior to the status quo and, ideally, can make first-best cooperation at the global level easier.

8.5.2 Monitoring and Coordination under the AFSD

In the wake of the 1997–1998 Asian financial crisis, the ADB partnered with crisis-affected economies to create the ASEAN Surveillance Process (ASP), which was designed to monitor the economic fundamentals of the ASEAN member states and provide an early warning mechanism. The ADB invested significantly in the ASP, including in terms of capacity building for the staff of finance ministries and central banks. In addition, the ADB's Asian Bond Monitor tracks not only movements in Asian bond markets, but also the economic fundamentals that drive them.

Expanding, deepening and nesting the activities of the ASP through a more comprehensive AFSD makes sense from a variety of economic perspectives. First, it would be an effective way to share information and promote dialogue across the finance ministries and central banks in the region. This would help in macroeconomic planning, particularly with respect to potential adverse movements in the markets. Second, an effective monitoring system would improve transparency and would reduce market uncertainty. Third, it could be used as a means of 'peer pressure' for economies that need to address underlying macroeconomic problems. Fourth, it could help the region develop joint positions that could reduce external imbalances. Fifth, it could be used as a means to coordinate responses to economic shocks and emerging crises (for example stimulus plans). Sixth, the AFSD could help Asian economies project joint positions in international forums. Finally, the AFSD could be used as a vehicle to enhance regional financial integration.

Importantly, coordination under the AFSD would be complicated. It is one thing to engage in dialogue and exchange information; it is another thing to impose any decisions and rules pertinent to coordination. As the region embraces a generally common set of macroeconomic goals, coordination in this area may not be as difficult as it would be in the area of financial regulatory measures and norms. The latter would have to be developed cautiously step by step, in order to create confidence and a solid foundation on which to build deeper forms of cooperation and coordination based on best practices and the common goal of systemic stability.

As the AFSD is a new concept, there is little relevant literature. One exception is a study by Setboonsarng (2009). He offers a suggested mandate and institutional structure for the AFSD. He suggests that the AFSD should report directly to the ASEAN+3 Summit and meet at least twice a year, and that the country chairing the AFSD should be same as that chairing the ASEAN+3 FMM. He also recommends the creation of a formal secretariat for the AFSD.

8.5.3 Interaction with the FSB

How would the AFSD relate to the FSB, formerly the Financial Stability Forum (FSF)? The goals of the FSF, which was founded in April 1999, were closely related to those of the AFSD for the Group of Seven (G7)[11] countries, namely to promote international financial stability. The FSF held regular meetings of national authorities of the G7 economies responsible for 'financial stability in international financial centers, international financial institutions, sector-specific international groupings of regulators and supervisors, and committees of central bank experts' (FSB 2009b: 3), to exchange information and engage in dialogue regarding financial supervision and surveillance issues. Three representatives from each of the G7 countries participated, along with representatives from each of the major international groupings and organizations concerned with financial regulation.[12] The FSF promoted the observance of the standards and codes of its compendium, which is a guide to more than 60 sets of standards and codes from a variety of international institutions. Many, including those relating to accounting and corporate governance, involve rules and norms that operate within private sector institutions as well as having a public sector dimension. Key developing countries were included in some of the working groups. For instance, two countries that had experimented with capital controls, Malaysia and Chile, were included in the Working Group on Capital Flows.

The FSB superseded the FSF with its inaugural meeting on 26–27 June 2009 in Basel, Switzerland. It has expanded membership and has a broader mandate to promote financial stability.[13] It now includes seven Asian economies: it has three participants each from Japan (Bank of Japan, Ministry of Finance and Financial Services Agency) and the People's Republic of China (PRC) (People's Bank of China, Ministry of Finance and Chinese Banking Regulatory Commission), one participant each from Singapore (Monetary Authority of Singapore) and Hong Kong, China (Hong Kong Monetary Authority), three participants from India (Ministry of Finance, Reserve Bank of India and Security and Exchange Board of India), two participants from the Republic of Korea (hereafter Korea) (Bank of Korea and Financial Services Commission), and one participant from Indonesia (Bank Indonesia). Most major international financial institutions, international standards-setting, regulatory and supervisory groupings, and committees of central bank experts, as well as the European Central Bank and the European Commission, are now members. According to the FSB's inaugural press release (FSB 2009a: 1):

> The FSB's mandate is to assess vulnerabilities affecting the financial system; identify and oversee action needed to address them; promote coordination and information exchange among authorities responsible for financial stability; monitor and advise on market developments and their implications for regulatory policy; advise on and monitor best practice in meeting regulatory standards; undertake joint strategic reviews of the policy development work of the international standards setting bodies; set guidelines for and support the establishment of supervisory colleges; manage contingency planning for cross-border crisis management; and collaborate with the International Monetary Fund (IMF) to conduct Early Warning Exercises.

In addition to an FSB plenary group, the new structure includes a steering committee and three standing committees on vulnerabilities assessment, supervisory and regulatory cooperation, and standards implementation. The FSB's first meeting focused on the global financial crisis, but was also forward-looking in consulting about exit strategies from the extraordinary monetary and financial policies put in place during the global financial crisis.

In sum, potentially there could be a good deal of overlap between the AFSD and the FSB. However, addressing such an overlap and issues of mutual interest at the regional level can have some additional advantages over cooperation at the global level, just as free trade areas may complement the World Trade Organization even though they should have the same goals. There is some common membership across the groupings and the objectives of the two groups are similar, though the AFSD would be more focused. Clearly, there would be a good deal of potential for collaboration on various financial stability and regulatory issues across the two groups. The AFSD would be able to give priority to issues that affect its member economies the most. For example, developing and applying best practices in regulatory regimes would obviously be a high priority in Asia.

A case in point regards the first missions of the FSB, which have been assigned by the Group of Eight.[14] The FSB and its chairman, Mario Draghi, were first tasked with investigating issues related to bonuses in the financial sector. This is certainly an important issue in light of the current global financial crisis and an obvious area in which the FSB should have expertise. But bonuses are not an issue for Asian financial policymakers. These latter policymakers may be much more concerned with financial issues related to rebalancing, the future role of the US dollar, concerted capital-market deepening, and the like. There are sufficient critical issues of high priority in Asia that are lower in importance at the global level, and vice versa, to justify an institutional cooperative structure such as the AFSD. The same is true in the context of EU economies: while the FSB is an important forum, it is complementary rather than competitive with the many EU bodies related to financial cooperation.

While AMRO, at the time of this writing, is not yet up and running, it has the potential to support the AFSD in terms of data collection and dissemination, research, analysis and evidence-based policy recommendations. AMRO's surveillance and monitoring functions, combined with its key objective of anticipating financial and macroeconomic problems in East Asia at the individual, country, subregional or even regional levels, will allow it to become an important depository of information, analytical capacity and expertise upon which the AFSD can draw.

8.6 RECOMMENDATIONS FOR IMPROVING REGIONAL MONITORING AND COORDINATION OF FINANCIAL REGULATION

A great deal of work needs to be done at the global, regional, national and firm levels in terms of improving the regulatory environment, supervision and best practices in the international financial system. So much went wrong during the global financial crisis that it is difficult to give a good summary of priorities in creating a more stable global financial regime. However, to summarize:

Capital flows are a necessary feature of the international financial system. They bring with them important economic benefits. However, there is a potential externality in terms of systemic risk when there are strong capital-flow reversals (referred to as financial pollution). Hence, there is a strong case to be made for close monitoring of capital flows at the national level and taking prudential measures to avoid excessive risks. In Asia, mechanisms have been put in place since the Asian financial crisis of 1997–1998 to avoid negative externalities associated with capital flows. These have not been tested recently due to the creditor status of Asian economies; however, the region needs to remain vigilant as its respective financial systems develop.

In order to improve the global regulatory and supervisory environment a number of issues need to be addressed, including better information dissemination and transparency, improved cross-border arrangements for financial transactions, better early warning systems and macroeconomic monitoring, new mechanisms to mitigate the procyclical nature of financial adjustments during crises, and the need to address the 'too big to fail' issue.

In terms of early warning systems and macroeconomic surveillance, it is not sufficient to identify emerging problems; there must be a system in place to deal with them. This is not an easy task, as it involves tackling the burden of adjustment problem. Regional economic cooperation can help in this area as it can facilitate concerted responses to emerging problems.

Given the growth trajectory of Asian economies and the importance of finance to the future development of the region, strengthening financial institutions and markets in Asia needs to be a priority. Moreover, the global financial crisis underscored the problems associated with relying largely on financial intermediation outside the region. Once again, regional cooperation can help in this regard.

An AFSD could help the region address many issues of interest to the region's economies in terms of improving financial stability, fostering development and helping Asia project its positions more forcefully in international forums. Moreover, emerging issues related to financial cooperation, coordination and integration should be key areas that the AFSD should include in its modus operandi.

But there are many other possibilities. As Asian economic cooperation and integration proceeds apace, the region will require additional means of boosting intraregional trade, investment and financial flows. In the area of finance, the CMIM and the Asian Bond Fund are two first (small) steps in this direction and others are in the works; at the subregional level, the AEC program includes financial-related measures, though it is mainly focused on the real sector. The case for closer cooperation at the regional and subregional levels, nested within the context of global forums, is strong and should continue, from concerted measures to strengthen local capital markets to initiatives that facilitate joint issuances of paper instruments.

Still, the emphasis needs to be placed on national financial development. While the financial systems of developing Asian countries have improved since the Asian financial crisis, much remains to be done in terms of improving national financial institutions, particularly the banking system. Moreover, the development and deepening of local fixed-income and equity markets need to be part of this process. While global, regional and subregional initiatives can help accomplish this, the most important reforms will have to be undertaken at the national level.

The global financial crisis has taken a horrific toll on global and regional economies. Hopefully the worst of the crisis is past. But policymakers need to learn from this crisis and put in place a more stable, resilient international financial regime. The financial boat has revealed many leaks that need to be repaired if it is not to sink when the next storm hits it.

NOTES

1. As is the case with all second-best policies, economic efficiency requires that the cure be less harmful than the externality itself.
2. One exceptional episode in December 2006, when the Thai government imposed capital controls pre-emptively in order to prevent further baht appreciation, had negative consequences.
3. See Kreinin and Plummer (2008) for a discussion.
4. There are many excellent surveys of financial cooperation in the Asian region, including Henning (2002), ADB (2008) and Hamanaka (2009).
5. The People's Republic of China (PRC), Republic of Korea (hereafter Korea) and Japan.
6. ASEAN member countries include: Brunei Darussalam, Cambodia, Indonesia, Lao People's Democratic Republic, Malaysia, Myanmar, the Philippines, Singapore, Thailand and Viet Nam.
7. That is, ASEAN plus the PRC, Korea and Japan.

8. That is, the original ASEAN countries (Indonesia, Malaysia, the Philippines, Singapore and Thailand) and Brunei Darussalam.
9. The AEC Blueprint was formally approved by the ASEAN heads of state on 20 November 2007.
10. This discussion borrows from Petri and Plummer (2009).
11. The G7 group is made up of the following economies: the US, Japan, Germany, France, the United Kingdom, Italy and Canada.
12. One representative each from Australia; Hong Kong, China; the Netherlands; and Singapore, which are not G7 countries, were also included.
13. Details can be found at its homepage: http://www.financialstabilityboard.org/. This section draws from information available at that web site.
14. The Group of Eight includes the G7 countries plus Russia.

REFERENCES

Abiad, A., E. Detragiache and T. Tressel. 2008. A New Database of Financial Reforms. IMF Working Paper WP/08/266. Washington, DC: IMF.

Adams, C. 2008. Emerging East Asian Banking Systems 10 Years after the 1997/98 Crisis. ADB Working Paper Series on Regional Economic Integration Number 16. Manila: ADB.

Andriztky, J., J. Kiff, L. Kodres, P. Madrid, A. Maecheler, A. Narain, N. Sacasa and J. Scarlata. 2009. Policies to Mitigate Pro-Cyclicality. IMF Staff Position Note SPN/09/09. Washington, DC: IMF.

Asian Development Bank (ADB). 2008. *Emerging Asian Regionalism*. Manila: ADB.

Association of Southeast Asian Nations (ASEAN). 2007. Declaration on the ASEAN Economic Community Blueprint. http://www.aseansec.org/21081.htm (accessed 18 June 2009).

Association of Southeast Asian Nations (ASEAN). 2009. Director: ASEAN+3 Macroeconomic and Research Office (AMRO). Job opportunity posting. http://www.aseansec.org/25193.htm (accessed 10 March 2011).

Bernanke, B.S. 2005. The Global Savings Glut and the US Current Account Deficit. Sandridge Lecture, Virginia Association of Economics, 10 March. http://www.federalreserve.gov/boarddocs/speeches/2005/200503102/default.htm.

Bhagwati, J. 2004. *In Defense of Globalization*. Oxford: Oxford University Press.

Edison, H.J., M. Klein, L. Ricci and T. Slok. 2002. Capital Account Liberalization and Economic Performance: Survey and Synthesis. IMF Working Paper WP/02/120. Washington, DC: IMF.

Financial Stability Board (FSB). 2009a. Financial Stability Board Holds Inaugural Meeting in Basel. Press release. 27 June.

Financial Stability Board (FSB). 2009b. Financial Stability Board Meets in Paris. Press release. 15 September.

Hamanaka, S. 2009. Re-considering Asian Financial Regionalism in the 1990s. ADB Working Paper Series on Regional Economic Integration 26. Manila: ADB.

Henning, C. 2002. *Policy Analyses in International Economics 68*. Washington, DC: Peterson Institute for International Economics.

International Monetary Fund (IMF). 2009. Initial Lessons of the Crisis for the Global Architecture and the IMF. Mimeo. Washington, DC: IMF.

Johnston, B., E. Psalida, P. de Imus, J. Gobat, M. Goswami, C. Mulder and F. Vazquez. 2009. Addressing Information Gaps. IMF Position Note SPN/09/06. Washington, DC: IMF.

Kawai, M. and M. Lamberte. 2008. Managing Capital Flows in Asia: Policy Issues and Challenges. ADBI Research Policy Brief 26. Tokyo: Asian Development Bank Institute (ADBI).

Kawai, M. and S. Takagi. 2008. A Survey of the Literature on Managing Capital Inflows. ADBI Discussion Paper 100. Tokyo: ADBI.

Kim, S.H., A. Kose and M.G. Plummer. 2001. Understanding the Asian Contagion. *Asian Economic Journal* 15(2): 111–138.

Klein, M.W. 2005. Capital Account Liberalization, Institutional Quality and Economic Growth: Theory and Evidence. National Bureau for Economic Research (NBER) Working Paper No. 11112. Washington, DC: NBER.

Kreinin, M.E. and M.G. Plummer. 2008. Global Trade Balances: Are They Sustainable? Traditional and New Remedies. *Global Horizons* 2(1): 13–27.

Naya, S.F. and M.G. Plummer. 2005. *The Economics of the ASEAN-US Initiative*. Singapore: Institute of Southeast Asian Studies.

Petri, P.A. and M.G. Plummer. 2009. The Triad in Crisis. Paper presented at a workshop on The People's Republic of China (PRC), Japan, and the United States: Deepening Integration, ADBI, Tokyo, 28–29 May.

Setboonsarng, S. 2009. Desirability of the Asian Financial Stability Dialogue. Paper presented at the Conference on Global Financial Crisis: Regional Cooperation and Architecture Policy Issues, Tokyo, ADBI, 16 July.

PART III

Financial Crisis Management and Resolution

9. The role of state intervention in the financial sector: crisis prevention, containment and resolution

Yoon Je Cho

9.1 INTRODUCTION

The underlying theme of this chapter is an old and familiar, yet unresolved one: the roles of the government and the market in relation to a stable financial system and economic growth. Times of crisis call for extraordinary government interventions in the market, often through the direct ownership of banks and non-bank financial institutions (NBFIs). But these interventions need to address the issue of moral hazard and reduce the likelihood of a subsequent crisis. Interventions should also protect the interests of taxpayers, impose losses on the responsible parties and use the market as much as possible to pick the winners and losers. The ultimate objectives of government interventions are to address failures of and imperfections in the market, but the exposure of interventions to the risk of government failure must be considered as well. When markets collapse in times of crisis, the government is the only remaining option. Nevertheless, government interventions should be complemented by market incentives and principles.

This chapter first briefly discusses the role of the state in crisis prevention (section 9.2), as crisis prevention is linked with containment and resolution. It then discusses the role of state interventions in the financial system for crisis containment and resolution (sections 9.3 and 9.4). The discussion of crisis resolution is based largely on the experience of the Republic of Korea (hereafter Korea) during the 1997–1998 Asian financial crisis. Finally, the chapter draws some lessons and recommendations from the Korean experience of financial crisis resolution (section 9.5).

9.2 THE ROLE OF THE STATE IN CRISIS PREVENTION

Access to credit and finance is crucial for industrial development, smoothing out consumption, supporting house purchases, international trade and economic growth. That is why the financial system is called the 'circulatory system' of the economy. The financial market is different from the goods market in that it sells and buys 'promise' and 'credit' (Stiglitz 1989; Bhagwati 1998). Today's transactions are always linked to the promise of future delivery. As such, the financial market is more fragile than the goods market. Therefore, the state's approach to the financial market has to be different from its approach to the goods markets.

One common goal of state intervention is to ensure the stability of the banking system. This has been done through the imposition of high entry barriers, restrictions on the types of products banks can deal with, and restrictions on deposit and lending competition, often through the adoption of interest rate regulations. Arguments are divided on whether these interventions have aided or impeded the growth of financial savings – and, as a result, access to finance by firms and households – and financial sector development.

When countries are moving toward financial liberalization and removing economic regulations, they tend to increase the risk of financial crisis. Most cases of homegrown financial crises in emerging market economies have taken place during or following financial deregulation and opening. The Asian financial crisis in 1997–1998, the financial crisis in the Nordic countries in the early 1990s, and the Latin American financial crisis in the 1980s (Diaz-Alejandro 1985) were all related to financial liberalization and opening. The United States' (US) subprime mortgage market debacle and the recent global financial crisis are also related to financial deregulations that had been introduced during the previous two decades. In the US, the separation of commercial and investment banking businesses was relaxed, regulations on new products became obscure and entry barriers were reduced.

This points to the importance of establishing an effective prudential regulatory system when a country is moving toward greater opening and liberalization of its financial system. Prudential regulation should have a broader scope in emerging economies than in advanced economies whose currencies are international reserve currencies (such as the US, the eurozone and Japan). Currency and maturity mismatches in foreign currency loans should be carefully monitored in emerging economies as the international financial market becomes more integrated and new types of interrelated transactions emerge frequently.

Macroeconomic stability, the introduction of proper rules and standards for supervision, and the building of a proper institutional framework and infrastructure for regulation are of paramount importance. The recent global financial crisis has also highlighted the importance of macroprudential regulation.

It is now generally recognized that actions for crisis prevention are required in five general areas: (1) the regulatory, supervisory and information perimeter needs to be broadened to ensure that all financial activities that pose systemic risks are adequately captured; (2) capital regulation, liquidity management and risk management need to reflect individual institutions' risk, but also their potential to form systemic risk; (3) regulatory approaches that more effectively dampen the procyclicality of financial markets need to be designed; (4) information disclosure and corporate governance practices need to be improved in order to enhance market discipline; and (5) greater coordination is needed within and across countries in the design of regulation and the monitoring of systemic crises (Claessens 2009).

9.2.1 Monetary Policies, Asset Prices and Macroprudential Regulation

Most financial crises have been caused by the boom and bust of asset markets, especially housing bubbles. Thus, one major policy question is: should the monetary authority respond systematically to inflation in asset markets?

In many emerging market economies, central banks have adopted inflation targeting as an anchor for their monetary policies during the last two decades. The conventional view of inflation targeting assigns no role to asset prices in the conducting of monetary policy, except to the extent to which the changes in asset prices signal changes in expected inflation (Bernanke and Gertler 2000). In line with this view, the authorities should deal with asset price bubbles only as their consequences, if any, arise in terms of the inflation objective, for example by supplying the needed liquidity in the event of a bubble burst (Demirguc-Kunt and Serven 2009).

An alternative view advocates a more proactive response of monetary policies to asset prices. Because asset prices may rise for many reasons, including changes in fundamentals, this view holds that monetary policy should react to deviations of asset prices from their underlying fundamentals rather than deviations from any particular target level. Formally, while the monetary authorities' objective functions should continue to be defined only in terms of goods inflation, their reaction function should include not only inflation forecasts and the output gap, but also measures of asset price misalignment – what has been labeled 'flexible inflation targeting' (Cecchetti et al. 2003).

It is difficult to judge which view is correct. The timing and magnitude of the effects of monetary policy on asset prices remain uncertain. As a consequence, raising interest rates may be an ineffective and costly way of dealing with bursting bubbles. The international evidence suggests that a very large interest rate increase may be necessary to stabilize housing prices – so large as to result in huge output losses (Assenmacher-Wesche and Gerlach 2008).

The political pressure not to raise interest rates to contain an asset bubble is also very strong (in every country). Even for the central bank, which enjoys the highest independence guaranteed by law or by tradition, it would not be easy to tighten policy pre-emptively. Given the constraints on using monetary policy to contain an asset bubble, an alternative response would be to use regulatory measures, such as loan-to-value and debt-to-income ratios, or some temporary tax measures. The Korean government adopted these measures when it was concerned about the overheating of the housing market during 2003–2007. While inflation was stable and there was no significant output gap, it was not deemed to be appropriate to use the interest policy to address the rapid housing price increase. It is not clear to what extent these measures helped to contain the bubble in the housing market. But they certainly helped to lower the vulnerability of bank loans to the risk of a housing market collapse.

9.2.2 Options Available to Emerging Market Economies to Stabilize Currency Markets

Most emerging market and developing economies' currencies are non-convertible. Thus, a substantial portion of their firms' and banks' transactions, as well as assets and liabilities, are denominated in a reserve currency, most notably the US dollar. Current international accounting rules require mark-to-market accounting on assets and liabilities reflecting the current exchange rate. This means that the balance sheets of big companies and financial institutions in these countries are highly vulnerable to changes in exchange rates. When there is a sharp depreciation of currency due to currency market instability, the debt ratio of firms and the capital adequacy ratio of banks are severely affected. This can further destabilize the financial and currency markets and may even lead to a crisis. Emerging market firms are becoming more integrated in the global economy in terms of foreign banks' share in their domestic banking industries, foreign investors' share in their domestic stock markets and the foreign trade share in their gross domestic products.

However, the international financial architecture is still far from institutionally matching the closely integrated financial system. This leaves national governments and central banks in a helpless position when they face dollar liquidity problems, unless they hold a large amount of foreign reserves. Thus, a new architecture for the international monetary system is urgently needed. In the meantime, swap arrangements with the central banks of international reserve currencies, such as the Federal Reserve Board and the European Central Bank, need to be extended to emerging and developing economies that are well integrated into the global financial system and have sound macroeconomic management records. Regional monetary arrangements may be another option. Otherwise, emerging economies will have to face increased risk of currency and financial crises, or reverse the opening of their markets, either by imposing capital controls or by reducing the pace of integration, neither of which would be desirable.

9.2.3 Early Warning System

It may be helpful to establish an early warning system to prevent crises. Korea developed such a system after the 1997 crisis. Initially, it was an early warning model focused on forecasting the developments of the foreign exchange market. The system was gradually expanded to include early warning models in the housing, labor and financial markets. These models were continuously refined. Then, in 2004, the government established a comprehensive early warning system that more clearly defined the responsibility of ministries and meetings that should monitor developments in each sector, the level of warning signals and the reporting system. For instance, the Bank of Korea (BOK) was responsible for monitoring foreign exchange flows, the Financial Supervisory Commission (FSC) for monitoring the development of non-performing assets of financial institutions, the Labor Ministry for monitoring the wage level and the situation of worker strikes, the Construction Ministry for monitoring the tightness of housing and land value movements, and the Ministry of Finance and Economy (MOFE) for making overall judgments and reporting to the President. The system established a round table meeting, the core members of which were the minister of finance and economy, the governor of the BOK, the head of the FSC, and the economic adviser to the president. These members met every week to check the market developments of the previous week.

The advantages of this system were to make the monitoring of market developments part of the regular business of each responsible staff and institution, to automatically call the authorities' attention to market developments based on the signal of quantified indicators (and, as a result, to enable them to consider proactive policy measures), to allow a coordinated response by different government bodies, and to keep the head of the government informed regarding developments in the economic situation.

9.3 THE ROLE OF THE STATE IN CRISIS CONTAINMENT

Crises should be prevented. But once a crisis develops, the government's job is to contain and resolve it. For successful resolution of a crisis, it is important for the government to understand the nature of the crisis and to have a clear vision about the new system it wishes to build from the collapsed system.

The measures and focus of government interventions need to be different according to the origin, nature and scope of the crisis. One of the first things that the government has to decide is its macroeconomic policy response. In general, weaknesses in the domestic financial system develop as a result of long-sustained economic recession or the burst of asset bubbles. Facing such a situation, the government has to determine whether expansionary macroeconomic policies are appropriate (as they would enable the financial system to tide over any disruptions), or whether some fundamental restructuring is needed. In the latter case, implementing low interest rates and expansionary policies would give the corporate and banking sectors reason to underestimate the seriousness of their problems and to delay the required restructuring.

Although every financial crisis is different, some common factors exist. Every crisis comes to the surface as a consequence of bank liquidity shortages. Banks facing shortages generally see their credit lines and the rollover of their debt reduced. Liquidity starts to dry up in the interbank market, and depositors start to withdraw their funds from banks and NBFIs. Runs can also involve the withdrawal of funds placed in off-balance-sheet instruments known as trust accounts, money desks, mutual funds and the like. In developing economies, this can develop in parallel with a shifting of local savings to foreign currency deposits at local banks, or to foreign-controlled banks. As currency speculation becomes widespread, strong pressures build in the currency market. Corporate firms rush to secure as much cash as their capacity allows, anticipating that their credit line will be inaccessible in the near future. Through the process of contagion – that is, increased uncertainty about bank solvency – funding pressures can spread from the weakest to the strongest banks.

Facing such a situation, the government and central bank are forced to intervene through various means. The central bank is the first line of defense in dealing with runs. If the efforts of the central bank prove insufficient, the government must step in. In this type of situation, the government can provide a blanket guarantee of bank deposits (sometimes covering most liabilities, including foreign debt), suspend or nationalize banks, and impose temporary capital controls. Concurrent with taking urgent steps to stabilize the economy, the government needs to lay the foundation for managing the crisis.

This section will address the issues related to: (1) the coordination of policy responses; (2) liquidity support; (3) government guarantees; and (4) effective communication with the market.

9.3.1 Coordination of Policy Responses

Effective crisis containment requires effective triage. There should be a clear coordination of policy responses among different government bodies, including economic ministries, the central bank and regulatory authorities. It would be ideal to organize a crisis management team that includes these bodies. An early task of such a team is to assess the scope of the problems facing individual banks and the overall financial system. An accurate diagnosis is necessary to determine appropriate mechanisms for stabilizing the exchange market, resolving distressed banks, determining the amount of support required by banks to be rescued and estimating the aggregate financing needed to resolve the crisis.

It is vital at this stage to assure market participants that the government is taking the situation seriously and is capable of dealing with the problems. If different views are voiced and inconsistent messages are conveyed by different organizations, possibly involving different ministries, the central bank and regulatory bodies, market confidence will be eroded and the crisis will intensify. The emergency team should be given a clear mandate with well-defined powers, and it is equally important to endow the team with experts in this area who are well insulated from conflicts of interest. Past experience suggests that in this early stage of a crisis, existing accounting and regulatory information is substantially misleading and that the crisis management team will have to devote a large portion of its time to developing and analyzing a substantial amount of information necessary to support sound decisions.

9.3.2 Liquidity Support

A financial crisis is typically triggered by runs on banks and a flight of funds from the financial system, and from the country. Facing liquidity problems, the central bank, as the first line of defense, is forced to provide liquidity support. It provides liquidity to the overall system or to specific banks. It uses tools such as open market operations, discount window lending, repurchase and reverse repurchase operations, overdraft lending and reduced reserve requirements to supply liquidity.

According to Bagehot's (1894) classic policy advice, during a systemic crisis the central bank may lend freely to solvent banks, but should minimize its subsidization of risk taking (moral hazard). In addition, loans should be made at a penalty rate and only on good collateral. This implies that the central bank should not provide liquidity support to insolvent banks or to those with poor collateral. In order to follow this principle, the central bank must be able to distinguish quickly between insolvent banks and solvent banks facing liquidity problems. However, in times of crisis, the central bank and the government are not often well situated to make a fair judgment in this regard due to lack of information. Therefore, if a bank that has systemic importance is facing liquidity problems, the central bank usually provides liquidity at this stage. Systemic importance usually has to be determined by the size of the bank and its interconnectedness to other financial institutions. But the central bank may soon realize that its initial liquidity support is insufficient to stabilize the situation. In such cases, the government should step in and issue extensive guarantees to bank liabilities, and/or suspend specific banks to stop runs.

In the case of a foreign liquidity crisis, the ability of the authorities to provide liquidity is constrained by the country's foreign reserve holdings and swap arrangements with other central banks. Facing a run by foreign creditors and speculative currency dumping, the authorities have to decide whether to defend the currency or to allow free floating. If the authorities have sufficient foreign reserves to comfortably cover the amount of short-term foreign debt, foreign portfolio investment and long-term debt falling due within a year, a commitment to defending the currency would be credible. Otherwise, they would have to reach a compromise between the goals of maintaining exchange rate stability and avoiding a currency crisis. If the crisis is homegrown, a credible domestic reform program should be framed and announced to support this commitment. If, given the amount of government-held foreign reserves, exchange rate depreciation could go beyond a level that can be accommodated by domestic companies and financial institutions, the authorities should not wait until that happens, but instead ask the International Monetary Fund for assistance.

9.3.3 Government Guarantees

When it is found that the central bank's liquidity support is insufficient to stabilize the market, the government has no choice but to issue a blanket guarantee on bank liability or suspend troubled banks. Although this measure is controversial due to its long-term moral hazard effect (Demirguc-Kunt and Serven 2009), it is unavoidable in order to stop a run from spreading to other institutions.

While the suspension of banks has the advantage of saving fiscal costs, it tends to undermine market confidence further, reduce the money supply, increase uncertainty and sometimes deepen a systemic crisis. Korea and Thailand suspended specific banks in an effort to stop runs during the 1997 crisis. Their experience suggests that, although suspension seems to be an expedient means for dealing with runs, it can exacerbate uncertainty and precipitate more runs (Scott 2002).

In principle, the government should avoid offering extensive bank liability guarantees, as they limit the government's flexibility in allocating losses and may create incentives for moral hazard. In practice, however, given the potentially systemic nature of financial crises and the ensuing loss of confidence, governments may have few options other than to offer a broadly based guarantee of most bank liabilities. Quickly restoring depositor confidence is important for minimizing the damage caused by a financial crisis. A time-bound blanket deposit guarantee was made in Asian countries including Korea, Indonesia and Thailand during the 1997–1998 Asian financial crisis. Korea and Thailand (though not Indonesia) achieved relatively positive results from providing such guarantees, but even they were ineffective with respect to foreign currency funding.

In the case of a foreign currency run, a government guarantee is credible only to the extent that the government holds a sufficient amount of foreign reserves or swap arrangements with foreign central banks to be able to honor such a guarantee. During the 1997 crisis, foreign creditors did not trust the information and statistics that the Korean government disclosed regarding the amount of usable foreign reserves and short-term foreign debts. This intensified the crisis in the currency market and eventually led to the International Monetary Fund bailout.

Even if the guarantees provided are deemed credible and the crisis is contained, governments still face another set of important challenges. These include the need to control the additional deposits or debts that insolvent institutions will continue to attract, to make sure the guaranteed institutions invest these new resources prudently, and to reduce or eliminate the guarantees once the containment stage of the crisis is over.

An extensive literature supports the position that in normal times overly generous safety-net policies and deposit insurance lead to moral hazard and financial instability (Demirguc-Kunt and Kane 2002; Demirguc-Kunt et al. 2008). The longer the guarantee remains in place, and the longer insolvent banks are allowed to operate, the more difficult it will be to curb these excessive risk-taking incentives. Thus, it is important to initiate quickly the resolution of insolvent banks and to have a timely exit from such guarantees.

9.3.4 Effective Communications and Building Confidence

Effective communication with market players is also critical in the stage of crisis containment. Sometimes it may be necessary to replace ministers who appear to be incapable of winning strong confidence from the market.

In order to add credibility to its messages, the government should prepare a comprehensive and consistent program, in both macroeconomic and sectoral terms, to deal with macroeconomic problems as well as financial and corporate sector problems, especially those responsible for the development of the crisis. Based on this program, the government should ask the parliament or congress for the approval of sufficient public funds to deal with impaired assets and recapitalization. Unless the government program is reliable and convincing, none of the measures discussed above (that is, liquidity supports, guarantees) will be of much help in containing the crisis. Once the program is prepared, it needs to be communicated to domestic creditors and investors as well as foreign ones in international money centers to earn their confidence. Communicating with the public is also crucial to mobilizing political support for the government's program.

9.4 THE ROLE OF STATE INTERVENTIONS IN CRISIS RESOLUTION

When the initial panic abates and market confidence gradually improves, the crisis moves into its resolution stage. A critically important decision revolves around which banks to bail out and which banks to let go under. While the government should be prepared to act in a systemic crisis, its approach needs to be designed to mitigate moral hazard and the possibility of a subsequent crisis. This should be done by imposing real costs on all responsible parties and putting resources back into productive use as soon as possible. Any government involvement should be designed to protect the interests of taxpayers, impose losses on the responsible parties and use the market as much as possible to pick the winners and losers.

In this section, the government approach to crisis resolution, based on the Korean experience during the 1997 crisis, will be discussed in terms of: (1) consolidating the crisis management team; (2) developing crisis resolution strategies; (3) diagnosing bank conditions; (4) mobilizing public funds; (5) resolving insolvent and capital-deficient banks; (6) managing nationalized banks and privatization; (7) resolving NBFIs; (8)

dealing with impaired assets; and, finally, (9) strengthening the regulatory framework.

9.4.1 Consolidating the Crisis Resolution Team

The formation of a specific-purpose crisis resolution team is necessary when a government is preparing a resolution strategy. The crisis management team organized in the contagion stage could be developed into a crisis resolution team, or an entirely new team could be created if the initial team has lost market confidence. Key objectives would be to consolidate responsibility, promote consistency of work and decisions, provide the necessary specialized skills and insulate the work from other official responsibilities and related conflicts of interest. This crisis management team should have a governing body to facilitate the implementation of its decisions through the various government agencies involved and to secure political support.

Officials or representatives from institutions that were responsible for creating and contributing to the development of the crisis should be excluded from the team, if possible. They tend to underestimate the size of the problem to justify past mistakes. In the case of Korea during the 1997 crisis, following the failures on the parts of the MOFE and BOK, and given the dwindling credibility of these organizations, the newly created FSC was charged with the role of crisis resolution as well as financial and corporate restructuring. The head of the FSC had not held a position in the government in the preceding 15 years and the commission recruited staff from outside the government. The emergency economic policy coordination meeting was created, chaired by the president himself and attended by key economic policymakers, including the minister of finance and economy, the governor of the BOK, the head of the FSC, the chief economic adviser to the president and other economic ministers.

One weakness in Korea's strategy of organizing the crisis resolution team during the 1997 crisis, however, was having placed it under the FSC. The coordination between the FSC and MOFE (which was responsible for mobilizing public funds and monitoring their use) was not smooth. Another weakness was that the dual roles of the FSC in crisis resolution and financial sector supervision often gave rise to serious conflicts of interest during the crisis period.

9.4.2 Developing Crisis Resolution Strategies

The first key task of a crisis resolution team is to develop a comprehensive and clear resolution strategy and then execute it. This can be problematic.

For example, solutions to financial problems in banks have implications for debt restructuring in corporate firms and vice versa. Steps taken in nationalizing banks have implications for the government's ability to privatize them (Scott 2002). Moreover, solutions to financial problems have to be tempered by the recognition of their political and social implications (for example unemployment, foreign entry and social instability). Failure to develop an explicit, comprehensive strategy is likely to result in actions and decisions that limit future scope for action, leading to partial and false solutions and, subsequently, to higher long-run costs.

The first step in defining the strategy is to obtain from senior political authorities clearly defined objectives for the crisis resolution team. Based on these objectives, the government or the team has to define in specific terms what is to be accomplished and avoided in the process of resolving the crisis. This serves as a mandate for the team driving the financial restructuring. These objectives then need to be translated into sector-specific goals for the banking system, the NBFI sector, the public sector and the structure of corporate finance.

The strategy needs to be flexible and requires continuous revision and enhancement as it proceeds. The senior political authorities and the crisis resolution team must have distinct roles to play in developing and executing a comprehensive strategy. A key task of the team is to maintain political consensus on the main elements of the strategy. This is important because the team is likely to encounter serious unforeseen problems, including lobbying by vested interests. Similarly, maintaining media and public support for the strategy needs to be included as part of the work program.

9.4.3 Diagnosis of Bank Conditions

It is important to distinguish viable banks from non-viable ones early in the crisis to prevent the wasting of funds. The government needs accurate information to determine appropriate resolution mechanisms for distressed banks and to estimate the potential requirements for funding the crisis resolution. However, it is likely that the authorities will not have access to accurate information regarding the financial condition of banks.

Contributing to the inaccuracy of accounting and regulatory information are the incentives presented to most stakeholders to underestimate the scope of financial problems, especially in the face of a systemic crisis. Bankers who face the risk of losing their jobs if their banks are assessed as insolvent are strongly inclined to underestimate the severity of their financial problems. Owners and managers of firms who risk losing control of their business or its assets if the firms are diagnosed as insolvent are likely to be motivated by a similar incentive. Supervisory authorities, which may expect to be held accountable for the current situation by politicians, the media and the public, also have incentives to downplay the scope of the problems (Scott 2002).

Regulatory indicators also have a number of weaknesses. The regulatory indicators that receive the most attention in a crisis are non-performing loans and bank capital. Because bankers are capable of manipulating accounting information to obscure the actual conditions of debtors, the regulatory measure of non-performing loans can be substantially underestimated (Scott 2002). The overstatement of asset values and understatement of liabilities mean bank capital can be substantially overstated. Therefore, early diagnosis tends to underestimate, to a large extent, the scope of the problems and the amount of financing that will be required of the government.

Korea's crisis resolution team, with the assistance of the World Bank, attempted to obtain better information on the conditions of banks in at least four ways: by hiring international accounting firms to perform diagnostic reviews of troubled banks; by requiring the banks to submit rehabilitation plans containing detailed information regarding their prospective financial and operating conditions; by commissioning major international firms to perform an industry analysis; and by commissioning a financial analysis model that could incorporate various inputs, including the results of the diagnostic reviews and the industry analysis, and project the future profitability and equity recapitalization needs of banks (Lee 2006; Scott 2002). These steps served to help identify clearly non-viable banks, which should be resolved as a priority, but they did not provide sufficient information regarding the capital shortfalls or the nature and consequences of operational weaknesses in the banks and, as a result, insufficient capital was injected in the initial round.

9.4.4 Mobilizing Public Funds

Securing sufficient public funds for financial crisis resolution depends on the political leadership, as well as on political consensus. Gaining quick political consensus on a financing package helped to restore confidence in the Korean economy and financial markets by bolstering the credibility of the government's statements and commitments. However, the Korean government faced difficulties in determining the appropriate size of the financing package. Initially, there was great uncertainty about the scope of insolvency and the amount of financing required. The government faced a trade-off between speed in arranging financing and certainty as to the amount of financing required. At the time, the government expected to run into difficulties in raising additional financing if the initial package proved insufficient. Thus, the initial package had to be sufficiently large to be credible to the market. To the extent that assets acquired by the government in the course of crisis resolution can be sold quickly, the proceeds can be used to reduce the size of the financing package.

The Korean government took quick action to intervene and stabilize banks. A number of banks, including the largest five, were nationalized. Rapid intervention and recapitalization helped to restore confidence quickly in the financial system and economic performance. Korean authorities were able to mobilize and allocate a substantial investment of public funds, equivalent to about 30 percent of gross domestic product, which was used to purchase impaired assets, recapitalize banks and pay out depositors of closed banks.

The government also used indirect methods of financing, such as issuing guarantees or writing put options as a substitute for issuing direct government debt. The possible danger in using these methods is that these obligations give rise to contingent liabilities and may obscure the cost of crisis resolution (Scott 2002; Calomiris et al. 2005). These financial liabilities have to be identified, monitored and managed in much the same manner as direct liabilities.

9.4.5 Resolving Insolvent and Capital-Deficient Banks

Three options for resolving insolvent banks were adopted in Korea: liquidation, business transfers (both asset and liability transfer) and nationalization. The Korean authorities tried to avoid liquidating failed banks unless they had little or no franchise value, but used liquidation to resolve small failed NBFIs. For small failed commercial banks, they orchestrated deposit and asset transfers to healthier banks; the largest banks were nationalized. Shareholders lost their investments, while creditors remained protected. The acquiring banks had access to the central bank's liquidity support to minimize the disruption of banking services for customers of the failed banks. They also received a put-back option on non-performing loans and capital injections to maintain their capital ratio at pre-acquisition levels. For the nationalized banks, top managers were removed and new managers were instructed to cut costs substantially.

In Korea, the largest banks had no controlling shareholders, which minimized the prospects for raising capital from existing shareholders. Also, acquisition by a sound domestic bank was difficult to envision in such circumstances, while large chaebol were restricted from owning banks and the government did not want to sell a large portion of the banking system to foreign investors. To the extent that private sector solutions could not be achieved, nationalization was required to sustain the core institutions of the banking system. The government also sought to use its provision of public funds to banks as an opportunity to promote consolidation within the banking system, as a means to increase the efficiency and competitiveness of Korean banks, and to generate public support for using public funds to recapitalize the banks.

It was almost impossible to make a clear estimation of the amount of losses, as uncertainty was still looming over the future value of corporate firms. The government opted for a gradualist approach to corporate debt restructuring, and this significantly undermined its bank resolution strategy. When big companies in the chaebol (including Daewoo) failed later, the government had to recapitalize the banks again.

9.4.6 Management of Nationalized Banks and Privatization

The nationalization of banks brought with it the major responsibility of exerting governance and overseeing bank restructuring. The government had to ensure that the support provided was put to good use in order to minimize potential demands for additional support, and to maximize the potential for prompt reprivatization. The principal tool for accomplishing this was performance contracts for the senior managers of nationalized banks. This effort, however, was hampered by the managers' lack of sufficient information on the quality of assets. Managers were most successful in their efforts to reduce staff expenses and close or sell branches, but in other areas they did not take much initiative beyond rapidly expanding loans to households and consumers.

Privatization turned out to be difficult to achieve. Chaebol were only allowed to hold 4 percent of banks before the crisis, although this was raised to 9 percent in 2009. Permitting foreign ownership helped the situation and three of the seven largest banks were purchased by foreign interests. However, the government was reluctant to see more of the sector come under foreign control. As a result, Woori Bank is still government owned.

9.4.7 Resolving NBFIs

While industrial chaebol have not been permitted to own commercial banks since the 1960s, they were permitted to own NBFIs, including securities firms and insurance companies. As a result, most NBFIs in Korea have been owned by chaebol or other private controlling shareholders. The Korean authorities limited the use of public funds in resolving NBFIs to what was required to meet the government guarantee on NBFI liabilities.

Existing shareholders were given a certain time period to recapitalize and restructure. If those efforts failed, the government then intervened. NBFIs were resolved by either business transfers to other institutions or liquidation. Few NBFIs were nationalized.

As a result, a number of banks and NBFIs exited the market. Many of them merged with or were taken over by others. The number of banks and NBFIs has been significantly reduced and the soundness of Korean banks has been much improved. The stability of the financial system was fully restored after two or three years. This was achieved in conjunction with a substantial improvement of the debt ratio as well as other financial indicators of the corporate sector.

9.4.8 Dealing with Impaired Assets[1]

To deal with impaired assets, the Korean government established the Non-Performing Asset Management Fund under the management of the Korea Asset Management Company (KAMCO) and raised funds through government guarantees. The government classified the impaired assets based on collateral availability, seniority and degree of impairment, and applied a consistent 'haircut' to assets within the same class.

The haircut used for the valuation of secured assets was based on the historic average of recovery rates less the portion given to senior lien holders. For unsecured assets, it was based on the historic non-performing loan recovery rates of KAMCO. Collateral value was appraised by professional third-party property appraisers to ensure the credibility of the pricing mechanism. Another notable aspect of Korea's case is that the Korean government used a post-settlement scheme to share the proceeds from the sale of impaired assets with financial institutions in order to build a relationship of trust and encourage the participation of such institutions.

Pricing impaired assets and removing them from the balance sheet is an important exercise in determining the financing requirements for the recapitalization of banks. In this regard, the task of preventing a potential conflict of interest was considered crucial, and the government sought not to delegate both functions to a single agency. The Korean government assigned KAMCO the role of relieving banks of impaired assets and the Korea Deposit Insurance Company (KDIC) the role of recapitalizing financial institutions. The rationale behind this decision was that a single agency endowed with both responsibilities would not be able to negotiate the lowest price for the impaired assets, largely because doing so would require a capital injection in the future. Recognizing a need for the coordination of both processes, the government established the Public Fund

Oversight Committee to control and supervise the operations of KAMCO and the KDIC.

Roughly two-thirds of banks' impaired assets were taken over by the government's asset management company (KAMCO) at discounted prices, and capital was injected by the KDIC through the issuing of bonds guaranteed by the government.

The Korean government also adopted various exit measures to minimize government intervention and revive the market functions, as well as to lessen the fiscal burden. Methods were adopted to dispose of acquired impaired assets quickly. These included conventional methods, such as court auctions, public auctions and direct sales, as well as less conventional international tenders, securitization, joint ventures and debt–equity swaps.

9.4.9 Strengthening the Regulatory Framework

Crisis resolution provides a unique opportunity to build a new system – a more robust and sound financial system. Political support for regulatory reform could never be stronger than in times of crisis. But in the course of strengthening the regulatory system, Korea also experienced several problems that it could have handled better (Cho 2002a). First, the unbalanced approach to strengthening the regulatory rules on banks and NBFIs led to a shift of funds from better-regulated banks to less-well-regulated or poorly regulated NBFIs, especially investment and trust companies (ITCs). Corporate firms with cash shortages sought other sources of finance and relied heavily on issuing bonds, which were purchased by ITCs that were still poorly supervised. Prevalent irregularities in the business operations of ITCs allowed heavy financing to risk-taking chaebol firms such as Daewoo, and when these firms got into trouble, the ITCs could not avoid a similar fate.[2] This required a second round of mobilization of public funds and financial restructuring by the government.

Second, the strengthening of banks' regulatory rules had a contractionary monetary effect. When banks had to maintain the required capital adequacy ratio under the new loan classification and provisioning rules, they could not increase their lending. This suggests that monetary policy and supervisory policy need to be well coordinated – not only in boom times but also in times of crisis – to reduce procyclicality.

9.5 LESSONS AND CONCLUSIONS

This chapter has discussed the role of the state in crisis containment and resolution, based mainly on the Korean experience of the 1997 financial crisis. The Korean government was not fully successful in dealing with the crisis, but it has drawn much attention from policymakers, as well as economists, as one of the more successful efforts. Although there is no one-size-fits-all solution for every crisis, we may be able to draw several lessons from the Korean experience. Chief among these lessons are the importance of the following.

9.5.1 Quality of Information

It is important to have a well-defined, comprehensive and integrated strategy for crisis resolution. The effectiveness of this strategy in quickly resolving troubled banks and restoring the banking system's stability depends on the availability of relevant information. Korea's financial restructuring was largely successful. But the government failed to inject a sufficient amount of capital in the initial round and had to repeat the process of recapitalization. It also underestimated the amount of public funds necessary to deal with the problems. When the government recapitalized the banks, it did not have sufficient information to assess banks' capital needs, especially information regarding losses in the loan portfolios. The lack of information also impaired the government's ability to define performance contracts for the managers of nationalized banks.

9.5.2 Political Support

Financial and corporate restructuring is bound to produce many losers. These potential losers include banks, NBFIs and big companies, which tend to have strong political connections and influence over the local media. They are likely to lobby hard against the decisions made by the crisis management team. Principles and fairness are important in the process of allocating losses. Once these are compromised, the government will be unable to drive the financial and corporate restructuring effectively. This means that strong political support for the crisis management team is critical. Times of crisis provide a rare opportunity for economic reform and restructuring.

9.5.3 Prompt Government Action

In times of crisis, when uncertainty is high and accounting data are not reliable, authorities face difficult choices as to whether they should quickly recapitalize to resume the normal function of banks, or wait (by granting banks forbearance) until the size of the problem becomes reasonably clear. The Korean government opted for the first option. This later required another round of recapitalization, and perhaps increased the ultimate cost of bank restructuring. However, its impact on the overall economic recovery was positive. Prompt action may increase the cost of financial restructuring but may reduce the overall cost to the economy in terms of lost employment and output.

9.5.4 A Balanced Approach to Strengthening Regulation

Korea's financial restructuring plan initially concentrated on the restructuring and reregulation of banks and merchant banks. Other financial institutions, including ITCs, remained beyond the scope of the strengthening of supervision or restructuring. As a result, these institutions took advantage of poor regulatory oversight and expanded rapidly (Cho 2002b).

This had both positive and negative impacts. The positive impact was immediate in that it mitigated the impact of the credit crunch in the banking sector. The negative impact was realized over time. When the ITCs imploded, the securities market collapsed, and this added to the ultimate number of non-performing loans, as well as to the taxpayers' burden (Cho 2002b).

9.5.5 Macroprudential Regulation: Coordination between Monetary and Supervisory Policies

The Korean experience showed that financial restructuring and the strengthening of regulatory rules have a strong contractionary effect by diminishing the money creation function of the involved intermediaries (Cho 2002a). During the time of bank restructuring and the strengthening of regulatory rules, the actual monetary stance was affected more strongly by the actions taken by the supervisory authorities – through the reduction of the money multiplier – than those taken by the monetary authorities. This suggests that there should be close coordination between the two authorities to avoid unintended consequences for the money supply during crisis resolution.

9.5.6 Conflicts of Interest: When the Regulatory Authority is a Main Driver of Crisis Resolution

The newly created FSC, the regulatory body, was empowered to become the main driver of crisis resolution, and a crisis resolution team was formed under its auspices. This had advantages and disadvantages. The dual role of crisis resolution and financial sector regulation gave rise to conflicts of interest during the time of bank restructuring. The FSC was forced to forbear on banks that could not meet the regulatory requirements due to problems caused by the actions of the crisis resolution team. This undermined the effective supervision and regulation of financial institutions. Another problem was policy coordination with the MOFE. The MOFE was mainly responsible for financial sector policies and the mobilization of public funds to address the financial crisis. The coordination and cooperation between the MOFE and the FSC, which was tasked with financial restructuring, was not always smooth. This proved costly, as the government was unable to act decisively and to speak with a single voice.

NOTES

1. This subsection is based on Ministry of Strategy and Finance of the Republic of Korea (2009).
2. See Cho (2002a) for a detailed discussion on irregularities of ITC business operations during this time.

REFERENCES

Assenmacher-Wesche, K. and S. Gerlach. 2008. Ensuring Financial Stability: Financial Structure and the Impact of Monetary Policy on Asset Prices. University of Zurich Institute for Empirical Research in Economics Working Paper 361. Zurich, Switzerland: University of Zurich Institute for Empirical Research in Economics.

Bagehot, W. 1894. *Lombard Street*. London: Kegan, Paul, Trench, Trubner & Co.

Bernanke, B. and M. Gertler. 2000. Monetary Policy and Asset Price Volatility. NBER Working Paper 7559. Cambridge, MA: National Bureau of Economic Research.

Bhagwati, J. 1998. The Capital Myth: The Difference Between Trade in Widgets and Trade in Dollars. *Foreign Affairs* 77: 7–12.

Calomiris, C., D. Klingebiel and L. Laeven. 2005. Financial Crisis Policies and Resolution Mechanisms: A Taxonomy from Cross-Country Experience. In *Systemic Financial Crises: Containment and Resolution*, edited by P. Honohan and L. Laeven. New York: Cambridge University Press.

Cecchetti, S., H. Genberg and S. Wadwhani. 2003. Asset Prices in a Flexible Inflation Targeting Framework. In *Asset Price Bubbles*, edited by W. Hunter, G. Kaufman and M. Pomerleano. Cambridge, MA: MIT Press.

Cho, Y.J. 2002a. What Have We Learned from the Korean Economic Adjustment Program? In *Korean Crisis and Recovery*, edited by D.T. Coe and S.J. Kim. Washington, DC: International Monetary Fund.

Cho, Y.J. 2002b. Financial Repression, Liberalization, Crisis and Restructuring: Lessons of Korea's Financial Sector Policies. ADBI Research Paper 47.

Tokyo: Asian Development Bank Institute. http://www.adbi.org/research-paper/2002/11/01/81.financial.repression/.
Claessens, S. 2009. Lessons from the Recent Financial Crisis for Reforming National and International Financial Systems: The Road Ahead to a Sustainable Global Economic System. Annual Bank Conference on Development Economics, World Bank and Government of Korea, Seoul, 22–24 June.
Demirguc-Kunt, A. and E. Kane. 2002. Deposit Insurance around the Globe? Where Does It Work? *Journal of Economic Perspectives* 16(2): 75–95.
Demirguc-Kunt, A., E. Kane and L. Laeven. 2008. Deposit Insurance around the World: Issues of Design and Implementation. Cambridge, MA: MIT Press.
Demirguc-Kunt, A. and L. Serven. 2009. Are All the Sacred Cows Dead? Implications of the Financial Crisis for Macro and Financial Policies. Policy research report. Washington, DC: World Bank.
Diaz-Alejandro, C. 1985. Good-bye Financial Repression, Hello Financial Crash. *Journal of Development Economics* 19(1–2): 1–24.
Lee, K.S. 2006. *Currency Crisis of Korea: Development, Overcoming, and After*. Seoul: Bakyoungsa (in Korean).
Ministry of Strategy and Finance of the Republic of Korea. 2009. Korea's Proposal for Addressing Impaired Assets. March.
Scott, D. 2002. A Practical Guide to Managing Systemic Financial Crises: A Review of Approaches Taken in Indonesia, the Republic of Korea and Thailand. Policy research paper. Washington, DC: World Bank.
Stiglitz, J.E. 1989. Financial Markets and Development. *Oxford Review of Economic Policy* 5(4, Winter): 55–68.

10. The role of the state in managing and forestalling systemic financial crises: some issues and perspectives

Charles Adams[1]

10.1 INTRODUCTION

This chapter reviews recent state interventions in financial crises, with particular emphasis on the Asian financial crisis experience in the late 1990s and the current turmoil. Based on these experiences, it outlines a number of lessons for the state's role in crisis management, while recognizing that the modalities of crisis resolution invariably differ across countries and crises. Section 10.2 reviews the official responses to the financial crisis that struck the region in the late 1990s and the ongoing global financial turmoil. For ease of exposition, crisis management is considered during the three key stages of any crisis – stabilization and containment, asset write-downs and absorption, and rehabilitation and normalization – with different tools and instruments at the forefront of each stage and different state entities in the driver's seat. Section 10.3 outlines a number of broad lessons that can help guide crisis management and argues for expanding the tools available to involve the private sector in crisis resolution, creating procedures to allow for the orderly closure of systemically important financial firms, and integrating more closely *ex ante* and *ex post* systemic risk oversight. Finally, section 10.4 argues for the creation of high-level systemic risk councils (SRCs) in each country to oversee systemic risk in both tranquil and turbulent times and coordinate the roles of various state bodies, including the central bank.

10.2 FINANCIAL CRISIS MANAGEMENT

The key features of the Asian financial crisis and the ongoing international turmoil have been extensively documented.[2] Both episodes have raised major challenges for policymakers in the region, even though the current turmoil has had much smaller effects on the region's financial systems than the crisis of the late 1990s.

The epicenters of the 1997–1998 financial crisis were the financial systems of a number of Asian economies that had extended excessive credit without due regard to risk.[3] Not only were the crises in these countries extremely severe, but they were also multifaceted in that they frequently involved balance-of-payments problems, domestic and external debt crises, financial system distress and, in some cases, political upheaval. The costs of the crises were extremely large, whether measured by (estimates of) the output losses incurred or by the fiscal costs of financial sector bailouts.[4]

Consistent with the pattern of many other emerging market crises, the Asian financial crisis was preceded by huge inflows of private capital and was triggered by both a sharp pullback of capital (sudden stops and reversals) and market doubts about the sustainability of relatively tightly managed exchange rate regimes (currency speculation) (International Monetary Fund, IMF, 1998, 1999, 2007). Even more than ten years after the crisis, key features of the crisis management strategies adopted – most notably the use of so-called high interest rate defenses, the handling of some bank closures, and the resort to capital and other direct controls – remain highly contentious.[5]

Whereas Asia was at the epicenter of the late 1990s crisis, it has largely been at the periphery of the recent turmoil. This is a reflection of the fact that the recent crisis erupted in the United States (US) and the financial spillovers to the region thus far have generally been relatively small. This has been the result, *inter alia*, of limited direct exposure to the 'toxic' products and institutions at the center of the crisis, a general strengthening of conditions and risk management in regional banking systems, and much stronger external macroeconomic fundamentals (Asian Development Bank, ADB, 2008a; Bank for International Settlements, BIS, 2009; Adams 2008). Spillovers, however, were substantial.[6] For the most part, the spillovers have been the result of real trade linkages and the high export orientation of many Asian economies. Only for a short period in late 2008, when international credit markets began to seize up, did foreign currency liquidity pressure become a significant issue for some countries in the region.[7]

Reflecting the key differences between the crisis of the late 1990s and the current turmoil, crisis managers in the region have thus far faced very different challenges during the two episodes. Most importantly, whereas the 1990s crisis called for the adoption of wide-ranging measures to manage collapsing financial systems in several countries, the key challenges during the current episode have involved taking pre-emptive measures to reduce crisis spillovers and efforts to keep credit flowing.[8] Exceptions are the cases of the Republic of Korea and Indonesia, which had US dollar liquidity shortages in late 2008 that needed to be addressed, and Japan, where banking system exposure to falling stock markets has been high (BIS 2009).

A range of orthodox and unorthodox measures has been taken to stabilize advanced-country financial systems during the recent turmoil, and the state has assumed – explicitly or implicitly – an important market-maker role (Buiter 2009). Some of the measures taken in the advanced countries – such as the resort to blanket guarantees and the nationalization of parts of financial systems,[9] may have added to pressures in the region by encouraging withdrawals of foreign currency. At the same time, especially in the case of countries in the region with a strong foreign bank presence, there were spillovers to domestic financial markets and institutions from distressed foreign financial firms, especially in the wake of the Lehman Brothers' failure in late 2008.

To facilitate exposition, the stages of crisis management are broken down into three phases: (1) stabilization and containment; (2) asset write-downs and absorption; and (3) rehabilitation and normalization.[10] In making the breakdown, the intention is not to suggest that crisis management is a clean and structured process that proceeds in clearly defined stages. By their nature, financial crises are messy and disorderly with unpredictable twists and turns (Hoelscher and Quintyn 2003). Every crisis, however, involves a number of critical stages during which certain key decisions need to be made and the breakdown facilitates the consideration of these decisions.

10.2.1 Stabilization and Containment Phase

This is the first and, arguably, the most important phase for systemic crisis management. Except in those instances where a major crisis erupts completely unexpectedly, crises frequently begin with the emergence of pressures in particular segments of financial systems or in particular financial institutions (the 'tremors' phase). In the recent turmoil, the warning signs began to emerge in the subprime segment of the US real estate market in 2006 as default rates began to increase (ADB 2009a; IMF 2008a, 2008b, 2008c). Even though these problems can be seen *ex post* as the starting point for a full-blown crisis, they are frequently not seen in such terms at the time they emerge. Either because the sectors facing difficulties are seen as too 'small' to have large spillovers, the excesses in these sectors are not judged to be symptomatic of wider problems, or as a consequence of political unwillingness to confront reality (the 'denial' phase), a relatively common response is to regard the first problems as 'isolated'.

At some point, the difficulties in particular segments of the financial system no longer remain contained. The crisis becomes systemic and an arsenal of policy and other instruments begins to be deployed to stabilize the financial system. Policy instruments that can be employed at this stage include central bank liquidity support operations, partial and blanket government guarantees of deposit and other liabilities and, in some instances, the use of direct measures such as deposit freezes, bank 'holidays' and capital controls.[11] And if balance-of-payments pressures accompany the financial crisis – as was the case during the Asian financial crisis – the government may seek the assistance of international financial institutions or regional partners (Boorman et al. 2000; Adams et al. 2000).

Numerous issues arise with regard to the roles of different policy instruments in containing the crisis during the first phase, and there is a need for a relatively high degree of coordination between various official agencies and the central bank in assessing and responding to problems. Typically, central banks play a major role as suppliers of domestic currency (and, perhaps, foreign currency) liquidity,[12] but finance ministries, supervisory and regulatory bodies and deposit insurance agencies may also play important roles. Generally, liquidity support operations are at the forefront of initial efforts and are undertaken by the central bank, implying that it absorbs the risks. Key operational issues include whether standing liquidity facilities are up to the task (including whether stigma effects limit their use), the terms and conditions for the liquidity provided (including collateral and counterparty requirements), and whether the central bank is able to channel the liquidity to where it is needed in the system (Hoelscher and Quintyn 2003; Boorman et al. 2000; Demirguc-Kunt et al. 2006; Demirguc-Kunt and Detragiache 1998, 1999). As evidenced during the current turmoil, some of the advanced countries, including the US, found it necessary to expand the counterparties eligible to use lender-of-last-resort facilities as liquidity seized up in both the capital markets and the banking system. New facilities were also created in some instances, either to address stigma effects, or to allow liquidity to be channeled to where it was needed.

Generally, the challenges associated with getting liquidity to where it is needed can be addressed under the flexibility provided by the 'exceptional' circumstance provisions of many central bank charters and, as necessary, new regulation or legislation can be enacted. Both during the recent crisis and during the Asian financial crisis, central banks were generally able to provide domestic currency liquidity to where it was needed, even though in some cases this called for the 'flexible' use of existing facilities and, in some instances, the liquidity was provided to institutions not usually covered under regular lender-of-last-resort facilities. Generally, the technical ability to inject domestic currency liquidity is not a problem, except perhaps in currency unions or where there are relatively rigid currency board-type arrangements, which limit domestic currency issuance.

In practice, a key challenge in providing liquidity support is to ensure that it does not compromise the overall macroeconomic policy stance. What this means is that the central banks must have the tools to 'sterilize' injections of liquidity to ensure that monetary and exchange rate policy are not compromised. The importance of sterilization depends on the scale of the liquidity support provided and the nature of the financial crisis. During the Asian financial crisis, sterilization operations were very important given external sector weakness and the so-called high interest rate defenses judged necessary to support the external sector (Adams 2003).

Additional important issues in liquidity provision include the conditions under which liquidity is provided and when the support should be backstopped by other measures. Even though prudence might dictate that liquidity support should only be provided to solvent institutions, it is very difficult in practice to distinguish between solvency and liquidity problems in the heat of a major crisis (Boorman et al. 2000). Very often, major crises tend to require central banks to loosen their collateral requirements and it may not be feasible to charge distressed financial institutions penal interest rates. Generally, as evidenced by the current crisis, the scale of central bank liquidity support can become very large and the credit quality of central bank balance sheets can deteriorate, especially in circumstances where the central bank seeks to circumvent breakdowns in financial intermediation (BIS 2009).

Generally, countries do not rely exclusively on liquidity support, except in the very short run before there is time to introduce other measures. Key complementary or alternative measures include the provision of partial or blanket government guarantees to the financial system and the introduction of direct controls on withdrawals from the banking system. As these measures typically require changes in government policy and may have implications for taxpayers, it is normal for finance and other ministries to play a key role in their introduction. At the same time, critical input and cooperation has also typically been required from a range of supervisory and regulatory agencies and deposit insurance funds in order to help assess the solvency of different financial institutions.[13]

Notwithstanding the existence of deposit insurance funds, a common response in many crises is the introduction of 'blanket' guarantees that expand the scope of deposit insurance coverage. By providing confidence that deposits (and, perhaps, other liabilities) will be covered by the state, policymakers intend to avoid wholesale or retail bank runs and reduce the pressure on the lender-of-last-resort function. All the countries at the center of the Asian financial crisis eventually introduced blanket deposit guarantees. Several countries in Asia have used blanket guarantees during the recent turmoil so as to limit contagion or in response to similar moves by their neighbors as discussed by the ADB *Monitor* (ADB 2008b, 2009b).

As in the case of liquidity support, experience shows that it is critically important that blanket guarantees do not compromise the overall macroeconomic framework. Given the potentially huge fiscal costs, blanket guarantees can easily raise questions of fiscal sustainability and, in the cases of heavily dollarized economies or where the guarantees cover external currency funding, may also threaten external sustainability (Collyns and Kincaid 2003). Based on these considerations, best practice in the case of low-intensity financial crises has typically been to use blanket guarantees very sparingly, and to employ them only after losses have been imposed on the stakeholders of troubled institutions (Boorman et al. 2000).

Even though blanket guarantees may be introduced to lessen the possibility of bank runs, their introduction can also play a potentially important stabilizing role by signaling that the state is prepared to absorb at least some of the financial system losses. As a result, guarantees can represent an initial critical stage in the process of allocating and distributing losses across different stakeholders and making clear that particular claimants (such as depositors) will be protected. The earlier blanket guarantees are introduced, the less likely it is that the state will have a full accounting of the scale of potential losses it will be covering and the fiscal implications. By signaling that certain deposits will be protected, the state is also making clear that other claimants, including capital owners, may not be covered.

Finally, should liquidity support and government guarantees not be sufficient to stabilize the financial system, the state may impose direct controls on the withdrawal of funds from financial institutions and, in extremis, bank 'holidays'. Even in the cases of very severe crises, these have typically been used as measures of last resort not only on account of their potentially damaging effects on confidence and efficiency but also because they can be very hard to administer. Realistically, however, it is important to recognize that some direct controls are frequently used during crises, but typically as a backstop to front-line efforts to control the crisis.

10.2.2 Asset Write-Downs and Absorption

Once the economy is stabilized (if not before), a comprehensive crisis management strategy is required to write down impaired assets, deal with troubled institutions and, eventually, bring more capital into the financial system. The modalities of such strategies differ widely across countries as a result of not only differences in legal and political systems, but also the nature of the crisis (in particular, whether it is an external as well as a domestic financial crisis), whether the financial system is mainly bank- or capital-markets-based, and the authorities' preferences as regards economic stability and growth.

One key shortcoming at this stage is that the state will often take a very long time to come up with a coherent and proactive crisis management strategy. This is arguably one of the key lessons the IMF has drawn from its crisis management experiences (Hoelscher and Quintyn 2003; Boorman et al. 2000; Collyns and Kincaid 2003). Typically, a key turning point in addressing the financial sector problems in many crises occurs when the authorities develop a comprehensive, forward-looking crisis management strategy.

From a narrow economic perspective, the optimal strategy for crisis resolution might appear to be one that involves taking the losses implied by the crisis as quickly as possible with a view to allowing for a speedy bounce-back. For a variety of reasons, however, the process of absorbing losses typically takes several years and the authorities invariably face numerous trade-offs in resolving a number of complex burden sharing and collective action problems. Experience shows, however, that the fact that the process may take several years does not obviate the importance of coming up with a crisis management strategy as early as possible (Hoelscher and Quintyn 2003; Boorman et al. 2000).

As during the first phase of a crisis, various government agencies and ministries are involved during the second stage, and the role of the central bank in providing emergency liquidity support may start to be reduced. Alternatively, as has been the case during the recent turmoil, central banks in some countries may assume a key role in allocating credit in response either to generalized credit crunches or to breakdowns in some aspects of the financial system 'plumbing'. A number of central banks in Europe and the US have arguably played an unprecedented role in the recent turmoil in seeking to circumvent the effects of perceived or actual breakdowns in credit provision. As a result, there have been large changes in the size and composition of central bank balance sheets during the recent turmoil (IMF 2008b; BIS 2009).

The implementation of any crisis resolution strategy will generally take a relatively long time. Most obviously, it is difficult to move very fast in writing down impaired assets because there will typically be considerable uncertainty in the heat of the crisis about how much assets are worth (price discovery) and in finding buyers. And, at least in the case of major systemic crises, the value of virtually all assets may be impaired to some degree. Uncertainty about asset values arose during the Asian crisis experience in the late 1990s, which was predominantly a bank-based crisis, and bedeviled the management of the recent crisis in the US and Europe, where capital markets have been more important and the market (were it working) could play a potentially important price discovery role.

Conventionally, valuing bank loans is seen as posing the toughest challenge because loans are typically held on bank balance sheets and are not traded (even if there is some potential to trade the underlying collateral) (Boorman et al. 2000). Another reason why it is difficult to move rapidly is the existence of negative feedback loops. As financial crises are inevitably preceded by excessive credit creation, there is a need for a period of deleveraging. Typically, deleveraging requires asset sales that tend to depress asset prices, which makes necessary further deleveraging and so on. A vicious circle can easily occur in which the process becomes destabilizing. Unfortunately, there are no easy solutions to this problem and, in practice, seat-of-the-pants judgments need to be made about how to navigate around the instability.

The likelihood that the markdown of impaired assets will lead to some financial institutions becoming insolvent also tends to slow down the process. Allowing all insolvent institutions to close immediately would be damaging for systemic stability, and the approach that is often taken is to close down only those whose 'departure' would not create large adverse spillover effects. As argued below, such an approach can create enormous moral hazard problems if the 'owners' of these institutions are bailed out and are not somehow required to take losses.

The process of valuing bank loans during a crisis is often assigned to the supervisors of banks working in close cooperation with bank management and staff. In many cases, asset management companies (AMCs) may also be set up to play a role in valuing bank loans as part of an effort to shift these assets off bank balance sheets (the 'good bank–bad bank' approach).[14] Practice varies across countries and crises, and a key challenge has typically been to try to establish 'fair' values for assets in stressed conditions. Given that banks and (private) AMCs will have different objective functions, price discovery can be very difficult (Boorman et al. 2000; Ingves et al. 2006). This conflict can be avoided to some extent when intervened banks sell their impaired assets to government-owned AMCs, but it is then important to avoid situations in which the AMCs overpay for assets and implicitly help recapitalize the banks. As during other crisis resolution stages, a high degree of transparency and independence has been found to be desirable in valuing impaired assets, as noted in particular by Boorman et al. (2000) and Ingves et al. (2006).

The crisis has demonstrated that the process of valuing securitized assets can also be extraordinarily difficult in circumstances where there is uncertainty about underlying asset values. In such circumstances, private buyers may be encouraged to bid for such assets to facilitate price discovery through explicit subsidies on risk taking. To this point, however, a proposed variant of such an approach that has been set up in the US – the private public partnership – has not yet been used and appears increasingly likely to fall by the wayside.

Following loan write-downs, banks or financial firms are often split into different groups according to their solvency and viability. Three main groupings are often identified: (1) firms that are adequately capitalized; (2) those that are undercapitalized but which are potentially viable over the medium term; and (3) those that are both undercapitalized and non-viable on account of either a lack of a profitable business model or an inability to raise fresh capital in the market (Hoelscher and Quintyn 2003). In some cases, as in the US and Europe during the recent turmoil, the classification of banks and other financial firms might also be based on stress tests in which their solvency or need for fresh capital is determined by the government on the basis of their ability to absorb various shocks (IMF 2008a, 2009a; BIS 2009).

Generally, intervention to banks and institutions in the third 'no-hope' group would be quick and, when systemic risk is not judged to be large, they would be closed immediately, albeit with arrangements typically made to transfer their guaranteed deposit liabilities to a viable institution. Banks in the second group would typically be encouraged to raise private capital, but if this is not possible, may receive injections of official capital. Banks in the first group may escape official intervention. Of course, for these approaches to be adopted, the state must have the authority to intervene in the troubled institutions. As illustrated by recent experience, the state frequently has 'special' powers to intervene in certain financial institutions such as banks, but may not have the authority in the case of other financial institutions.

Key operational questions also concern the basis on which institutions intervened by the state should be operated (and by whom) and the conditions that banks receiving public monies (preferred or common equity) should be asked to meet. Based on experience, best practice in the former area tends to suggest that intervened banks should be run on commercial grounds with a view to minimizing losses, and then privatized or closed down as soon as feasible without creating systemic risk (Collyns and Kincaid 2003). In some cases, independent managers with banking experience are put in charge of these banks, whereas in other cases, their supervisors may be put in control. Experience suggests that the intervened institutions should be protected from political influence and patronage.

Generally, injections of public capital into potentially viable banks – whether in the form of preferred or common stock – should be accompanied by time-bound conditionality as regards restructuring and, in some cases, by the requirement to raise private capital. More controversially, some countries have sought to require recapitalized banks to undertake new lending. Experience suggests, however, that such requirements should generally be used sparingly as the resumption of new lending too quickly may delay the return to financial health. As evidenced during the recent turmoil, however, there may be strong political pressure for banks that receive public monies to engage in new lending.

10.2.3 Rehabilitation and Normalization

The third and final phase involves the ongoing restructuring and strengthening of financial firms and the gradual unwinding and withdrawal of the special measures taken earlier. Even though the state will continue to play a critical role in this stage, the nature of its role will evolve and tend to become less hands-on as temporarily nationalized financial firms are reprivatized and non-performing loans and assets held by state-run AMCs are slowly divested.

Even though the structure of the newly emerged financial system will generally be determined by the market, it will also be influenced importantly by changes in financial structure as a result of state actions during the crisis. In addition, as was the case following the Asian financial crisis in the late 1990s, the state may develop financial action plans to help guide the direction in which financial systems develop; including, for example, with regard to the degree of concentration in the banking sector as well as seeking to grow local currency financial markets and the supporting infrastructure.[15]

Two key operational issues in the third phase concern the speed with which the state should pull back from its management of supported financial firms and how quickly impaired assets should be sold by state-run AMCs. Even though there is a presumption that the moves in these areas should be rapid, there is generally a need to balance several competing objectives.[16] And, in those cases where non-financial corporate restructuring is a key component of the effort, it has had to be recognized that such restructuring generally takes a long time to complete. Ultimately, it is the 'quality' of the adjustments made that will determine the success of the restructuring efforts and 'good' operational restructuring will necessarily take time (Adams et al. 2000; Pomerleano and Shaw 2005).

Generally, states have sought to divest themselves of stakes in financial firms relatively rapidly. In those cases where firms have been temporarily intervened ahead of their orderly closure, the key steps have typically involved transferring some of their assets and liabilities to other institutions and/or mergers with stronger firms. The argument for moving quickly in the case of these institutions is that their continued operation may create unfair competition for viable firms and may involve substantial taxpayer costs. Provided the firms can be unwound in an orderly manner, they are typically allowed to exit as soon as possible. Nationalized and viable banks will also need to be privatized, but the speed with which this occurs is also influenced importantly by how quickly their balance sheets can be cleaned up and by the availability of private capital. Moving rapidly can imply that these firms will be bought up at 'fire sale' prices and can generate political backlashes.[17]

How rapidly the assets held by state AMCs are sold to the market involves balancing several competing objectives. With a view to maximizing recovery value (and minimizing taxpayer costs), governments may choose to avoid selling assets quickly and wait for markets to recover (Ingves et al. 2006). Such approaches were quite common in the wake of the Asian financial crisis and led to many AMCs being in operation several years after the crisis.[18] On the other hand, to the extent to which the state AMCs are sitting on a large stock of assets, the effect may be to delay the bottoming out of asset prices and their eventual recovery. Some balance is necessary between competing objectives.

10.3 CRISIS MANAGEMENT LESSONS

Reflecting differences in political, economic and legal systems, as well as the nature and scope of different crises and the availability of different tools, a single template for crisis management cannot be outlined. There is no 'good housekeeping' book on crisis management, even though the crisis management experience does suggest that there are pitfalls to be avoided. In addition, it is not easy to place the approaches to crisis management into simple boxes such as 'market-friendly' or 'state-led' or 'fast-track' versus 'slow-track'. Crises by their nature are highly complex, a mix of different approaches is usually taken to manage them and there is no single one-size-fits-all template for crisis management.

Based on crisis experience, it is possible to note a number of broad but important lessons that can guide crisis management, as well as some key areas where the strengthening of crisis resolution frameworks would be desirable. Key general principles or lessons for crisis management that can be distilled from the very large number of recent crises are as follows:[19]

1. The need for a correct early diagnosis of the nature of the crisis and the adoption of a consistent overall crisis strategy that has the support of the highest level of government.
2. The importance of the crisis resolution strategy being cast within a sustainable macroeconomic framework.
3. The need for the state to have adequate tools and instruments to intervene in the system where and when necessary.
4. The importance of recognizing losses, writing down impaired assets, and facilitating the injection of new capital as needed.
5. The importance of a high degree of transparency and independence in the key decisions regarding the allocation of losses, intervention of firms and injection of official capital.
6. The need for the independence of the crisis management strategy from vested political and financial interests.
7. The need for a high level of cooperation, coordination and information sharing among key state agencies, ministries and the central bank.
8. The need for a clear exit strategy for the orderly unwinding of extraordinary measures.

There are also three aspects of crisis management that could be strengthened: (1) the tools and instruments available to involve the private sector in crisis resolution; (2) the ability to impose losses credibly on systemically important financial institutions while keeping them afloat; and (3) the approaches used to identify and manage systemic risk.

The ability to involve the private sector in crisis resolution (and avoid bailouts) will depend ultimately on there being sufficient capital in the system to absorb losses. Accordingly, progress in this area is linked closely to ongoing efforts with regard to capital adequacy and ensuring that the capital involved is 'real'. The second key area is with regard to the tools and instruments for dealing with systemically important financial institutions. Arguably, the increased resort to guarantees, bailouts and liquidity support during the recent crisis has reflected both the assessment that the systemic risk implications of allowing certain financial firms to fail are too high and, in some cases, a lack of instruments to allow for their orderly unwinding. One possible approach, suggested by King (2009), is that if an institution is judged to be too important systemically to fail, then it should not be allowed to operate.[20] Such an approach seems unlikely to be workable in practice, however, and could imply forgoing the economies of scale and scope of large financial institutions. Either because the too large or too interconnected to fail problem is unlikely to go away, or because it is only during a crisis that it becomes clear what is too important to fail, an approach is needed to deal with systemically important firms that run into difficulty. One possibility is the 'living will' approach in which systemically important financial firms are required to draw up plans regularly for their orderly termination (King 2009; Buiter 2009). But this may not go far enough and would require a correct *ex ante* identification of systemically important firms. What would arguably be more desirable (and feasible) would be to set up crisis resolution systems in which the owners of systemically important financial institutions could be forced to take large losses (and ultimately fail) even while the business operations of these firms could be wound down in a slow and orderly manner. Or, alternatively put, these financial firms must be made 'safe to fail'. The key elements of such an approach would be: (1) the creation of special crisis resolution regimes in which the state is provided with flexible powers to intervene in a timely manner in all systemically important financial institutions (based on an *ex ante* or *ex post* determination of systemic importance) and, if necessary, keep them afloat; (2) the existence of real[21] capital and other cushions in these institutions that are sufficiently large to absorb losses in extreme events and which can be written down even as the firms are kept on life support; and (3) the ability to provide assistance flexibly to innocent bystander financial firms that are adversely affected by spillovers and collateral damage from the financial firms in distress.

An essential ingredient in crisis avoidance and management is the early detection and containment of systemic risk.[22] Against this background, there is an urgent need to strengthen the oversight and understanding of systemic risk. Since the current turmoil erupted, there has been a considerable amount of work done on how frameworks for macroprudential surveillance could be strengthened and systemic risk better assessed.

For the most part, the work program on systemic risk has been directed toward *ex ante* crisis prevention. But very clearly, financial crises will invariably occur and there can be important pay-offs in better managing them when they arise. Arguably, therefore, there would also be benefits to addressing systematically the links between systemic risk in normal times (*ex ante*), the particular crisis management strategies adopted (*ex post*) to deal with the realization of systemic risk, and how crisis management strategies influence systemic risk in the future. In addition, account can usefully be taken of how alternative crisis management strategies will impact on systemic risk in the future through moral hazard and other effects. Arguably, assigning the same state entity overall responsibility for systemic risk may facilitate the linking of *ex ante* and *ex post* oversight.

Under most current structures, such an assignment of responsibilities does not appear to be common (Davies and Green 2008).

10.4 SYSTEMIC RISK RESPONSIBILITY

A case can be made for assigning both *ex ante* (surveillance) and *ex post* (crisis management) oversight to the same state body. Which state body should have these responsibilities is not clear, however, and most countries currently involve a number of different state entities in decisions with actual and potential systemic risk implications.

Given their existing roles in macroprudential surveillance and crisis management, central banks might appear to be the natural candidates for a central role in systemic risk oversight. As documented by Schinasi (2006), ADB (2008b) and Davies and Green (2008), many central banks already have mandates for macroprudential or *ex ante* systemic risk oversight and are well positioned to track the build-up of risk on account of their 'need to know' the markets in order to implement monetary policy. And, in many countries, central banks still play a role in the micro supervision of banks. In addition, by virtue of their lender-of-last-resort and other related functions, central banks frequently play a major role in systemic crisis management, as documented in previous sections. From these perspectives, at least, central banks would appear to be well positioned to assume the dual roles of both *ex ante* and *ex post* systemic risk overseers.

Against the arguments for providing central banks with a central role in systemic risk oversight, there are a number of important caveats. These include the possibility that the role of systemic risk overseer will distract central banks from their focus on monetary policy; lead to them becoming excessively politicized, as many decisions will need to be made about liquidity and other forms of support to financial firms; and, more generally, that it might involve central banks in many actual or quasi fiscal activities.[23] Moreover, given that micro-based supervision and regulation in several countries has already been moved outside the central bank – in one or more variants of the mega or integrated regulator model (Davies and Green 2008) – the proposal might require partially reversing this shift as central banks would either need to acquire comprehensive information on the financial system directly in order to perform their expanded mandates, or information-sharing agreements with financial regulators would need to be strengthened.

Alternatively, the systemic risk overseer role could be assigned to a mega financial regulator (outside the central bank), but this would immediately run into the difficulty that mega regulators do not normally have the lender-of-last-resort function or the other tools central banks have to manage crises. While it might be possible to provide the mega regulator with a lender-of-last-resort fund on which it can draw during a crisis, this could seriously impede its flexibility to respond to shocks. Another possibility would be to assign the responsibility for systemic risk oversight to the ministry of finance based, *inter alia*, on its taxing responsibilities. This, however, could create a similar issue due to missing policy instruments as well as information-sharing problems with the central bank and/or regulatory bodies. In short, there does not seem to be a simple solution to the issue of which entity should play the role of overall systemic risk overseer.

Against this background, this chapter proposes a compromise structure in which a single new state body is created to assume overall responsibility for *ex ante* and *ex post* systemic risk oversight even as the implementation of key policies with systemic risk implications remain the responsibility of the central bank, the ministry of finance and relevant regulatory bodies. As envisaged, a high-level SRC would be established in each country and would have the ultimate responsibility for systemic risk oversight and for setting macroprudential and crisis management policies. Under the envisaged structure, relevant state bodies, such as regulatory agencies, would continue to play important roles in micro-based supervision and regulation, central banks would continue to serve as lenders of last resort, and deposit insurance funds would discharge their mandates. What would be different would be that the activities and actions of these agencies as they relate to systemic risk would be under the direction and control of the SRC. Effectively, the SRC would be the one-stop shop coordinating agency for systemic risk oversight and control.

The power of the SRC would derive from its vested authority to require other state bodies, including the central bank, to implement the macroprudential and crisis resolution measures regarded as necessary to contain or manage systemic risk.[24] To these ends, the SRC would need to have its own independent staff to assess and monitor systemic risk, be headed by an official with rank at least equal to the heads of relevant state agencies under its direction, and have the authority to request from other state bodies the information required to perform its functions.[25]

The key defining features of the SRC would be as follows:

- The SRC would be the ultimate point of responsibility for systemic risk oversight and management.
- The SRC would monitor actual and imminent threats to systemic financial stability and have the responsibility to determine the appropriate pre-emptive macroprudential policy responses that would be implemented by other state bodies.

- The SRC would address unfolding systemic risks during crisis periods and have the responsibility for determining the macroprudential measures and state interventions required to address these risks in order to support financial stability.
- The SRC would help coordinate the roles of the various state bodies and agencies as regards systemic risk (including the central bank) and help avoid duplication and overlap.

As envisaged, the SRC would address the key concerns associated with assigning systemic risk oversight to the central bank, while recognizing that several state bodies will invariably need to be involved in systemic risk issues. Most importantly, the SRC structure would help protect the monetary independence of the central bank and ensure that any quasi-fiscal actions (including lender of last resort) that the central bank undertakes to contain systemic risk are implemented on behalf of the SRC with the risk borne by the SRC (and ultimately the government). Beyond these advantages, the SRC would also be better positioned than the ministry of finance to decide when taxpayer funds should be used to address systemic risk concerns during a crisis. This is because the SRC, under its mandate, would be looking at systemic risk in deciding whether the use of public monies was warranted. And, the establishment of the SRC would imply that the micro regulatory body (or bodies) would not need to focus on systemic risk or make decisions about the use of taxpayer funds in any bailouts during a systemic crisis.

NOTES

1. The author would like to thank participants at the ADB Institute conference on Global Financial Crisis: Financial Sector Reform and Regulation, in Tokyo on 21–23 July 2009, for comments and suggestions on the chapter and, in particular, David Mayes and Biswanath Bhattacharyay for their insightful suggestions.
2. The references on both crises are numerous and still growing. The Asian financial crisis is well covered in various IMF reports and papers – including Boorman et al. (2000) – while the key features of the recent turmoil are discussed in IMF (2009a), BIS (2009) and ADB (2008a, 2009a). See also Bordo (2008) for a historical perspective.
3. Even though most of the region was affected, Indonesia, the Republic of Korea, Malaysia, the Philippines and Thailand were at the heart of the crisis. Japan was still dealing with the effects of the bursting of a real-estate bubble at the time of the Asian crisis. See Boorman et al. (2000).
4. See ADB (2009b) and Adams (2008) for a review of East Asian banking systems ten years after the crisis.
5. See Boorman et al. (2000) and Adams (2008).
6. See the discussion of ADB's *Asia Economic Monitor* in 2008 and 2009 (ADB 2008b, 2009a).

7. Notably the Republic of Korea and Indonesia, as discussed in the IMF's *World Economic Outlook* and *Global Financial Stability* reports (IMF 2009a, 2009b).
8. Across the region, some pressures have been evident in short-term interbank markets related to arbitrage across different funding sources. See BIS (2009) for further discussion.
9. See the IMF's *Global Financial Stability Report* (IMF 2008a) and BIS (2009).
10. This is essentially the breakdown used by a number of IMF studies, albeit with somewhat different terminology used. See Hoelscher and Quintyn (2003), Collyns and Kinkaid (2003), Boorman et al. (2000) and Laeven and Valencia (2008).
11. For further discussion see the IMF studies by Hoelscher and Quintyn (2003) and Collyns and Kincaid (2003).
12. Either using own reserves or by activating currency swap lines as during the recent global crisis. See *World Economic Outlook* (IMF 2008d) and BIS (2009).
13. The degree of cooperation required from deposit insurance agencies depends on the nature of their role and whether they have supervisory functions in addition to a pay-box role. See Hoelscher and Quintyn (2003).
14. Numerous mechanisms and structures typically play a key role during the second phase. In many crises, new vehicles such as asset management companies (AMCs) may also begin to play a role as efforts are made to deal with impaired assets. Very often these AMCs are creations of the state but their precise structure and ownership, as well as their funding and mandates, tend to differ across crisis experiences. And, whereas some countries have created very centralized AMCs to which all banks can transfer impaired assets, some countries have created decentralized AMCs that are linked directly to particular banks. See Adams et al. (2000).
15. For a discussion of the implications of such plans, see Adams (2008).
16. See Ingves et al. (2006).
17. See Adams et al. (2000).
18. See *Asia Economic Monitor* (ADB 2008b).
19. See Hoelscher and Quintyn (2003), Collyns and Kincaid (2003) and Boorman et al. (2000).
20. See comments on the Bank of England web site by King (2009).
21. Note the emphasis on real capital, which could be Tier 1 capital as defined by the Basel Capital Standards. For further discussion, see Basel Committee on Banking Supervision (2004).
22. A key recent example might be the Lehman Brothers' bankruptcy in late 2008. See BIS (2009) and IMF (2009a, 2009b).
23. This has clearly been the case during the recent turmoil as discussed earlier in this chapter and in BIS (2009).
24. In *ex ante* terms, these would include discretionary actions such as changes in capital requirements, stepped-up macroprudential supervision, and more rules-based approaches such as dynamic provisioning. *Ex post*, they would include decisions on how to respond to systemic stress and whether, for example, to bail out financial firms and/or provide liquidity support.
25. Kawai and Pomerleano (2009a, 2009b) stress the importance of an independent view of systemic risk.

REFERENCES

Adams, C. 2003. The IMF Approach to the Asian Currency Crises: An Alternative View. In *Exchange Rate Regimes and Macroeconomic Stability*, edited by L.S. Ho and C. Yuen. Dordrecht: Kluwer Academic Publishers.

Adams, C. 2008. East Asian Banking Systems Ten Years After the 1997–98 Crisis. ADB Working Paper No. 16. Manila: ADB.

Adams, C.F., R.E. Litan and M. Pomerleano. 2000. *Managing Financial and Corporate Distress: Lessons from Asia*. Washington, DC: Brookings Institution Press.
Asian Development Bank (ADB). 2008a. *Asia Economic Monitor*. July. Manila: ADB.
Asian Development Bank (ADB). 2008b. *Asia Economic Monitor*. December. Manila: ADB.
Asian Development Bank (ADB). 2009a. *Asia Economic Monitor*. July. Manila: ADB.
Asian Development Bank (ADB). 2009b. *Asian Development Outlook 2009*. Manila: ADB.
Bank for International Settlements (BIS). 2009. The International Financial Crisis: Timeline, Impact, and Policy Responses in Asia and the Pacific. Mimeo. Hong Kong, China.
Basel Committee on Banking Supervision. 2004. *International Convergence of Capital Measurement: A Revised Framework*. Basel: Bank for International Settlements. http://www.bis.org/publ/bcbs107.pdf.
Boorman, J., T. Lane, M. Schulze-Ghattas, A. Bulír and A.R. Ghosh. 2000. Managing Financial Crises The Experience in East Asia. IMF Working Paper No. 00/107. Washington, DC: IMF. http://papers.ssrn.com/sol3/papers.cfm?abstract_id=879684.
Bordo, M.D. 2008. An Historical Perspective on the Crisis of 2007–2008. National Bureau of Economic Research Working Paper No. 14569. Cambridge, MA: National Bureau of Economic Research.
Buiter, W. 2009. Regulating the New Financial Sector. Vox web site, 9 March. http://www.voxeu.org/index.php?q=node/3232.
Collyns, C. and G.R. Kincaid. 2003. Managing Financial Crises: Recent Experience and Lessons for Latin America. IMF Occasional Paper No. 217. Washington, DC: IMF.
Davies, H. and D. Green. 2008. *Global Financial Regulation*. London: Wiley.
Demirguc-Kunt, A. and E. Detragiache. 1998. The Determinants of Banking Crises in Developing and Developed Countries. *IMF Staff Papers* 45(1): 81–109.
Demirguc-Kunt, A. and E. Detragiache. 1999. Monitoring Banking Sector Fragility: A Multivariate Logit Approach. IMF Working Paper 99/147. Washington, DC: IMF.
Demirguc-Kunt, A., E. Detragiache and P. Gupta. 2006. Inside the Crisis: An Empirical Analysis of Banking Systems in Distress. *Journal of International Money and Finance* 25(5): 702–718.
Hoelscher, D.S. and M. Quintyn. 2003. Managing Systemic Banking Crises. IMF Occasional Paper No. 224. Washington, DC: IMF.
Ingves, S., S.A. Seelig and D. He. 2006. Issues in the Establishment of Asset Management Companies. In *Bank Restructuring and Resolution,* edited by D. Hoelscher. New York: Palgrave Macmillan.
International Monetary Fund (IMF). 1998. International Capital Markets. Developments, Prospects and Key Policy Issues. World Economic and Financial Surveys. Washington, DC: IMF.
International Monetary Fund (IMF). 1999. International Capital Markets. Developments, Prospects and Key Policy Issues. World Economic and Financial Surveys. Washington, DC: IMF.
International Monetary Fund (IMF). 2007. Reaping the Benefits of Financial

Globalization. IMF Discussion Paper. Washington, DC: IMF. http://www.imf.org/external/np/res/docs/2007/0607.htm.
International Monetary Fund (IMF). 2008a. *Global Financial Stability Report (April)*. Washington, DC: IMF.
International Monetary Fund (IMF). 2008b. *Global Financial Stability Report (October)*. Washington, DC: IMF.
International Monetary Fund (IMF). 2008c. *World Economic Outlook: Financial Stress, Downturns and Recoveries, World Economic and Financial Surveys*. Washington, DC: IMF.
International Monetary Fund (IMF). 2008d. *World Economic Outlook: Rapidly Weakening World Economic and Financial Surveys*. Washington, DC: IMF.
International Monetary Fund (IMF). 2009a. *Global Financial Stability Report (April)*. Washington, DC: IMF.
International Monetary Fund (IMF). 2009b. *World Economic Outlook: Crisis and Recovery (April)*. Washington, DC: IMF.
Kawai, M. and M. Pomerleano. 2009a. Bolstering Financial Stability Regulation. *Economists' Forum* blog, 28 August. http://blogs.ft.com/economistsforum/2009/08/bolstering-financial-stability-regulation/.
Kawai, M. and M. Pomerleano. 2009b. Financial Stability Regulator. Vox web site, 14 August. http://www.voxeu.org/index.php?q=node/3872.
King, M. 2009. Untitled. Speech to Scottish business organizations in Edinburgh. http://www.bankofengland.co.uk/publications/speeches/2009/speech406.pdf.
Laeven, L. and F. Valencia. 2008. Systemic Banking Crises: A New Database. IMF Working Paper 08/224. Washington, DC: IMF.
Pomerleano, M. and W. Shaw, eds. 2005. *Corporate Restructuring: Lessons from Experience*. Washington, DC: World Bank Publications.
Schinasi, G.J. 2006. *Safeguarding Financial Stability: Theory and Practice*. Washington, DC: IMF.

PART IV

Promotion of Asian Bond Markets

11. Developing Asian local currency bond markets: why and how?

Mark M. Spiegel

11.1 INTRODUCTION

Since the 1997–1998 Asian financial crisis, there has been a perception that Asian financial markets would be aided by the existence of developed local currency bond markets. In part, this perception stretches back to former Federal Reserve Chairman Alan Greenspan's 'spare tire' argument that bond markets would provide alternative vehicles for intermediation in the event that primary sources of financing, such as bank and equity finance opportunities, were disrupted (Greenspan 1999). While others have expressed skepticism at this argument, it is generally agreed that the absence of well-developed domestic and regional bond markets exacerbated the 1997–1998 crisis (Park and Park 2003). At a minimum, the opportunity to issue in local currencies would mitigate currency mismatch difficulties. Indeed, International Monetary Fund (IMF) conditionality requirements during the 1997–1998 crisis included explicit calls for the development of local currency bond markets in some countries, such as Thailand (Batten and Hoontrakul 2008).

In response, Asian governments have adopted initiatives to promote local currency bond finance through their initial Asia Bond Markets Initiative (ABMI) and through the Asian Bond Funds 1 and 2 (ABF1 and ABF2). While Asian bond markets have grown markedly since the launch of these initiatives, there is still a perception that the region is underserved by domestic bond markets (Eichengreen and Luengnaruemitchai 2006). Moreover, progress to date has been heterogeneous within the region.

In part, local currency bond market development has been hindered by the lack of sufficient economies of scale, due to insufficient demand for assets denominated in the local currencies of smaller Asian economies. In response, efforts have been made to coordinate policies at the regional level to achieve the scale economies needed for viable bond market activity.

This chapter reviews the arguments for intervention in favor of the development of regional bond markets and assesses the progress on these initiatives to date. Roughly five years passed between the launch of the ABMI and the onset of the global financial crisis. It would seem reasonable to expect some improvement in market liquidity and depth over this period of relatively uninterrupted global expansion, and indeed, it is apparent that much success was achieved. In the first five months of 2009, Chinese companies issued United States (US)$82 billion in debt, far outpacing the Japanese US$51 billion in issuance over the same period (Balfour 2009).

However, the recent global financial crisis begs for a reassessment of both the merits of efforts to encourage local currency bond market development and the degree of success that has been achieved to date. This event challenges our understanding of the functioning of financial markets and their roles in economic activity. The collapse of the asset bubble of the previous decade has revealed that a substantial share of investment during the boom years was misplaced, often undertaken in an effort to 'chase yields' in an environment of ever increasing risk tolerance. There can be no doubt that some of the capital allocated to Asian emerging market economies falls into this category.

As such, the recent financial crisis provides a good opportunity to re-examine the merits of the Asian bond initiatives. The analysis conducted for this study suggests that the bulk of policy conclusions one would be likely to have held going into the crisis are still likely to be valid. However, one should be cautious in concluding that the efforts to promote regional bond markets have been an unqualified success. While there is no doubt that the progress to date has resulted in a dramatic increase in local bond market volumes in some countries in the region,[1] there is still much heterogeneity across the region in the pace of market deepening and in the speed of regulatory reforms. Moreover, the crisis itself demands a reassessment of what constitutes a successful domestic bond market. These considerations will be reviewed and suggestions made as to which policies are likely to remain conducive to the pursuit of successful domestic bond markets going forward, and which now appear to be anachronistic.

The remainder of the chapter has five parts. Section 11.2 discusses the motivation for intervention in favor of local currency bond market development. Section 11.3 discusses regional efforts prior to the global financial crisis. Section 11.4 assesses the success of these initiatives. Section 11.5 discusses the implications of the global financial crisis for the merits of regional local currency bond market initiatives, and provides an early review of regional policy responses to the crisis. Lastly, section 11.6 provides some policy conclusions.

11.2 MOTIVATION FOR ENCOURAGING LOCAL CURRENCY BOND MARKETS

11.2.1 Enhanced Financial Stability

One major conclusion drawn from the 1997–1998 Asian financial crisis was that the crisis was exacerbated by excessive reliance on bank lending. Indeed, then-Chairman Alan Greenspan (Greenspan 1999) characterized a well-functioning bond market as a potential 'spare tire' that might have allowed for continued intermediation and mitigated economic turmoil after banks had stopped lending in Thailand.

Over time, this notion of bond markets as spare tires has largely been discredited. It has been widely observed that the development of successful banking sectors and domestic bond markets are complements, rather than substitutes. However, well-functioning bond markets can be more efficient than banks for some forms of intermediation. While banks are more adept at lending to smaller, more opaque firms, bond markets enjoy a comparative advantage in servicing larger, more established companies (Eichengreen 2006b).

A more enduring lesson of the 1997–1998 Asian financial crisis was of the danger of exposure to currency risk. During that crisis, devaluations decimated the balance sheets of firms and financial institutions. The opportunity to issue in local currencies allows firms to avoid currency mismatches. The desire to mitigate firm currency risk exposure remains one of the primary motivations for the development of local currency bond markets in Asia (Kwon 2006).

11.2.2 Achieving Economies of Scale

Another motivation for encouraging the development of local currency bond markets is that it allows markets to reach transaction volumes sufficient to achieve economies of scale and reduce funding costs for issuing domestic firms. The size of the underlying economy plays a key role in the determination of the depth of local bond market activity.

One benefit to bond markets of exhibiting scale economies is that smaller markets can suffer from illiquidity. Asian bond markets are commonly regarded as less liquid than those in the US. For example, Hale and Spiegel (2009) found that there was a 35.3 percent increase in the probability of issuing in euros relative to pre-union national currencies among non-financial firms in international bond markets subsequent to the launch of the European monetary union. Presumably, that increase was attributable to the far greater size of the eurozone economy relative to any of its national counterparts. Increased size implies that firms can attract more analyst coverage and face deeper markets.

Two features drive the perception that domestic Asian bond markets could achieve greater scale economies. First, many Asian bond markets are small relative to the size of their economies. Second, as a region, Asia runs a large trade surplus with the rest of the world. This is partly financed through the issuance of bonds, with the result that agents in Asia have acquired large stocks of foreign bonds, particularly US Treasuries. There is a perception that instead of following this pattern, capital could be profitably recycled within the region to local issuing firms. It has therefore been argued for some time that the development of local currency bond markets could play a role in alleviating global imbalances (Park and Rhee 2006).

Another motivation for encouraging the development of local currency bond markets is that current transaction volumes are inadequate to generate a desirable level of coverage by global rating agencies. It has long been understood (Park and Park 2003) that the successful development of Asian local currency bond markets would require the existence of both regionally specialized rating agencies, as well as rating activity from global firms. These rating agencies provide the analysis that investors require to feel secure about assessing the risks associated with foreign bond purchases, and the spreads required for issuance in the absence of their coverage may prove to be prohibitive to many potential issuing Asian firms. In response, Asian groups have actively encouraged additional coverage by both global and regional rating agencies.

However, many bond issuers in Asia are still not covered by these agencies. This immediately reduces the potential investor base for Asian issues, as many large Western institutional investors, such as pension funds, require that the bonds included in their portfolios be rated at some level by international credit rating agencies. This calls into question the wisdom of encouraging rating agencies solely at the regional level. These regional agencies are likely to encourage additional clients from the region itself, but may leave it difficult to attract foreign purchasers, as these institutions may not recognize the ratings generated by these regional agencies.

The superiority of global rating agencies over their national counterparts in Asia has also been questioned. National rating agencies are supposed to have access to superior information concerning the underlying fundamentals of issuing firms. However, global rating agencies are supposed to enjoy superior international credibility, as they are generally considered to be more independent. A recent study by Ferri et al. (2009) sheds doubt on the superiority of global rating agencies in the Republic of Korea (hereafter Korea), as downgrades from a national rating firm generated deeper negative responses on average than downgrades from its global affiliate counterparts.[2] As such, additional coverage by both regional and global agencies is likely to be desirable.

11.2.3 Anomalies and Imperfections in Less-Developed Markets

There is a widespread perception that less-developed bond markets exhibit anomalies and other distortions in their yield curves. When well behaved, bond yield curves can provide important information concerning the degree to which investors discount future payment streams. Yield curves have been shown to provide important information concerning agents' discount and expected inflation rates. For example, Gürkaynak et al. (2005) demonstrate that bond yield curves are useful in gauging investors' long-term inflation expectations, as long-term yields appear to respond to current data.

Distortions in yield curves can arise for a wide variety of reasons, including liquidity premia, hedging demand, demand for deliverability into futures contracts, desirability for use in repurchase markets, or differences in bid–ask spreads or non-synchronous quote times (Gürkaynak et al. 2007). Anomalies can make it difficult to estimate the rate of discount. First, as bonds do not exist at all maturities, the estimation of yield curves must entail some degree of interpolation. This can introduce errors depending on the underlying causes of observed anomalies: some might reflect actual differences in rates of discount, while others might reflect more market-based sources of heterogeneity. The inability to identify the true rate of discounting of bonds at various maturities can make it hard to gauge, for example, how well inflation expectations are anchored, and thereby hinder the ability of bond yields to be used in the conduct of monetary policy. Second, to the extent that anomalies reflect difficulties in settlement or other financial frictions, they represent additional costs of intermediating through the bond market. As such, it is more costly to conduct transactions. Since mitigating risk often requires the ability to open and close positions at various maturities, these costs may discourage bond issuance not only at the maturities exhibiting the observed anomalies, but also in the market exhibiting these anomalies as a whole.

However, liquidity discrepancies can lead to some lack of smoothness in even the most developed markets. In their estimation of the US Treasury yield curve from 1961 to 2006, Gürkaynak et al. (2007) found that while they could fit a curve that matched the data well using only six parameters, they still found maturities that were off their fitted curve, most notably at two and three-year maturities. Nevertheless, yield curve anomalies appear to decline with bond market development.

Yield curve anomalies also appear to arise during temporary episodes of financial turbulence. These anomalies are likely to reflect the lack of liquidity in issues at specific maturities. For example, Gürkaynak et al. (2007) found increases in liquidity premia of on-the-run ten-year US Treasury yields relative to synthetic off-the-run US Treasury securities with comparable maturity dates and coupons during episodes of financial turmoil, such as the 1987 stock market crash and the fall 1998 seizing-up of financial markets following the Russian ruble crisis.

Even among developed economy bond markets we see evidence that increased depth and liquidity in domestic bond markets can reduce the magnitude and incidence of anomalies. For example, Ehrmann et al. (2007) examined the case of bond markets in the eurozone before and after the advent of the European monetary union. They found that the advent of the euro led to substantial convergence of levels and co-movements of yields across these markets, suggesting that investors tended to treat the eurozone bond market as a single market, notwithstanding the differences in perceived default risk among eurozone member countries. Indeed, Manganelli and Wolswijk (2007) found evidence that heterogeneity in the pricing of government bond yields after the launch of the euro was attributable to differences in bond credit ratings, which are supposed to be based solely on default risk. As such, it appears that net of default risk and differences associated with legal regimes, the eurozone was treated as a single local currency bond market after the launch of the monetary union.[3]

Given the efforts made in encouraging the development of Asian local currency bond markets, we would expect to observe a decline in yield curve anomalies over the time period where these efforts were taking place. That appears to be the case, as evidenced by the fitted Korean yield curves in Figure 11.1.[4] At the launch of the ABMI in 2003, the Korean government securities yield curve exhibited a number of anomalies, including a notable inversion at the two-year horizon. Four years later, this was replaced by a relatively smooth upward-sloping yield curve. Recently, despite the financial turbulence experienced in that country, the Korean yield curve has failed to exhibit any inversions, although the medium maturities deviate substantially from levels that would be consistent with a smooth fitted yield curve.

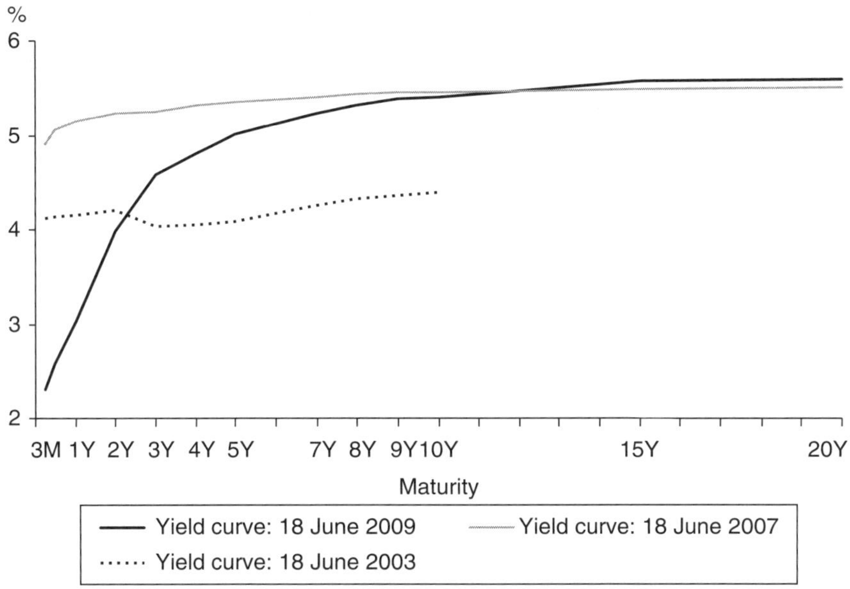

Source: Bloomberg database, http://www.bloomberg.com/markets/.

Figure 11.1 Korea: government securities yield curves, 2003, 2007, 2009

11.3 REGIONAL EFFORTS TO ENCOURAGE BOND FUND DEVELOPMENT

Because of awareness of the issues raised above, discussions about regional cooperation in Asia concerning the promotion of local financial markets have been going on for quite a while. However, efforts to promote local bond markets really took off subsequent to the 1997–1998 Asian financial crisis. Early in the process, few of the Asian emerging market economies were prepared to issue bonds in their own currencies. The memory of the 1997–1998 crisis led many countries to fear that excessive holdings of local currency issues by foreign speculators could 'erode control over monetary policy and expose them to currency speculation' (Park and Park 2003: 4). Efforts were therefore launched under a number of regional groups to facilitate the development and depth of Asian financial markets. Most notable among these were the ABMI, which sought to develop the infrastructure for the Asian bond markets and to introduce issuance on local currencies, the Chiang Mai Initiative (CMI), which sought to mitigate, among other things, the risk of illiquidity through a series of swap

Table 11.1 Pre-crisis Asian regional bond market initiatives

Date	Event
2003	Executives' Meeting of East Asia Pacific Central Banks (EMEAP) announces creation of ABF1, consisting of US$1 billion in sovereign and quasi-sovereign Asian bonds.
	ASEAN+3 launches ABMI: six voluntary working groups established to discuss issues relevant to the development of domestic and regional bond markets. Groups include securitization, credit guarantees, local currency bonds, credit ratings and foreign exchange transactions.
2004	Japan Bank for International Cooperation (JBIC) guarantees baht-denominated bonds issued by Thai firm Tri Petch Isuzu.
	'Pan-Asian bonds' issued by Japan and Korea: senior debt issued by 46 small and medium-sized Korean firms with guarantees from JBIC and Industrial Bank of Korea.
	Ringgit-denominated Malaysian bonds issued by the Asian Development Bank (ADB) and the International Finance Corporation (IFC).
	EMEAP announces ABF2, consisting of a Pan-Asian Index Fund (PAIF) and eight single-market funds.
2005	Release of ABMI 'roadmap' for gathering and sharing information, as well as studies concerning issuing Asian currency basket bonds, regional efforts at promoting liquidity and cross-border trading, alternatives for tax treatment, and 'Asian bond standards'.
	EMEAP announces implementation of ABF2.
2007	CMI bilateral swap arrangements increased to US$80 billion. Agreement on self-managed reserve pooling arrangement.

Sources: ASEAN+3 (2003, 2008, 2009) and Jang and Hyun (2009).

arrangements, and the ABF1 and ABF2, which sought to increase demand for Asian bonds. The chronology of these initiatives is shown in Table 11.1; in this section, each of them will be reviewed in turn.[5]

11.3.1 ABMI and Currency Swaps

In August of 2003, the Association of Southeast Asian Nations (ASEAN)+3 Finance Ministers Meeting in Manila announced the ABMI, aimed at improving regional medium and long-term financial conditions. Six voluntary working groups were established to discuss issues relevant to the development of domestic and regional bond markets. These groups examined securitization, credit guarantees, local currency bonds, credit ratings and foreign exchange transactions (ASEAN+3 2003).

Regional issuance activity grew in 2004. In June, the Japan Bank for International Cooperation (JBIC) (formerly the Export–Import Bank of Japan) guaranteed baht-denominated bonds issued by Thai firm Tri Petch Isuzu. This was followed at the end of the year by the issuance of 'pan-Asian bonds' (collateralized bond obligations) by Japan and Korea. Under this program, senior debt was issued by 46 small and medium-sized Korean firms with a guarantee from the Industrial Bank of Korea. Bonds guaranteed by JBIC and backed by these pan-Asian bonds were then issued on the Singaporean exchange, promoting the creation of a regional collateralized debt obligation (CDO) market (Japan International Cooperation Agency 2004). At the same time, the Asian Development Bank (ADB) and the International Finance Corporation issued ringgit-denominated Malaysian bonds.

The progress was codified in the release of the 'roadmap' for gathering and sharing information, as well as studies concerning the issuing of Asian currency basket bonds, regional efforts at promoting liquidity and cross-border trading, and alternatives for tax treatment.

In May of 2008, efforts were increased with the release of the second ABMI roadmap, creating task forces for the promotion of issuance and demand for local currency bonds, and improvements in regulatory frameworks and institutional structures. In addition, member countries were asked to develop references for self-assessment to serve as their benchmarks (ASEAN+3 2008).

In addition to the ABMI, the CMI, which was launched in May 2000, set up a network of bilateral swap arrangements among the ASEAN+3 countries. Under these swap arrangements, countries requesting support could immediately access 20 percent of their facility, while the remaining 80 percent was to be disbursed under an IMF program. The motivation for linking the disbursement to an IMF program, and hence to IMF conditionality restrictions, was to address the region's 'current limited capacity to produce and enforce effective adjustment programs' (Kawai 2007: 26).

11.3.2 ABF1 and ABF2

In June of 2003, the Executives' Meeting of East Asia Pacific Central Banks (EMEAP)[6] announced the creation of the ABF1 under the management of the Bank for International Settlements (Bank for International Settlements 2003). The ABF1 consisted of US dollar-denominated sovereign and quasi-sovereign Asian bonds equal to approximately US$1 billion issued by the EMEAP countries with the exception of Australia, Japan and New Zealand. The ABF1 was one vehicle designed to encourage the development of Asian bond markets and reduce the region's perceived excessive reliance on bank financing (Kawai 2005).

From the beginning, it was understood that the ABF1 was aimed at retaining some of the region's reserves within the region in an effort to encourage the development of local capital markets. It was also apparent that true traction in affecting the development of local capital markets would require that the regional fund hold securities denominated in local currencies. It was announced at the outset that such activity was planned for the EMEAP.

With the launch of the ABF2, the EMEAP moved toward the inclusion of instruments denominated in local currencies in the Asian bond funds. The ABF2 invests in local currency issues from EMEAP countries other than Japan, Australia and New Zealand. There are two components of the ABF2, the Pan-Asia Index Fund (PAIF), which invests in sovereign and quasi-sovereign issues from eight EMEAP countries, and the Fund of Bond Funds, which invests in eight single-market funds that hold sovereign and quasi-sovereign local currency bonds. Both the PAIF and the Fund of Bond Funds had initial allocations equal to US$1 billion (Jang and Hyun 2009).

11.3.3 Regional Credit Rating Agencies

Many bond issuers in Asia remain uncovered by credit rating agencies. This reduces the potential investor base for Asian issues, as many large Western institutional agencies, such as pension funds, require that the bonds included in their portfolios be rated. One strategy to alleviate this problem is the two-tiered securitization process. Under this procedure, local currency bonds are aggregated into two pools. The senior bonds are sold to an offshore special-purpose vehicle, with prices based on their ratings. The special-purpose vehicle repackages them and issues asset-backed securities. These asset-backed securities are then sold at a price based on their credit rating. Ample coverage and common standards by rating agencies are therefore required for such transactions to take place.

Efforts have been made to encourage additional coverage by both regional and global agencies. The Association of Credit Rating Agencies in Asia (ACRAA) contains rating agencies from 20 Asian nations that meet regularly to encourage cooperation on rating standards. However, many have called for a regional rating agency (Park and Rhee 2006), particularly to encourage rating coverage of local currency bonds.

Among the firms that are rated by both, there was initially a systemic discrepancy in the ratings assigned by domestic and international agencies, with those from the international agencies almost invariably being lower. International rating agencies rate foreign issues for many issuers as simply one notch below the ratings given to the sovereign debt issued in their home country, which themselves are often below investment grade. Large investors – who commonly face restrictions against purchasing securities below investment grade – are often precluded from purchasing these bonds.

There was hope that the ABMI would reduce this gap by 'uncovering' creditworthy private borrowers in the region (Park and Park 2003). This was based on the notion that agencies would be better informed about the macroeconomic conditions of local economies, as well as firm-specific information about the issuers themselves, and therefore base their ratings less on the ratings earned by the sovereign issues of firms' countries of origin.

Moreover, the existence of a deep regional bond base would allow for the creation of regionally specialized rating agencies, which would presumably have superior information concerning the conditions of issuing firms. There would therefore be a benign feedback to regional bond market development, as the creation of deeper bond markets could enhance the profitability of rating agencies covering such markets, while the greater coverage would encourage more firms to issue in these markets, leading to further deepening.

While the ABMI explicitly called for the development of domestic credit rating agencies in Asia in 2003, ACRAA has been acting since 2001 to pursue harmonization of rating standards within the region. However, these efforts are often hampered by differences in legal systems and accounting standards followed across the region, as well as the reality that capital markets are in quite different stages of development (Imai 2004). To address these differences, ACRAA has created a 'best practices' committee that compares the practices of rating agencies across the region. ADB recently issued its *Handbook on International Best Practices in Credit Rating* (ADB 2008), which aims to harmonize and improve standards across the region. There have also been efforts within the region to cooperate in the formation of a rating agency. For example, in 2006, India, Malaysia and Indonesia announced efforts to promote a regional rating agency.

11.4 SUCCESS OF REGIONAL BOND INITIATIVES

Many characterize Asian bond markets as 'underdeveloped' relative to other countries' financial systems. One basis for this assessment is the fact that intermediation through bond markets as a share of gross domestic product (GDP) is far lower in emerging Asia than in major financial centers such as the US and Japan. Another reason is that the share of private borrowing is still small relative to the share of government issues, as private firms in Asia still borrow extensively through banks and also raise capital through equity markets. Finally, there is a perception (Jang and Hyun 2009) that because of Asia's status as a surplus country in trade, it is generating capital that could profitably be 'recycled' within the region, rather than used to finance foreign issues.

Asian bond markets exhibit a diverse set of circumstances. Some markets in Asia exhibit greater liquidity and narrower bid–ask spreads (Jiang and McCauley 2004). These tend to be markets with larger average issue size. However, the region also contains less liquid markets that exhibit wider bid–ask spreads and higher yields. In particular, the size of local currency bond markets pales relative to their more developed counterparts in the US and Japan.

Another characteristic of Asian bond markets is the small share of private issuance, as corporate financing remains dominated by equity and bank financing. Because private issuance tends to be in foreign currencies, while public issuance tends to be in local currencies, the share of domestic currency issuance in Asian markets usually exceeds that of hard currency issuance. This feature suggests that private firms in Asia may be excessively reliant on bank lending for their financing.

Efforts to encourage bond market development in the past decade have been quite successful. Volumes more than doubled in the region prior to the onset of the global financial crisis, with increased corporate participation and decreasing risk premia. However, the pace of advancement has been heterogeneous. Bond markets in Korea and Malaysia have achieved corporate market penetration comparable to that in the US (Batten and Szilagyi 2007), while the pace of advancement in other nations has lagged.

For example, see Figure 11.2. As a share of GDP, the local currency bond markets of Korea, Malaysia and Singapore are most prominent, while those of India and Viet Nam are notably lagging behind. To some extent, this discrepancy clearly reflects the relative level of development these countries have achieved. However, it is also interesting to see which countries have succeeded in increasing their local currency bond issues as a share of GDP between 2002 and 2008. Only Korea, Singapore, Thailand and Viet Nam appear to have made much progress in this area over this period.

While Asian bond markets are quite heterogeneous, and the success of efforts to date to promote bond markets in the region is mixed, some broad generalizations can be made. The first concerns size. It is clear that the regional bond market has grown dramatically since the 1997–1998 financial crisis. It also appears to be the case that Asian bond markets have become more liquid, as evidenced from declines in average bid–ask spreads. However, a look at the raw size of Asian bond markets (Figure

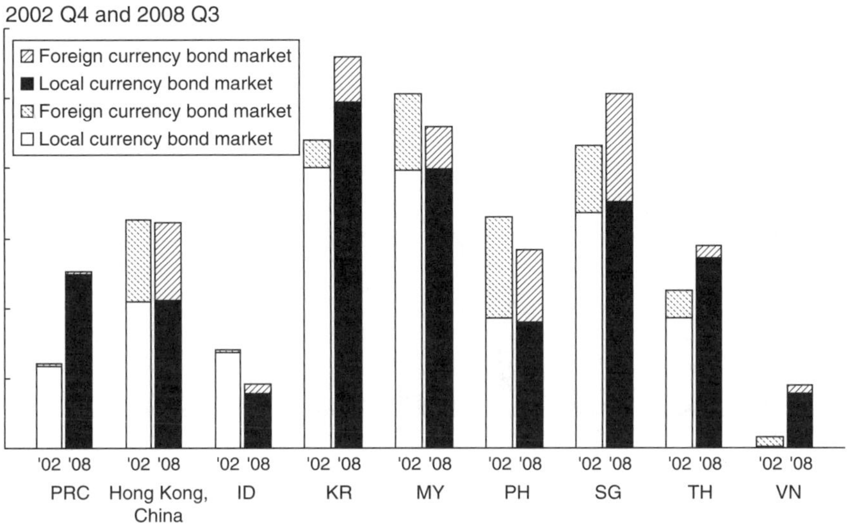

Notes:
Size is defined as the absolute amount of bonds outstanding in US$.
Country abbreviations: ID = Indonesia; MY = Malaysia; SG = Singapore; TH = Thailand; VN = Viet Nam.

Source: ADB Asian Bonds Online database, http://asianbondsonline.adb.org/regional/data.php, author's calculations.

Figure 11.2 Size of Asian bond markets as a percentage of GDP

11.3) reveals a much different picture. In value terms, the People's Republic of China (PRC) and Korean bond markets dwarf those of their emerging Asia counterparts. This suggests that for many of these countries, improvements are unlikely to leave many individual markets sufficiently efficient to reach the scale economies necessary to achieve the cost reductions that are adequate to compete successfully with offshore bond markets. Instead, the achievement of scale economies is likely to require cooperation at the regional level.

Moreover, the large volumes observed in the PRC are misleading, as the market is dominated by sterilization bonds. Some authors (Lardy 2008) have argued that increased issuance of sterilization bonds actually has a negative impact on the development of the PRC bond market, as the need to continue to issue sterilization bonds to pursue its exchange rate goals gives the PRC government an incentive to discourage the development of the rest of the bond market in an effort to maintain low funding costs.

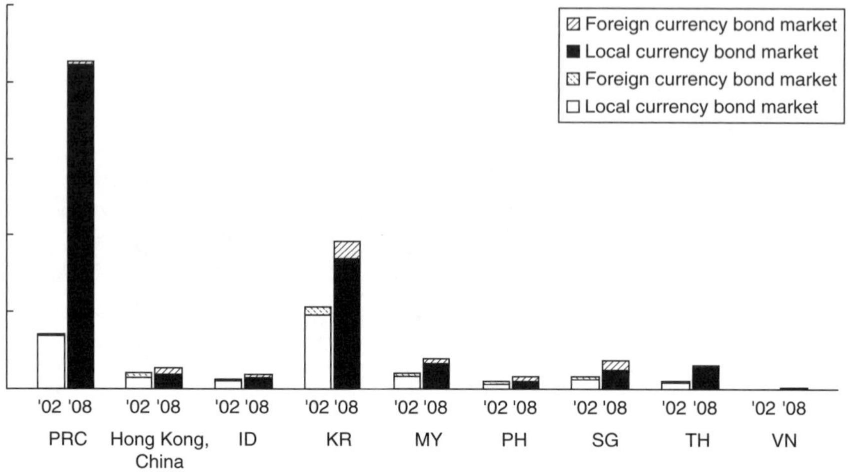

Notes:
Size is defined as the absolute amount of bonds outstanding in US$.
Country abbreviations: ID = Indonesia; MY = Malaysia; SG = Singapore; TH = Thailand. VN = Viet Nam.

Source: ADB Asian Bonds Online database, http://asianbondsonline.adb.org/regional/data.php, author's calculations.

Figure 11.3 Size of Asian bond markets (US$ billion)

A related question concerns the penetration of local currency bond markets. As a share of total regional issuance, the growth of the local currency bond market has been substantial, as the share has increased from 42.8 percent at the launch of the ABMI in 2003 to 54.5 percent in the third quarter of 2008 (see Table 11.2). Moreover, in value terms, the growth has been even more dramatic, as corporate issuance of local currency debt has more than doubled in value over this period while government issuance has almost tripled.

Figure 11.4 displays foreign securities holdings both within and outside the Asian region.[7] Holdings from other Asian nations grew dramatically within the region between 2003 and 2007, going from US$25.0 billion to US$48.5 billion. However, those holdings were not sufficient to close the gap on holdings of securities issued outside the region, which grew over the same period by 52 percent from US$212.0 billion to US$322.3 billion. Similarly, Figure 11.5 reports the overall shares of holdings both within and outside the region. Again, it can be seen that the share of foreign

Table 11.2 Size of local currency (LC) and foreign currency (FC) bond markets

(Values in billions of US$)	2002	2003	2004	2005	2006	2007	2008
Size of LC bond market	1167.8	1349.1	1700.1	2106.1	2663.8	3393.1	3694.1
Corporate	455.8	463.8	518.9	596.6	755.1	928.9	947.0
Government	712.0	885.3	1181.2	1509.5	1908.8	2464.2	2747.1
Size of FC bond market	171.1	191.3	225.4	252.9	280.0	311.8	–
(As a percentage of GDP)	2002	2003	2004	2005	2006	2007	2008
Size of LC bond market	40.9	42.8	46.2	50.4	53.7	55.8	54.5
Corporate	16.0	14.7	14.1	14.3	15.2	15.3	14.0
Government	24.9	28.1	32.1	36.2	38.5	40.5	40.6
Size of FC bond market	6.0	6.1	6.1	6.1	5.6	5.1	–

Note: Country group: PRC; Hong Kong, China; Indonesia; Korea; Malaysia; the Philippines; Singapore; Thailand; Viet Nam.

Sources: ADB Asian Bonds Online database, http://asianbondsonline.adb.org/regional/data.php; author's calculations.

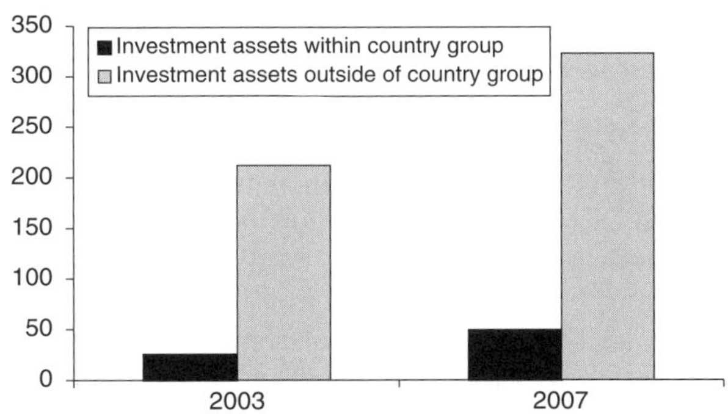

Notes:
Country group: Hong Kong, China; Indonesia; Korea; Malaysia; the Philippines; Singapore; Thailand.
IMF Coordinated Portfolio Investment Survey (CPIS) database reports portfolio investment assets by economy of non-resident issuer.
Investment assets within an individual country's own country are not included in sum of investment assets within the country group.

Source: IMF CPIS database Table 1.2.A, http://www.imf.org/external/np/sta/pi/part.asp, and Table 12.1, http://www.imf.org/external/np/sta/pi/global.htm (accessed 12 June 2009), author's calculations.

Figure 11.4 Reported portfolio investment assets: long-term debt securities (US$ billion)

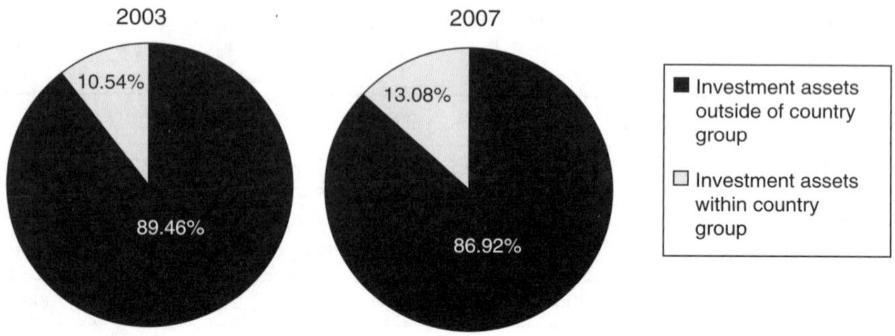

Notes:
Country group: Hong Kong, China; Indonesia; Korea; Malaysia; the Philippines; Singapore; Thailand.
CPIS database reports portfolio investment assets by economy of non-resident issuer. Investment assets within an individual country's own country are not included in sum of investment assets within the country group.

Source: IMF CPIS database Table 1.2.A, http://www.imf.org/external/np/sta/pi/part.asp, and Table 12.1, http://www.imf.org/external/np/sta/pi/global.htm (accessed 12 June 2009), author's calculations.

Figure 11.5 Reported portfolio investment assets: long-term debt securities (US$ billion)

holdings from within the country group increased by a substantial amount, from 10.5 percent to 13.1 percent from 2003 to 2007, but this only represented a modest reduction in the share of holdings from outside the region, from 89.5 percent to 87.0 percent.

Finally, the issue of the systematic discrepancies between global and regional credit rating agencies that many claimed existed at the launch of the ABMI will be revisited here. To a large extent they no longer seem to exist (for example, see Table 11.3). A comparison was made between the long-term sovereign debt ratings of nine Asian nations by global rating agency Standard & Poor's (S&P) and Japanese rating agency Risk and Investment (R&I). It can be seen that foreign currency ratings by R&I in 2000 were generally modestly higher than those given by S&P. However, consider current ratings by both agencies. If anything, S&P ratings of both local and foreign currency bonds tend to be higher, with a small number of exceptions.

11.5 IMPACT OF THE GLOBAL FINANCIAL CRISIS

11.5.1 Asian Bond Market Performance During the Crisis

While the 2007–2009 financial crisis originated in the US, it quickly disrupted financial markets across the globe, including those in Asia. As volatility spread, Asian markets seized up along with their counterparts in the rest of the world. Asian bond funds exhibited increased bid–ask spreads as markets became increasingly illiquid (Figure 11.6).

Table 11.3 Long-term sovereign debt ratings

Local currency						
Country	S&P			R&I		
	Current	2005	2000	Current	2005	2000
PRC	A+	A−	BBB	AA−	N/A	N/A
Hong Kong, China	AA+	AA−	A+	AA+	AA	AA
Indonesia	BB+	BB	B	N/A	N/A	N/A
Korea	A+	A+	A	AA−	N/A	N/A
Malaysia	A+	A+	A	A+	N/A	N/A
Philippines	BB+	BB+	BBB+	N/A	N/A	N/A
Singapore	AAA	AAA	AAA	AAA	AAA	AAA
Thailand	A−	A	A−	A−	N/A	N/A
Viet Nam	BB+	BB	N/A	N/A	N/A	N/A
Foreign currency						
Country	S&P			R&I		
	Current	2005	2000	Current	2005	2000
PRC	A+	A−	BBB	A+	A	A+
Hong Kong, China	AA+	AA−	A	AA+	AA−	AA−
Indonesia	BB−	B+	B−	BB+	BB−	B−
Korea	A	A	BBB	A+	A	BBB+
Malaysia	A−	A−	BBB	A	A−	BBB+
Philippines	BB−	BB−	BB+	BBB−	BBB−	BBB−
Singapore	AAA	AAA	AAA	AAA	AAA	AAA
Thailand	BBB+	BBB+	BBB−	BBB+	BBB+	BBB
Viet Nam	BB	BB−	N/A	BB	N/A	N/A

Note: R&I is a Japanese rating company named Risk and Investment Incorporated.

Source: Bloomberg database, http://www.bloomberg.com/markets/.

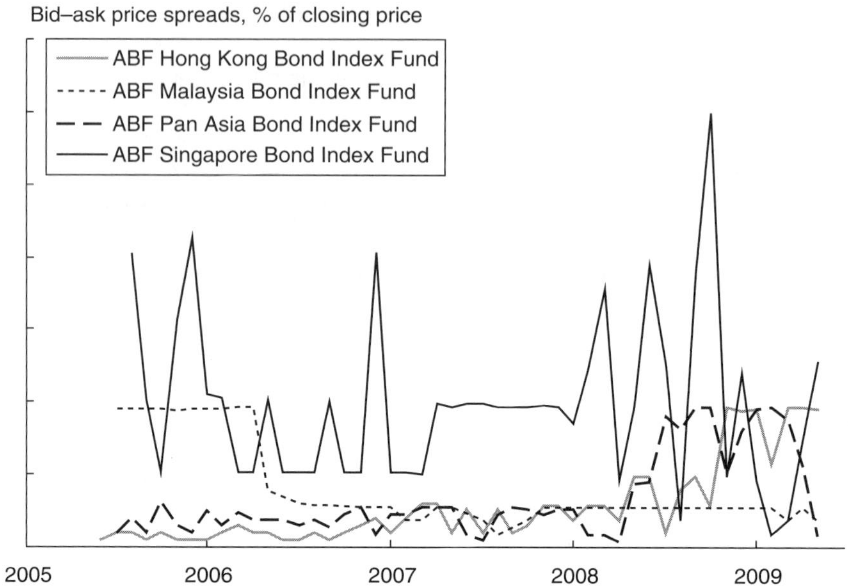

Note: Closing price is a 3-month moving average centered on second month.

Source: Bloomberg database, http://www.bloomberg.com/markets/, author's calculations.

Figure 11.6 Asian bond funds

An assessment of regional performance over this period requires some sort of benchmark. One piece of evidence might be the relative severity of yield curve anomalies exhibited during the height of the crisis. As argued above, yield curves for less-developed bond markets are likely to exhibit more severe anomalies. As a benchmark, the yield curves of both the US and Germany have been included as the financial turbulence in the US probably leaves it a poor benchmark despite that market's greater transaction volume.

Yield curves for 1 October 2008 are shown in Figures 11.7 and 11.8. Deviations from a smoothed yield curve are displayed for all of the countries in the first panel. However, the deviations are much larger for the smaller local currency bond markets of Singapore and Hong Kong, China. The emerging-market-country local currency bond markets exhibit even more aberrant behavior in the second panel. Many of the economies exhibit higher yields at the short end, consistent with deteriorating borrowing conditions. In particular, the Vietnamese curve is actually inverted, with very high short-term rates that reflect steep premia on

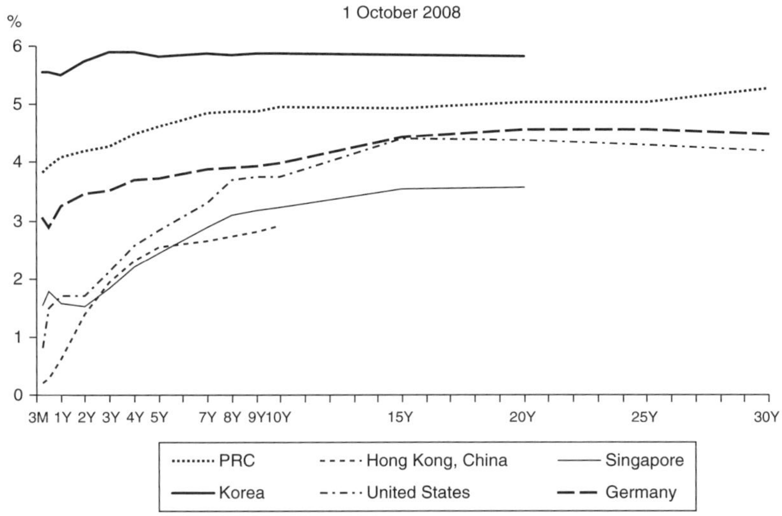

Source: Bloomberg database, http://www.bloomberg.com/markets/.

Figure 11.7 Government securities yield curves

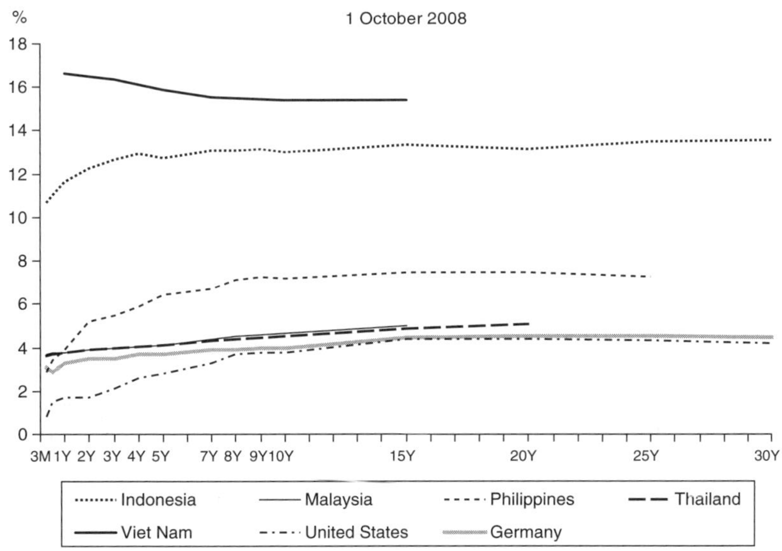

Source: Bloomberg database, http://www.bloomberg.com/markets/.

Figure 11.8 Government securities yield curves

short-term borrowing during the crisis. However, most of the other curves also exhibit high short-term rates, reflecting a decreased supply of short-term funds.

It is difficult to say whether these pictures indicate that Asian government securities markets performed well over the course of the crisis. This period was a volatile one where investors' taste for emerging-market paper of any kind was changing rapidly. As such, one would expect some anomalous behavior to appear in any market.

As financial markets recovered, yield curves did as well. As of 18 June 2009, for example, the Vietnamese yield curve was no longer inverted, although one-year yields were the highest in the region.[8] At the short end, yields recovered dramatically. For example, the three-month Korean Treasury yield fell by 325 basis points to 2.3 percent, while the three-month yield on US Treasuries fell 61.9 basis points over the same period.[9]

11.5.2 Reassessment of Bond Market Promotion

It is clear that the current global financial crisis has affected our understanding of the role of financial markets in economic activity, and the role of bond markets in particular, in fundamental ways that are as yet incompletely understood.

Some lessons are apparent. One is that the 'spare tire' argument does not hold under sufficiently severe disruptions. As Eichengreen (2007) notes, there is no guarantee that bond markets will continue to function as the banking sectors around them collapse. In the US, bank lending seized up during the crisis precisely at the point when difficulties arose in using CDOs as collateral. The lesson is that well-functioning bank and bond markets tend to go together.

The recent financial crisis also demonstrates that bond market characteristics can create new problems during financial disruptions. For example, the diversification achieved through bond markets is a welcome source of reduced idiosyncratic risk, but it weakens the incentives faced by creditors to gather information about their borrowers. This could lead to more imprudence in lending. Moreover, once a default does take place, the dispersion of credit claims leaves it more difficult to restructure debt obligations.

Other issues raised by the financial crisis remain unresolved. For example, many conclude that the recent global financial crisis revealed that the growth in financial intermediation going into the crisis period was excessive. Authors such as Rose and Spiegel (2009) found that those countries with the greatest leverage in financial institutions going into the crisis experienced the deepest downturns in economic performance and equity returns. However, much of the literature on the implications of the global financial crisis (Jang and Hyun 2009) has concluded that the global crisis provides evidence of the 'clear need' for well-functioning bond markets in Asia.

This raises the following question: if the global financial crisis revealed that intermediation worldwide was excessive, should Asian governments continue promoting increased bond market activity? In particular, how do we know that previous benchmarks that were used to assess the viability of the levels of activity in Asian markets, for example by comparing volumes in Asian bond markets to those in developed economies, were accurate?

One answer is that the difficulties associated with the run-up to the global financial crisis stemmed more from flaws in the financial system than from excessive intermediation volumes. However, some of the steps that have been advocated in response to these flaws may exacerbate the difficulties associated with the lack of scale economies in smaller Asian economies, as these efforts may increase the cost of intermediation. As a result, we may experience some declines in volumes in these markets, moving them even further below levels associated with achieving viable economies of scale. Another answer is that the importance of regional efforts has increased. As it becomes ever more difficult for individual country local currency bond markets to 'go it alone', the potential for welfare-improving outcomes from coordination at the regional level are enhanced. For example, the poor performance of rating agencies in classifying the underlying risk in securitized debt raises, rather than lowers, the demand for quality rating services.

11.5.3 Official Responses to the Global Financial Crisis

A number of official responses to the global financial crisis have been announced since the beginning of 2008. Following the May 2008 ASEAN+3 Finance Ministers Meeting, it was announced that efforts were being made to strengthen financial cooperation in the region. The group reiterated its commitment to the CMI Multilateralization (CMIM) under a self-managed reserve pooling arrangement in a single contractual agreement. The group raised the total size of the CMIM to US$80 billion. It also agreed to implement measures to facilitate monitoring and surveillance of economic and financial conditions under the ASEAN+3 Economic Review and Policy Dialogue and agreed to explore the role of the international financial institutions in providing information.

In efforts to promote the ABMI, the group endorsed the release of the second ABMI roadmap, which argues for the promotion of issuance and demand for local currency bonds as well as improvements in regulatory frameworks and institutional structures. The group also agreed to make periodic self-assessments of their progress to undertake voluntary efforts to promote the ABMI. A private sector group was also launched to discuss facilitating cross-border transactions.

The ASEAN+3 finance ministers met in Phuket, Thailand in a special meeting in February 2009, convened in response to the global financial crisis. At that meeting, the total size of swap arrangements under CMIM was increased from US$80 billion to US$120 billion. The finance ministers also agreed to establish an independent regional surveillance unit to promote the monitoring of economic conditions. Finally, the group called for an immediate and substantial capital increase for ADB.

The regular May ASEAN+3 meeting also included a number of notable announcements, both concerning addressing the current crisis and in terms of fostering the development of regional financial markets. The group announced agreement on all of the main components of CMIM, including individual country contributions, borrowing limits and surveillance mechanisms, with the scheme to be implemented before the end of the year. In addition, Hong Kong, China was welcomed into CMIM.

The May ASEAN+3 Finance Ministers Meeting also endorsed the establishment of a Credit Guarantee and Investment Mechanism as a trust fund of the ADB with an initial capital outlay of US$500 million to support private local currency bond issuance in the region. Some details, such as the scope of coverage, leverage ratios and country limits, were to be resolved by the 2010 meeting.

The group also agreed on the proposed provision of technical assistance from ADB for cross-border bond issuance of Lao People's Democratic Republic government debt in Thailand. The group took note of private sector efforts on cross-border transactions and settlements issues.

Overall, it is clear that the bulk of official responses to date have moved toward more regional cooperation and greater efforts to encourage local bond markets. However, not all policies remain unchanged. For example, the Basel Committee has changed its proposed treatment of securitized assets, such as CDOs and asset-backed securities, in response to the changed perception of the relative riskiness of securitized assets in the wake of the financial crisis (Bank for International Settlements 2009). Presumably, the crisis will lead to similar reassessments among the regional Asian groups.

11.6 POLICY CONCLUSIONS

The experience over the previous decade was one of rapid growth and development of local currency bond markets within the region. Moreover, while the advent of the global financial crisis has required that we reassess many of policy conclusions that were held going into the crisis, it appears that most of them remain intact.

First and foremost, the global financial crisis does not refute the merits of pursuing the development of local currency bond markets. It is true that the crisis revealed many institutions to be overleveraged, suggesting that a reduction in overall issuance volumes worldwide might be desirable. However, the crisis also demonstrated the perils of currency mismatch.

The crisis also supports the pursuit of initiatives at the regional level. Mitigating currency risk exposure among firms from smaller emerging-market economies can only be satisfied through regional efforts. These economies are too small to achieve economies of scale in debt issuance in their domestic currencies, and their best prospect would be some kind of regional currency basket that would mitigate their exposure, although not eliminate it entirely. A viable arrangement for debt issuance of that form would only be feasible through coordination at the regional level.

Small movements toward monetary integration may have benign implications for the development of local currency bond markets. As Eichengreen (2006a) noted, one result of the path toward monetary integration in Europe was the increased issuance of European Currency Unit (ECU) bonds. The ECU was a basket of European community currencies that countries were encouraged to stabilize their currencies against, beginning in 1979. While the bulk of transactions in Europe were still conducted in national currencies during this time, the development of the ECU bond market presents an alternative for Asia, as the adoption of a similar parallel currency (that is, an Asian currency unit) might encourage increased local currency issuance within the region.

Second, the effort to encourage greater coverage by regional rating agencies is also of primary importance. While there were many disappointments with the performance of the rating agencies during the crisis, the problems illuminated that the need for quality ratings was stronger than previously believed, not weaker.

Finally, we must also reassess the conclusion that regional efforts to promote local currency bond issues were an unqualified success based on the astronomical growth in issues observed over this period. In retrospect, it is clear that a portion of these issues were motivated by an unhealthy and unrealistic appetite for risk in world financial markets.

A number of other policy conclusions are worth mentioning. First, it remains of primary importance that countries maintain macroeconomic stability and the financial infrastructure needed for successful intermediation in their domestic markets. On the macro policy side, it has been well documented that emerging market economies that exhibit macroeconomic stability are more successful in developing their domestic financial markets (Burger and Warnock 2007).

It is also important to develop a robust and safe domestic financial system. Such a system would allow firms to issue offshore, as well as in foreign currencies. Many market imperfections in Asian markets are self-induced. For example, withholding taxes and legal constraints combine to segment markets from global capital (Jiang and McCauley 2004). These policy-induced distortions raise the cost of intermediation through local bond markets, and drive issuers to alternative financial instruments or to alternative jurisdictions.

Countries may also expand their domestic financial depth by encouraging foreign borrowers to issue domestically in local currency. Asian markets are already making headwind along these lines, such as in the Korean 'Arirang' bond market, which reached US$2.7 billion in 2006 (Batten and Szilagyi 2007).[10] Attracting foreign issuers may be a desirable way to encourage increased volume in the domestic market.

There is a logical disconnect in the notion that the capital surpluses built up in Asia are somehow available for 'recycling' by domestic Asian borrowers. The build-up of capital is a result of large current account surpluses, the financing of which requires a net surplus of external lending. However, if a portion of this foreign borrowing can be channeled to domestic local currency bond markets, it can play a positive role in increasing domestic currency issue volumes to levels sufficient to achieve economies of scale. Indeed, as noted by Hoschka (2005a), the presence of highly rated multinational corporations may actually 'crowd in' local issuance, because they will deepen markets.

A successful program of encouraging local currency issues by foreigners would require liberalization. A primary source of foreign issuance is through the multilateral development banks (Hoschka 2005b), which typically require compliance with liberalized regulatory conditions.

Finally, one of the primary forces limiting the development of Asian bond markets is that the large current account surpluses enjoyed by Asian nations are financed in large part through offshore bond issuance. If trade were more balanced, there would be less excess demand for credit from the rest of the world, and the borrowing terms faced by Asian issuers would be enhanced, holding all else equal.

NOTES

1. In this chapter, 'the region' is defined as the Association of Southeast Asian Nations (ASEAN)+3 group, unless constrained otherwise by data availability. This includes Brunei Darussalam, the People's Republic of China (PRC), Cambodia, Indonesia, Japan, Republic of Korea (hereafter Korea), Lao People's Democratic Republic, Malaysia, Myanmar, the Philippines, Singapore, Thailand and Viet Nam.
2. The rating agencies in question in the study were Korea Investors Service and Korea Ratings Corp., which have been subsidiaries of Moody's and Fitch, respectively, since 2001, and National Information & Credit Evaluation, Inc., which is a rating agency with solely Korean ownership.
3. To the extent that a bailout of a defaulting eurozone member carried positive probability, convergence in perceived default risk would be expected as well. This suggests that not all of the changes in spreads can be ascribed to convergence due to greater liquidity in these markets.
4. Each yield curve in Figure 11.1, and the other curves displayed in this chapter, contains all of the maturities listed on the x-axis. The 2003 curve does not extend beyond the ten-year maturity.
5. These comments concentrate on official regional cooperative efforts. Private entities have also played a central role in encouraging regional demand for equity finance.
6. The 11 nations in the EMEAP are Australia; the People's Republic of China (PRC); Hong Kong, China; Indonesia; Japan; Korea; Malaysia; New Zealand; the Philippines; Singapore; and Thailand.
7. These figures do not include national holdings of securities issued in the home country.
8. Longer-term yields were actually higher in Indonesia.
9. Of course, the movement in yields is not only attributable to the changes in liquidity in these markets and the appetites for these types of paper, but also to the unprecedented steps taken by central banks over the period to ensure adequate liquidity levels and stimulate their economies.
10. At that size, Batten and Szilagyi (2007) noted that the Arirang market still only accounted for 1.7 percent of Korea's corporate bond issuance.

REFERENCES

Asian Development Bank (ADB). 2008. *Handbook on International Best Practices in Credit Rating*. http://www.asianbondsonline.adb.org/features/credit_rating_practices/OREI_Handbook_on_International_Best_Practices_WEB.pdf.

Association of Southeast Asian Nations (ASEAN)+3. 2003. Joint Ministerial Statement of the ASEAN+3 Finance Ministers Meeting, Makati, Philippines, 7 August. http://www.mof.go.jp/english/if/as3_030807e_01.htm.

Association of Southeast Asian Nations (ASEAN). 2008. Joint Statement of the 11th ASEAN+3 Finance Ministers Meeting, Madrid, 4 May. http://www.mof.go.jp/english/if/as3_080504.htm.

Association of Southeast Asian Nations (ASEAN). 2009. Joint Statement of the 12th ASEAN+3 Ministers Meeting, Bali, Indonesia, 3 May. http://www.aseansec.org/22536.htm.

Balfour, F. 2009. In China, a Burst of Corporate Bonds. *Business Week*, 25 June. http://www.businessweek.com/magazine/content/09_27/b4138025154217.htm.

Bank for International Settlements (BIS). 2003. Launch of the Asia Bond Fund. BIS Press Release. 2 June.

Bank for International Settlements (BIS). 2009. Proposed Enhancements to the Basel II Framework. Consultative document. Basel Committee on Banking Supervision, January.

Batten, J.A. and P. Hoontrakul. 2008. What are the Next Steps for Bond Market Development in Thailand? *International Finance Review* 8: 497–519.

Batten, J.A. and P.G. Szilagyi. 2007. Domestic Bond Market Development: The Arirang Bond Experience in Korea. *The World Bank Research Observer* 22(2): 165–195.

Burger, J.D. and F.E. Warnock. 2007. Foreign Participation in Local Currency Bond Markets. *Review of Financial Economics* 16: 291–304.

Ehrmann, M., M. Fratzscher, R.S. Gürkaynak and E.T. Swanson. 2007. Convergence and Anchoring of Yield Curves in the Euro Area. Federal Reserve Bank of San Francisco Working Paper 2007-24. http://www.frbsf.org/publications/economics/papers/2007/wp07-24bk.pdf.

Eichengreen, B. 2006a. The Parallel-Currency Approach to Asian Monetary Integration. *American Economic Review* 96(2): 432–436.

Eichengreen, B. 2006b. The Development of Asian Bond Markets. In *BIS Papers No 30 – Asian Bond Markets: Issues and Prospects*. Basel: BIS.

Eichengreen, B. 2007. The Mother of All Emerging Market Crises. Mimeo. 22 August. http://www.econ.berkeley.edu/~eichengr/mother_all_emerging.pdf.

Eichengreen, B. and P. Luengnaruemitchai. 2006. Why Doesn't Asia Have Bigger Bond Markets? In *BIS Papers No 30 – Asian Bond Markets: Issues and Prospects*. Basel: BIS.

Ferri, G., T.S. Kang, P. Lacitignola and J.Y. Lee. 2009. Foreign Ownership and the Credibility of National Rating Agencies: Evidence from Korea. Paper presented at the Conference on Credit Ratings, Credit Rating Agencies, and their Development in Asia, Asian Development Bank Institute, Tokyo, 1–2 July.

Greenspan, A. 1999. Do Efficient Financial Markets Mitigate Financial Crises? Speech before the 1999 Financial Markets Conference of the Federal Reserve Bank of Atlanta, Sea Island, GA, 19 October.

Gürkaynak, R.S., B. Sack and E.T. Swanson. 2005. The Sensitivity of Long-Term Interest Rates to Economic News: Evidence and Implications for Macroeconomic Models. *American Economic Review* 95(1): 425–436.

Gürkaynak, R.S., B. Sack and J. Wright. 2007. The US Treasury Yield Curve: 1961 to the Present. *Journal of Monetary Economics* 54(8): 2291–2304.

Hale, G.B. and M.M. Spiegel. 2009. Who Drove the Boom in Euro-Denominated Bond Issues? Federal Reserve Bank of San Francisco Working Paper 2009-20. San Francisco, CA: Federal Reserve Bank of San Francisco.

Hoschka, T.C. 2005a. Developing the Market for Local Currency Bonds by Foreign Issuers: Lessons from Asia. ADB Economics and Research Department Working Paper 63. Manila: ADB.

Hoschka, T.C. 2005b. Local Currency Financing: The Next Frontier for MDBs? ADB Economics and Research Department Working Paper 68. Manila: ADB.

Imai, K. 2004. ACRAA and Harmonization Under Asian Bond Market Initiative. Paper presented at 6th Tokyo Roundtable on Capital Market Reform, Tokyo, 28 September. www.oecd.org/dataoecd/6/19/33735708.pdf.

Jang, H.B. and S. Hyun. 2009. A Way Forward for Asian Bond Fund Development. Bank of Korea Institute for Monetary and Economic Research Working Paper 383. Seoul: Bank of Korea Institute for Monetary and Economic Research.

Japan International Cooperation Agency. 2004. Guarantee for Korean

Collateralized Bond Obligations (Pan-Asian Bond). Press Release. 8 December. http://www.jica.go.jp/english/news/jbic_archive/autocontents/english/news/2004/000074/index.html.

Jiang, G. and R. McCauley. 2004. Asian Local Currency Bond Markets. *BIS Quarterly Review*. June: 67–80.

Kawai, M. 2005. East Asian Economic Regionalism: Progress and Challenges. *Journal of Asian Economics* 16: 29–55.

Kawai, M. 2007. Evolving Economic Architecture in East Asia. *Kyoto Economic Review* 76: 9–52.

Kwon, T. 2006. For the Advent of a Promising and Sound Asian Bond Market. In *BIS Papers No 30 – Asian Bond Markets: Issues and Prospects*. Basel: BIS.

Lardy, N.R. 2008. Financial Repression in China. Peterson Institute for International Economics Policy Brief PB08-8. Washington, DC: Peterson Institute for International Economics.

Manganelli, S. and G. Wolswijk. 2007. Market Discipline, Financial Integration and Fiscal Rules: What Drives Spreads in the Euro Area Government Bond Market? ECB Working Paper 745. Frankfurt: European Central Bank.

Park, D. and C. Rhee. 2006. Building Infrastructure for Asian Bond Markets: Settlement and Credit Rating. In *BIS Papers No 30 – Asian Bond Markets: Issues and Prospects*. Basel: BIS.

Park, Y. and D. Park. 2003. Creating Regional Bond Markets in East Asia: Rationale and Strategy. Paper presented at 2nd Annual Conference of the PECC Financial Forum, Hua Hin, Thailand.

Rose, A. and M.M. Spiegel. 2009. Cross-Country Causes and Consequences of the 2008 Financial Crisis: Early Warning. NBER Working Paper 15357. Cambridge, MA: National Bureau of Economic Research.

12. Foreign bond markets and financial market development: international perspectives

Jonathan A. Batten, Warren P. Hogan and Peter G. Szilagyi

12.1 INTRODUCTION

A key aspect of financial market reform following the 1997–1998 Asian financial crisis was the development of national and regional bond markets as an alternative to bank financing.[1] It was hoped that the development of alternative financial markets could provide a means of avoiding the 'double mismatch' of currency and maturity in the balance sheets of local corporations (Tan et al. 2001). Initially, attention was paid to markets where governments issued and traded, and subsequently to markets where industrial and financial corporations issued and traded (Schinasi and Smith 1998; Kim 1999; Batten and Kim 2001).

Academic attention and discussion by policymakers and practitioners has centered on an extensive range of regulatory and infrastructure initiatives that involve: improving regulation and the rule of law; enhancing financial market transparency; providing stronger investor protection and rights; improving clearing system performance and the reputation of local rating agencies; and providing the necessary stable macroeconomic policies to encourage investment. Recent policies that have been adopted include: the Asian Bond Markets Initiative; the formation of the Asian Bond Fund;[2] specific local market deregulation aimed at improving institutions; and proposals to enhance foreign participation by both investors and issuers in local markets.

The objective of this chapter is to add to the discussion of foreign participation by investigating the contribution it makes to domestic bond markets. The focus is on foreign participants as issuers, adding to the existing literature that investigated their role as investors (Bae et al. 2006). It is important to note that both foreign issuers and investors assume foreign exchange and possibly interest rate (maturity) risk as a result of these investments or liabilities. Despite some reservations arising from the level of risk management infrastructure present in the Asia and Pacific region, it will be argued that this largely overlooked segment is the best prospect for elevating regional and domestic bond markets to the global plane advocated by McCauley and Park (2006).

Previous literature that provided blueprints for bond market reform generally focused on two key aspects of market development: facilitating the demand and supply of bond issues, and overcoming structural impediments, such as the absence of financial market technology, that may impede the development agenda (Walter 1993; Schinasi and Smith 1998; Kim 1999; Rhee 2000, 2004; Lejot et al. 2006; Park and Park 2005; Arner et al. 2006). While governments and local corporations have typically supplied new bonds, in some markets international organizations have also been involved. These non-resident bond issues in a domestic bond market are termed foreign bonds, and their issuance has been linked to the long-term development of these markets (Hoschka 2005; Inoguchi 2007).

The development of a foreign bond market is consistent with the three-tiered bond market described by McCauley and Park (2006): first, there is a series of domestic markets in which domestic investors provide funds to domestic issuers; second, a regional bond market denominated in regional currencies with regional investors and issuers; and third, a global market in which a region's borrowers and possibly investors are minor players. Therefore, the ultimate objective when developing a national bond market should be integration into a global securities market (Batten and Szilagyi 2007). In turn, a regional bond market would compete with the alternative funding and investment opportunities provided by banks individually, or as syndicates, and existing debt securities, such as Eurobonds and other foreign bonds offered in large financial markets, such as those present in Japan or the United States (US).

This chapter will examine factors that have facilitated non-resident involvement in other financial markets and identify impediments that may prevent the application of these same factors to other local market segments, notably the corporate bond market. The scope of this chapter includes all key foreign bond markets other than those in the US, whose scale and institutional environment warrants separate analysis. Particular attention is paid to the enabling role of supranational corporations, such as the World Bank, in facilitating corporate bond market development. Thus, the chapter also adds to the analysis of Hoschka (2005) and Inoguchi (2007), which discussed the importance of multilateral development banks, especially the Asian Development Bank (ADB), in helping expand nascent bond markets.

Using information from the Thomson Reuters Fixed Income (RFI)

Database[3] on 3132 foreign bonds issued in 14 different markets since 1928, insights will be offered into the scale and scope of this segment, with particular attention paid to the characteristics of issuers. Overwhelmingly, this market consists of sovereign, supranational and major international bank issuers with high credit quality. Although there is a significant corporate presence, usually by non-bank financial institutions, issuance by this sector tends to have a shorter maturity and generally carries lower credit ratings. Local institutional investors appear to have a preference for simple fixed-rate coupons, which can then be swapped using foreign exchange and interest rate derivatives into the currency and coupon type of choice. Pricing and arbitrage between alternate products are therefore important drivers of foreign bond issuance.

The long-term viability of this segment appears linked to the presence of: highly liquid foreign exchange and derivatives markets that facilitate risk management and transformation; regulation that facilitates cooperation with market participants; and benchmark issues and competitive pricing between markets. This analysis will be of interest and value to those nations undertaking financial market reform to develop domestic markets or provide alternative funding mechanisms through improving issuance by domestic corporations in international bond markets (Jiang and McCauley 2004).

The chapter is structured as follows: section 12.2 provides a brief background on recent developments in international banking, international debt securities and syndicated loan markets with an emphasis on the implications that changes in the scale and scope of these markets may have for domestic bond market development in the Asia and Pacific region; section 12.3 focuses on key trends in the bond markets of the Asia and Pacific region; section 12.4 provides a detailed perspective on the characteristics of international issuers in foreign bond markets and discusses the implications of these characteristics; and section 12.5 highlights policy recommendations that must be undertaken to develop foreign bond markets further in the Asia and Pacific region and elsewhere.

12.2 INTERNATIONAL DEVELOPMENTS

Although bond markets in the Asia and Pacific region have had some successes, they remain underdeveloped for the size of the region's economies. Thus, despite roadmaps to develop bond markets being adopted at the highest level of government (Lejot et al. 2006), and extensive policy reforms (Leung 2006), the 'missing market' described by Herring and Chatusripitak (2000) remains.

Recent developments in international banking and international securities markets reported in data from the Bank for International Settlements (BIS) offer explanations to the possible reasons for and consequences of this underdevelopment (BIS 2009). According to data from banks reporting to the BIS,[4] total lending in all markets covered increased 194 percent to US$24.5 trillion (falling slightly during the 2007–2009 crisis period), whereas lending to developing economies increased 157.8 percent to US$1.9 trillion. Lending to economies in the Asia and Pacific region grew slightly less at 153 percent to US$608 billion, though it suffered a large decrease from 1995 to 2000 (31.9 percent) due to the Asian financial crisis of 1997–1998.[5] In addition, while the Asia and Pacific region had the highest level in bank loans outstanding in 2007, lending to the region decreased 3.6 percent during the financial crisis of 2007–2009, whereas lending to other regions, especially Europe, increased.

BIS data on bank deposits are also enlightening (BIS 2009). Of the developing regions that reported, it is not surprising that Africa and the Middle East (which includes key oil-rich nations) provided the most deposits to banks in 2007 at US$867 billion, although the Asia and Pacific region was a close second at US$832 billion. Within the Asia and Pacific region, the People's Republic of China (PRC) and Taipei,China provided nearly US$444 billion in deposits in 2008 that, combined with the totals from Hong Kong, China and Singapore, total US$1.36 trillion, almost double the deposits from Japan (US$769 billion).

However, it is the net positions from BIS data that are of most interest to the current discussion on the scale and scope of the Asia and Pacific region's bond markets. In 2008, Australia was an important net recipient[6] of bank lending at US$50.1 billion, as was India (at US$78.8 billion), Indonesia (at US$39.4 billion) and the Republic of Korea (hereafter Korea) (at US$74.3 billion). However, overall, the region reported deficits of US$68.7 billion. In 2007, the net deficit was a staggering US$223.2 billion, with the largest deficits coming from the PRC and Taipei,China. Notably, Japan changed from a net receiver of funds in 1995 (US$229.7 billion) to a net lender of funds in 2008 (US$234.9 billion).

Overall, international bank lending to developing Asia remains below lending to other regions, especially compared with lending to developing Europe. At the same time, regional deposits with banks in developing Asia exceeded loans during 2000–2008. Thus, savings from the Asia and Pacific region continue to support international bank lending, despite regional policymakers' efforts to direct these funds to regional economic and infrastructure development.

The promotion of regional bond markets and the development of domestic corporate and foreign bond markets is not inconsistent with improving access to international debt markets through syndicated bank loans or international bond issues (such as Eurobonds). Chakraborty and Ray (2006) and others recommended a two-tiered approach to financial market development with complementary bank and bond market reform as the best strategy for long-term economic development. Burger and Warnock (2006) mentioned that necessary financial market reform would provide improved services, more efficient financial and legal institutions, better protection for investors, and sound fiscal and monetary policy management by government, which would benefit bond market development and improve access to international investment or lending.

When considering the direction of international lending to the Asia and Pacific region in the form of international securities or syndicated loans, it is useful to note that issues from all the markets covered by the BIS grew 250 percent over 2000–2008 to US$23.9 trillion (BIS 2009). For the first time, this sum exceeded international bank lending, which was US$22.5 trillion. This suggests a global trend toward disintermediation, which may have been accelerated by the 2007–2009 financial crisis. Apart from the US and the United Kingdom (UK), which issued 37 percent of the total international debt securities in 2008, the important issuers were in the Asia and Pacific region: Australia with US$468 billion, Japan with US$398 billion, and Korea with US$109 billion.

Sums reported for syndicated loans were much less. From 2007 to 2008, syndicated loans fell 55 percent to US$297 billion, highlighting the fact that these markets (whose loans tend to be based on the London Interbank Offered Rate, LIBOR) were particularly affected during the financial crisis. During the same time, syndicated lending in the Asia and Pacific region fell by 65.4 percent to only US$13.7 billion, with Korea experiencing the largest reduction (86.9 percent to just US$1.6 billion). Reductions of this magnitude last occurred during the Asian financial crisis of 1997–1998 and highlight the implications of dependency on bank-based lending.

Comparing these data also highlights the beginnings of disintermediation with new lending in the Asia and Pacific region favoring international securities issues over syndicated and direct bank lending. This is consistent with the development of the region's issuers since the Asian financial crisis of 1997–1998, as local corporations are now more prepared to meet the information disclosure requirements of international investors. Issuers also need to comply with international accounting standards and obtain credit ratings. Nonetheless, much more needs to be done to ensure continued financial stability and successful participation in global markets by the region's major economies (Blommestein and Santiso 2007; Tovar and Quispe-Agnoli 2008).

Table 12.1 Total domestic bonds outstanding in key developed and Asia and Pacific region markets (billions of US$)

	Total domestic bonds outstanding				% change		
	1995	2000	2007	2008	1995–2000	2000–2007	2007–2008
Developed markets							
Australia	221.5	217.3	806.9	637.4	−1.9	193.4	−21.0
Canada	580.6	662.2	1 206.3	1 034.5	14.1	56.2	−14.2
France	1 338.1	1 125.2	2 817.4	2 921.1	−15.9	159.6	3.7
Italy	1 523.7	1 327.8	3 039.4	3 261.8	−12.9	145.6	7.3
Germany	1 922.5	1 715.7	2 634.4	2 592.8	−10.8	51.1	−1.6
Japan	4 648.6	5 701.9	8 855.7	11 076.8	22.7	94.3	25.1
New Zealand	19.8	14.2	23.5	18.3	−28.0	28.6	−22.3
Switzerland	225.1	157.7	242.8	259.0	−29.9	64.2	6.7
UK	564.6	688.3	1359.0	1 223.2	21.9	77.7	−10.0
US	10 209.1	13 738.2	23 303.6	24 621.6	34.6	79.2	5.7
Asia and Pacific region							
PRC	46.6	202.3	1 687.3	2 209.5	334.1	992.1	31.0
Taipei,China	85.7	123.1	199.4	205.7	43.6	67.1	3.2
Hong Kong, China	23.8	44.1	51.4	50.2	84.9	14.0	−2.3
India	70.6	113.6	458.4	426.7	60.9	275.8	−6.9
Malaysia	69.2	78.9	184.6	199.1	14.0	152.3	7.9
Pakistan	22.6	26.7	42.6	41.4	18.4	54.7	−2.8
Philippines	25.9	20.9	54.2	52.0	−19.5	149.3	−4.0
Singapore	22.8	41.9	97.2	101.9	83.9	142.9	4.8
Korea	274.2	377.7	1 076.6	863.5	37.7	128.6	−19.8
Thailand	15.1	30.8	140.2	146.1	104.4	374.2	4.2
Asia and Pacific region	656.6	1 060.0	3 991.8	4 296.1	161.4	244.2	7.6
All BIS Markets	24 598.7	29 177.0	56 210.7	59 666.0	18.6	104.5	6.1
Asia and Pacific region/BIS markets	2.7%	3.6%	7.1%	7.2%			

Note: Data as of December for each year.

Source: BIS (2009).

12.3 DOMESTIC BOND MARKETS IN THE ASIA AND PACIFIC REGION

Table 12.1 shows the growth of domestic bond markets from 1995 to 2008 using BIS data on domestic bonds outstanding in 20 markets. The top panel provides data from ten key developed countries, and the bottom panel provides data from the ten countries in the Asia and Pacific region that report to the BIS.

The last row shows that the Asia and Pacific region's share of the total domestic bonds outstanding in all markets covered by the BIS was 2.7 percent in 1995 and 7.2 percent in 2008. Total domestic bonds outstanding in the Asia and Pacific region grew from US$656.6 billion in 1995 to US$4.3 trillion in 2008, reflecting the development of the PRC's domestic bond market over the period, which grew more than any other market. The PRC had a 51.4 percent share of the Asia and Pacific region's domestic bonds outstanding, with a market size comparable to France and almost twice that of Canada or the UK.

While the size of all bond markets covered in Table 12.1 increased from 2000 to 2007, the average of growth rates reported by the Asia and Pacific region markets (244.2 percent) was higher than the average of growth rates reported by the developed markets (95.0 percent) and the average of growth rates reported by all markets covered by the BIS (104.5 percent). Notwithstanding the important contribution made by the PRC, these numbers say much for the success of efforts by policymakers to develop Asia and Pacific region bond markets after the 1997–1998 Asian financial crisis.

Table 12.1 also shows the impact of the 2007–2009 financial crisis on the domestic bond markets, which was most pronounced in Korea. Total domestic bonds outstanding in Korea fell 19.8 percent over 2007–2008. The economic effect of a withdrawal of this magnitude (US$213.1 billion) cannot be understated; this amount is equal to the entire bond market of Malaysia (US$199.1 billion) and is significantly larger than the market of Thailand (US$146.1 billion). Other countries in the Asia and Pacific region experienced more moderate declines in domestic bonds outstanding (typically less than 10 percent), with some experiencing an increase (especially the PRC, Malaysia, Singapore and Thailand). Thus, disintermediation activity by the Asia and Pacific region issuers did not suffer as much as direct lending by individual banks or syndicates during the 2007–2009 financial crisis. This suggests that regional securities markets functioned efficiently even when others, especially those in the major financial centers of the UK and US, were in disarray.

Table 12.2 shows changes in the composition of the same domestic bond markets in Table 12.1 during 1995–2008. Table 12.2 compares the average annual compound growth rates from 1995–2008 with the share of bonds outstanding that were government issued and the share of bonds outstanding that had short-term maturities. The bottom row reports the averages for all markets covered by the BIS, where bond markets grew at a compound rate of 7.05 percent from 1995–2008, and were mostly comprised

Table 12.2 Change in composition of domestic bond markets in key developed and Asia and Pacific region markets (%)

	Average annual compound growth rate 1995–2008	Share of bonds issued by government		Share of bonds with short-term maturities	
		2000	2008	2000	2008
Developed countries					
Australia	8.5	32.0	16.1	58.3	65.1
Canada	4.5	65.4	64.8	28.1	28.8
France	6.2	52.9	49.2	33.8	37.4
Italy	6.0	73.1	54.6	22.8	14.0
Germany	2.3	34.7	52.6	25.7	46.8
Japan	6.9	63.5	82.3	26.2	28.5
New Zealand	−0.6	100.0	100.0	31.2	17.4
Switzerland	1.1	33.8	46.3	10.5	13.8
UK	6.1	61.9	67.6	40.7	41.4
US	7.0	29.9	32.0	26.9	24.2
Asia and Pacific region					
PRC	34.6	54.7	64.1	5.5	41.1
Taipei,China	7.0	37.3	57.0	46.0	18.1
Hong Kong, China	5.9	34.6	41.8	72.6	55.2
India	14.9	98.2	90.9	5.0	16.1
Malaysia	8.5	36.0	38.5	18.9	12.8
Pakistan	4.8	100.0	100.0	45.3	58.5
Philippines	5.5	99.0	97.1	53.1	41.5
Singapore	12.2	59.6	71.4	43.8	46.5
Korea	9.2	30.6	39.1	35.4	40.5
Thailand	19.1	54.3	66.6	16.1	37.7
All BIS markets	7.1	45.4	49.9	27.0	27.7

Source: BIS (2009).

of government issues and issues with long-term maturities. Over the 2000–2008 period, the government share of domestic bond markets in all BIS markets increased 4.6 percent (from 45.4 percent to 49.9 percent), whereas the share of bonds with short-term maturities increased 0.7 percent (from 27.0 percent to 27.7 percent).

There is considerable diversity in these statistics across domestic markets, although with the exception of Japan, the larger bond markets tended to have a government share of issues less than 50 percent (for example the US has around 30 percent). A significant government sector, which may crowd out corporate issuers, is linked to the underdevelopment of some bond markets (for example in India, New Zealand, and Pakistan).

In Australia, the presence of fiscal surpluses from 2000–2007 enabled the government to repay debt, with the government proportion of bonds issued declining to 16.1 percent, the lowest proportion recorded. The reverse situation of increasing government share occurred in Germany (17.9 percent), Japan (18.8 percent) and Taipei,China (19.7 percent). For some domestic bond markets (for example in the Philippines) development coincided with a decline in the share of short-term bonds (in the case of the Philippines, from 53.1 percent to 41.5 percent). This is consistent with a more benign macroeconomic setting with reduced inflationary and exchange rate pressures that encouraged investors to hold longer dated securities.

12.4 KEY FEATURES OF FOREIGN BOND MARKETS

In this section, information will be provided on the scale and scope of select foreign bond markets and key features will be identified that may offer insights into their development. As noted earlier, a foreign bond is a security issued in a domestic market by a non-resident corporation and usually sold to domestic investors. These securities differ from bonds issued in international markets (for example Eurobonds) because they are subject to the regulations of the country of issuance.[7] The US market will be excluded owing to its size and level of sophistication, and instead the focus will be on smaller markets to identify characteristics that may provide insights for bond market development in developing economies.

Data were drawn from the Thomson Reuters RFI database, which provides details on the terms and conditions of 3132 bond issues. Key features of these bonds (such as market of issue, credit rating and industry sector of the issuer) were cross-tabulated with maturity. An analysis of variance *F*-test was then applied to provide a statistical measure of the presence of differences between the bond categories. The analysis of variance *F*-tests were conducted on only 3105 bonds as the dataset included 27 perpetual bonds. Coupons on the bonds analyzed were typically linked to a floating rate benchmark, such as the LIBOR.

Table 12.3 reports the number of bonds issued and the average maturity of each issue in major non-US foreign bond markets. The foreign bond issues were denominated in the local currency. However, in some markets other denominations are permitted. In such cases, issues in local and foreign currencies are usually named differently. For example, in the

Table 12.3 Number and maturity of foreign bonds by market of issue

Market of issue	Date of first issue	First issuer in market	Bonds issued		Bond maturity (years)	
			#	% of total sample	Average	Standard deviation
Australia – Kangaroo	17-01-1992	EUROFIMA	339	10.8	5.9	2.8
Canada – Maple	12-12-1989	Bowater Inc	43	1.4	9.6	6.5
PRC – Panda	14-10-2005	ADB	3	0.1	9.0	1.7
European Union	01-07-1928	Majzen	98	3.1	12.7	19.8
Greece	30-09-1991	Entreprise Publique D'Electricité	5	0.2	2.9	1.8
Japan – Samurai/ Shogun	04-08-1972	World Bank	1161	37.1	8.3	6.2
Eurobond	18-09-2002	World Bank	767	24.5	3.8	2.4
Netherlands – Rembrandt	15-12-1982	Commonwealth of Australia	13	0.4	9.8	2.2
New Zealand – Kauri	11-05-1995	Eurostate Securitized Rated Assets SA	37	1.2	6.5	5.2
Portugal – Navigator	28-07-1989	European Investment Bank	20	0.6	4.5	2.4
Spain – Matador	05-08-1987	EUROFIMA	107	3.4	5.3	1.8
Switzerland – Alpine	22-09-1994	Kun Young Construction Co. Ltd	516	16.5	1.7	1.3
Taipei,China – Formosa	02-08-1995	ADB	2	0.1	7.0	0.0
UK-Bulldog	04-08-1971	Republic of Ireland	21	0.67	13.1	11.9
Total			3132	100%	5.9	6.1

Notes:
1. Date format is day-month-year.
2. Sample includes all non-US foreign bonds in the RFI database issued from 1 January 1928 to 30 June 2009 (N = 3132).

EUROFIMA = European Company for the Financing of Railroad Rolling Stock.

Source: Thomson Reuters RFI database, http://thomsonreuters.com/products_services/financial/content_update/content_overview/content_fixed_income/.

Japanese market issues in the local currency (yen) are termed Samurai bonds, while issues in US dollars are termed Shogun bonds.[8] The data include all foreign bonds issued from 1 January 1928 to 30 June 2009 as recorded in the RFI database (N = 3132). There are 14 foreign bond categories or markets of issue. The largest market of issue was the Samurai/Shogun bond market in Japan (1161 bonds or 37.1 percent of the sample), followed by: the Eurobonds market[9] (767 bonds or 24.1 percent of the sample); the Swiss Alpine bond market (516 bonds or 16.5 percent of foreign bonds); and the Australian Kangaroo market (339 bonds or 10.8 percent of foreign bonds).

The remaining 11.5 percent of bonds covered a range of smaller markets, including issues in the legacy currencies of Europe prior to the introduction of the euro on 1 January 1999 and recent issues in markets such as the PRC (termed Panda bonds) and Taipei,China (Formosa bonds). As shown in Table 12.3, supranational or quality sovereign issuers played an important role in these markets, as they tended to be the first issuers. The first two Panda bonds were issued in October 2005 by the World Bank and ADB (1.1 billion yuan of ten-year bonds at a 3.4 percent yield, and 1 billion yuan of ten-year bonds at a 3.34 percent yield).

The F-statistic for differences in the average bond maturity of the different markets of issue ($F = 65.09$, $p = 0.000$, $N = 3105$) is consistent with variation in the average maturity of each of these markets. The two longest average bond maturities were in the UK (Bulldog issues) with a maturity of 13.1 years and the European Union with 12.7 years. The shortest maturities were in Switzerland (1.7 years) and Greece (2.9 years).

Table 12.4 reports the top 20 of the 445 foreign bond issuers in the sample, along with average and standard deviation of the maturities of the issuers' bonds. The most important issuer was the World Bank–International Bank for Reconstruction and Development (IBRD) (472 issues or 15.1 percent of the sample total), followed by the United Bank of Switzerland (UBS) (305 issues or 9.7 percent of the sample total) and the European Bank for Reconstruction and Development (EBRD) (102 issues or 3.3 percent of the sample total). While the UBS issues tended to have shorter maturities (average of 1.5 years) with very little variation (standard deviation of 0.8), the World Bank–IBRD and the EBRD tended to have longer maturities (averages of 6.3 and 9.9 years, respectively) with considerable variation (standard deviations of 6.2 and 7.2, respectively). This variation suggests that these issuers looked to maximize pricing opportunities that arose along the entire yield curve in a specific country of issue rather than restricting themselves to a specific maturity bucket. Nonetheless, the F-statistic for differences in the average bond maturity of the various single issuers ($F = 8.72$, $p = 0.000$, $N = 3105$) suggests

Table 12.4 Top 20 issuers of foreign bonds

Issuer	No. of bonds issued	Bond maturity (years)	
		Average	Standard deviation
World Bank–IBRD	472	6.3	6.2
UBS Aktiengesellschaft (Jersey Branch)	305	1.5	0.9
EBRD	102	9.9	7.2
International Finance Corp.	83	6.1	6.6
Clariden Leu Aktiengesellschaft and Nassau Branch	81	1.0	0.3
ADB	58	7.6	5.3
Inter-American Development Bank	52	8.5	5.0
Kommunalbanken Aksjeselskap	47	3.6	2.3
Svensk Exportkredit Aktiebolag	43	4.0	2.7
Merrill Lynch and Co. Inc.	40	5.6	2.4
European Investment Bank	39	5.2	2.9
Bank Vontobel Cayman Islands	38	1.1	0.1
Kuntarahoitus Osakeyhtio	37	3.0	1.8
Citigroup Inc.	36	8.1	6.3
European Company for the Financing of Railroad Rolling Stock	32	8.2	4.1
Korea Development Bank	32	5.6	2.3
Toyota Motor Credit Corp.	28	3.1	1.0
Kommuninvest I Sverige Aktiebolag (KIS AB)	27	3.0	1.4
Bank of America Corp.	25	6.5	2.1
Morgan Stanley	25	5.3	1.7
Total	3132	5.7	6.1

Note: Sample includes all non-US foreign bonds in the RFI database issued from 1 January 1928 to 30 June 2009 (N = 3132).

Source: Thomson Reuters RFI database, http://thomsonreuters.com/products_services/financial/content_update/content_overview/content_fixed_income/.

significant variation among the maturity choices of each issuer. This is consistent with issuers capitalizing upon the unique institutional aspects of each market (such as the presence of investors requiring long-term issues) or their own unique aspects.

The obvious differentiator between issuers is their degree of credit quality. This affects investor decisions to buy the securities regardless of the maturity preferences of investors. This appears to be the most important factor driving issuer maturity choice, as issuers with slightly lower credit ratings (for example in Table 12.4, Clariden Leu Aktiengesellschaft, Bank Vontobel and Morgan Stanley are all single A-rated) tended to have the lowest variation in the maturities of their issues (standard deviations of 0.3, 0.1 and 1.7, respectively). This effect is better illustrated for two issuers with similar numbers of bond issues but slightly different credit ratings. For example, Toyota and Kommuninvest I Sverige Aktiebolag (KIS AB) both issued similar amounts of bonds (28 and 27, respectively) with similar average maturities (3.1 and 3.0 years, respectively). However, AA-rated Toyota had a standard deviation of 1.0, whereas higher, AAA-rated KIS AB had a much higher standard deviation of 1.4. This is consistent with KIS AB having greater choice, or more opportunities, in foreign bond markets due to its better quality rating.

The RFI database classifies five bonds issued by Majzen (Ferrocarriles) from 1928–1952 (maturity 2022–2025) as foreign bonds. In 1971 the Republic of Ireland issued a foreign bond in pounds sterling in the UK. Later in 1971, the World Bank, ADB and other sovereigns issued a series of yen-denominated bonds in Japan (Samurai bonds). From 1976, foreign bond issues became more frequent, with the number of issues rising steadily. Despite the 2007–2009 financial crisis, the number of bonds issued in the period from 2006 to 2010 (1193 bonds as of June 2009) still exceeded the number issued in the period from 2001 to 2005 (827 bonds). Interestingly, in the period from 1985, the number of foreign bonds issued increased while the average bond maturity declined. This is likely the consequence of a developing market, which accommodates issuers with a variety of credit ratings, not just supranationals and high-quality sovereign issuers.

Table 12.5 presents a summary of the key features of foreign bonds in the sample. The most prominent feature of these bonds is the fact that 88.2 percent were fixed rate with simple pricing features. Only a very small proportion of bonds carried option features (8.2 percent were callable, 16.4 percent were convertible, 5.2 percent were dual currency and 0.7 percent were puttable[10]). More than half of the bonds (58.7 percent) were bearer securities (24.5 percent were bearer Eurobond issues), although a significant amount (36.8 percent) were also listed on the various stock exchanges of their home countries, or required registration (14.9 percent of these were issues in Australia, which prohibited bearer securities). In addition, other than a very small amount of bonds that were either secured (8.5 percent) or asset backed (1.3 percent), most were unsecured, placing the significant burden of credit risk assessment on investors, who rely upon rating agencies to perform this task.

The simplicity of the coupon structures places the responsibility of interest rate risk and, ultimately, currency risk (as, by definition, the

Table 12.5 Key features of foreign bonds

Foreign bond feature	No. of bonds issued	% of total sample
Asset-backed securities	40	1.3
Bearer	1838	58.7
Callable	256	8.2
Convertible	514	16.4
Dual currency	162	5.2
Exchange listed	1151	36.8
Fixed rate coupon-'Plain Vanilla'	2763	88.2
Floating-LIBOR or equivalent	331	10.6
Guaranteed	124	4.0
Indexed	34	1.1
Medium-term notes	1035	33.1
Mortgage-backed securities	23	0.7
Perpetual	26	0.8
Private placements	487	15.6
Puttable	22	0.7
Registered	468	15.0
Secured	267	8.5
Sinking fund	246	7.9
Warrants	3	0.1

Note: Sample includes all non-US foreign bonds in the RFI database issued from 1 January 1928 to 30 June 2009 (N=3132).

Source: Thomson Reuters RFI database, http://thomsonreuters.com/products_services/financial/content_update/content_overview/content_fixed_income/.

denomination of a foreign bond is not the reporting currency of the issuer) on the issuer. This burden can only be accommodated if there are deep and liquid foreign exchange markets to facilitate risk transformation and risk management, including: floating rate interest rate products (specifically forward rate agreements, FRAs; interest rate futures contracts; and interest rate swaps); currency swaps or currency options; and spot or forward foreign exchange markets. These last two markets are critical given that currency swaps require cash exchange at the inception and conclusion of the contract. A key feature of foreign bond markets where there is some scale (for example in Australia, Canada, Japan and Switzerland) is the presence of both over-the-counter derivatives markets and deep foreign exchange spot and forward markets (see BIS 2007). The absence of risk transformation capabilities appears to be a major deterrent to issuance.

Analysis of the issuance data offers insights into the number and maturities of bonds by type of issuer for all bonds. The market may broadly be divided into three main groups: corporations (51.1 percent), supranationals (28.8 percent) and sovereign issuers (20.1 percent). Based on these classifications, the supranational issues tended to have the longest maturities (7.0 years), followed by those of the sovereign issuers (6.6 years) and those of the corporation category (4.9 years). Maturity is clearly linked to rating quality, as the average credit rating was AAA for supranationals, AA for sovereigns and single-A for corporations. The F-statistic for differences in the average bond maturity for each type of issuer ($F = 26.32$, $p = 0.000$, $N = 3105$) confirms that these differences are statistically significant.

Within the corporation category banks and non-bank financial corporations were the most important, comprising 26.2 percent and 14.9 percent of all issues, respectively. Issues by banks had the shortest maturities of all the classifications, while utilities and railways had the longest (9.6 and 9.3 years, respectively). The supranational group showed the greatest variation with a standard deviation of 6.1, which is consistent with issuance designed to maximize comparative advantage given market conditions at the time of issuance, rather than a predefined or restricted issuance requirement.

12.5 LESSONS AND CONCLUSIONS

Over the last decade domestic bond markets have developed considerably as an alternative form of financing, with total bonds in all markets covered by the BIS reaching US$59.7 trillion in 2008 (BIS 2009). With a few exceptions, domestic bond markets remain dominated by government issuers and issues carrying long-term maturities. The trend toward disintermediation has been accompanied and facilitated by: improvements in domestic bond trading and settlement infrastructure; the development of spot and forward foreign exchange markets; and the development of currency and interest rate derivatives markets (specifically cross-currency swaps and FRAs).[11] Products in these markets facilitate risk management and risk transformation for the assets and liabilities held by investors and issuers, thus providing a means for avoiding the double mismatch problem (Tan et al. 2001).

The expansion of both the scale and scope of bond markets offers considerable benefits to issuers by diversifying funding possibilities and creating opportunities to offer a range of products that better match the needs of investors. Generally, at the early stage of bond market development the aim is simply to facilitate the exchange of funds between domestic issuers and domestic investors. The next stage requires international participation. For non-resident investors and issuers to become involved in domestic markets, they must have the means to manage and transform currency and interest rate risks associated with their foreign currency assets and liabilities. This implies having access to both foreign currency and interest rate derivatives and related cash-based hedging products. In the case of foreign bonds, issuers typically hedge the foreign exchange risk associated with the domestic issue via a currency swap into their home currency, and then transform the cash flows from the bond coupons to either fixed or floating via an interest rate swap (Worzala et al. 1997). Ideally, these transactions are undertaken simultaneously.

The presence of credit ratings and improvements in financial statement reporting has encouraged new issuance in international securities markets, with bonds outstanding totaling US$23.8 trillion in all markets covered by the BIS in 2008. The internationalization of securities issuance offers both investors and issuers the opportunity to diversify currency risks, although international issues tend to be hedged to eliminate likely currency, interest rate and, occasionally, credit risks. The recent development of sophisticated foreign exchange, interest rate and derivatives markets in the major financial centers of the Asia and Pacific region (especially Australia; Hong Kong, China; and Singapore) appears linked to the needs of international investors, such as sovereign and hedge funds, whose risk appetites vary. Growth in international syndicated bank lending appears to have suffered as a consequence of this trend toward disintermediated financing, especially since 2007. This is likely due to a combination of lenders experiencing difficulties in hedging credit risks, and issuers being reluctant to borrow using volatile floating rate benchmarks such as the LIBOR. As a result, syndicated loans outstanding in all markets covered by the BIS in 2008 fell to US$297 billion, a level not seen since the late 1990s.

The development of foreign bond markets in a number of smaller financial centers outside of the US, the UK and Japan with different legal traditions and degrees of supporting financial market infrastructure, offers hope to other countries seeking to expand the scope of their domestic financial markets. Attention should be drawn to the development of these markets in economies as diverse as Australia and Switzerland. The development of these markets is more reflective of financial participants leveraging unique country-specific features in conjunction with enabling legislation and the proactive involvement of government, rather than them adhering to a rigid or predefined checklist of requirements.

Nonetheless, the desire by a government to develop its financial services sector into a world-class financial trading and investment center will be difficult without the proactive involvement of market participants. For example, Korea failed to develop a viable foreign bond trading and issuance market despite the best efforts of its policymakers, providing valuable lessons for others (Batten and Szilagyi 2007).

In conclusion, the Asia and Pacific region, excluding Japan, Australia and New Zealand, has benefited from recent developments in financial infrastructure and trading, with its domestic bond markets now standing at US$4.3 trillion. However, given that this represents just 7.2 percent of the worldwide total, the region's bond markets remain underdeveloped – or at least offer scope for considerable further development – relative to the region's weight in the world economy. The development of foreign bond markets seems to offer the best hope for the next stage of regional market development. Below are listed a number of critical features of these markets that have emerged from the earlier analysis.

12.5.1 There is a Natural Evolution to the Sequence – and Time it Takes – for Market Forces to Drive Foreign Bond and Corporate Bond Market Development

It is difficult both to accelerate the speed of foreign bond market development and regulate for the risks associated with domestic development. For example, on average, the largest markets outside the US first issued bonds between 1984 and 1989. Thus, a step-by-step approach is recommended, which establishes: technical infrastructure (for example trading and settlement systems for bond trading and adequate benchmark bonds to enable corporate bond pricing); sufficient market access by investors and issuers (and the legal apparatus to support this); and the presence of additional products in other market segments (such as interest rate and exchange rate derivatives) to enable risk management and risk transformation. With respect to the last category, the importance of FRAs and swaps for managing interest rate and currency risks cannot be understated, although there must also be sufficient depth in spot and forward foreign exchange markets to ensure that exchange rate distortions are minimized. Deep, liquid and diverse products crossing a host of derivative and cash-based markets are necessary to ensure low-cost arbitrage and enable risk transformation. One key aspect of countries with developed bond markets (for example Australia, Japan and Switzerland) was deep foreign exchange and derivatives markets. The inability to offset risk via deep derivatives markets may account for the limited foreign bond market development in Korea.

Over-the-counter products, especially swaps and FRAs, are now well established, with standardized supporting legal documentation and settlement procedures. Thus, these products would be the easiest to introduce into a market, with the possibility of related exchange-traded products (for example interest rate futures) being introduced later on as markets unfold. Invariably, developing products for risk management requires international participation in domestic financial markets by foreign banks and financial institutions, regulatory changes to accommodate derivatives trading, and the removal of capital control restrictions (Forbes 2005).

Eichengreen and Luengnaruemitchai (2004) highlighted several obstacles to the development of bond markets within the Asia and Pacific region, including the slow development of private debt markets and the need to reform simultaneously other supporting aspects of financial markets. Such reforms include: creating bankruptcy legislation; reducing corruption; creating reliable securities market regulation; eliminating or reducing capital controls so there is free movement of currency; and adopting international accounting standards. In addition, there are necessary regulatory reforms linked to improving corporate governance (Nestor and Thompson 1999; Thompson 1999; Thompson and Poon 2000; Jiang and McCauley 2004; Park and Park 2005). All of these reforms are important and are difficult to achieve, even over several decades. Importantly, while risk management and trading skills may be imported to help kick-start a local development agenda, bringing about a comprehensive shift in business attitudes to risk management will require a much longer-term investment in training local employees.

12.5.2 Government Consultation with Industry is Crucial to the Development of Foreign Bond Markets

One should not underestimate the commitment required from industry, and financial intermediaries in particular, to support the markets in their embryonic stage. The presence of foreign institutions with existing skills in these areas is also a vital ingredient to this process. A noteworthy example of cooperation between industry and government arose when the governments of Australia and New Zealand withdrew from their respective bond markets in the period before 2008 due to the presence of ongoing fiscal surpluses. The governments and industries agreed to the use of high-credit-quality foreign bonds as substitutes for repurchase agreements to avoid liquidity and related benchmark pricing issues. The presence of foreign bonds also offered local pension funds the ability to buy the long-dated securities necessary to manage new asset–liability matching regulations, international accounting standards and risk-based regulations for insurance companies (Blommestein 2007). Blommestein argued that this will lead to a long-term demand for very long (20–30 years) and ultra long (30-plus years) term bonds, and foreign bond issuers will likely meet this investment demand.

12.5.3 Not all Financial Risk can be Managed through Government Intervention

Some risk can be avoided through appropriate accounting and risk management standards set by government. However, the human proclivity to gamble is difficult, if not impossible, to control or eliminate, as the losses suffered by traders in the most sophisticated financial firms can attest. This further emphasizes the need for consultation with industry in any development agenda.

12.5.4 An Ordering of Issuance Helps Build Confidence at the Nascent Stage of Foreign Bond Market Development

Almost without exception, as foreign bond markets develop, the highest credit quality issuers or sovereigns issue first, followed by quality banks and some multinationals. The foreign bond market appears to require an order of issuance. This particular order seems linked to the need for intermediaries to guide pricing (for example through benchmark bonds at long maturities) and related issues.

Although the presence of enabling infrastructure is important, it does not guarantee that corporate and foreign bond markets will develop. It appears that the right mix of issuer supply and investor demand is also needed to reach a take-off point for market development.

12.5.5 There is an Ongoing Need to Maintain Liquidity in all Markets, and Especially for Benchmark Bonds

Risk-free benchmarks remain an integral and necessary part of the corporate bond market for pricing and hedging purposes. The theoretical and practical aspect of this issue concerns trading and risk management based on credit spreads, where the risk-free government bond is the benchmark. Thus, it is critical that governments (and local central banks) recognize the need to maintain adequate liquidity irrespective of fiscal requirements. Alternatively, in the absence of this type of bond, governments can formally state that high-quality foreign bonds can act as credit substitutes, as occurred in Australia and New Zealand.

NOTES

1. Post-crisis, many governments in the Asia and Pacific region specifically set about developing local and regional bond markets as an alternative to traditional forms of intermediated (bank) financing (see Kim 1999; Rhee 2000; Thompson and Poon 2000; Park and Park 2005; Arner et al. 2006).
2. See BIS (2003).
3. See http://thomsonreuters.com/products_services/financial/content_update/content_overview/content_fixed_income/.
4. In the data used for this study, central banks in 42 of the major developed and developing economies reported their aggregate national locational data to the BIS. For more details see http://www.bis.org/statistics/bankstats.htm.
5. Note that these totals do not include contributions from Singapore and Hong Kong, China due to their status as financial centers.
6. That is, lending to banks via deposits exceeded loans made from banks.
7. For example, the largest foreign bond market is the Yankee market in the US, where securities are subject to the registration requirements of the Securities Act of 1933 (US Securities and Exchange Commission 1933), which importantly requires bonds to carry a credit rating if they are publically sold.
8. See Honda (2003) for a discussion of the process of financial market reform in Japan.
9. Bonds in this market are issued as part of global bond issuance programs and have a domestic component (for example a significant number of these bonds were Japanese Uradashi bonds issued in the high-yielding currencies of South Africa, Australia and New Zealand).
10. Callable bonds are bonds that may be bought back by the issuer at specific call dates, whereas puttable bonds are those that may be sold back to the investor at specific put dates.
11. See BIS (2007) for information on the scale and scope of the foreign exchange and interest rate derivatives markets.

REFERENCES

Arner, D., P. Lejot and G. Rhee. 2006. Developing Regional Market: Essential National Changes in Law and Regulation. In *Asia's Debt Capital Markets: Prospects and Strategies for Development*, edited by D. Arner, J. Park and P. Lejot. New York: Springer.

Bae, K.H., Y.S. Yun and W. Bailey. 2006. Determinates of Bond Holdings by Foreign Investors. In *Asian Bond Markets: Issues and Prospects*. BIS Papers 30. Basel: BIS.

Bank for International Settlements (BIS). 2003. Launch of the Asian Bond Fund. BIS press release, 2 June. http://www.bis.org/press/p030602b.htm.

Bank for International Settlements (BIS). 2007. *Triennial Central Bank Survey*. Basel: BIS.

Bank for International Settlements (BIS). 2009. *Quarterly Review: International Banking and Financial Market Developments*. Basel: BIS (various months).

Batten, J. and P. Szilagyi. 2007. Domestic Bond Market Development: The Arirang Bond Experience in Korea. *World Bank Research Observer* 22: 165–195.

Batten, J. and Y. Kim. 2001. Expanding Long-Term Financing Through Bond Market Development: A Post Crisis Policy Task. In *Government Bond Markets in Asia*, edited by Y. Kim. Manila: ADB.

Blommestein, H. 2007. Pension Funds and the Evolving Market for (Ultra-)Long Government Bonds. *Pensions: An International Journal* 12(4): 175–184.
Blommestein, H. and J. Santiso. 2007. New Strategies for Emerging Domestic Sovereign Bond Markets. Organisation for Economic Co-operation and Development (OECD) Development Centre Working Paper 260. Paris: OECD.
Burger, J. and F. Warnock. 2006. Foreign Participation in Local Currency Bond Markets. National Bureau of Economic Research (NBER) Working Paper 12548. Cambridge, MA: NBER.
Chakraborty, S. and T. Ray. 2006. Bank-Based Versus Market-Based Financial Systems: A Growth-Theoretic Analysis. *Journal of Monetary Economics* 53(2): 329–350.
Eichengreen, B. and P. Luengnaruemitchai. 2004. Why Doesn't Asia Have Bigger Bond Markets? NBER Working Paper 10576. Cambridge, MA: NBER.
Forbes, K. 2005. Capital Controls: Mud in the Wheels of Market Efficiency. *Cato Journal* 25(1): 153–167.
Herring, R.J. and N. Chatusripitak. 2000. The Case of the Missing Market: The Bond Market and Why it Matters for Financial Development. ADB Institute (ADBI) Working Paper 11. Tokyo: ADBI.
Honda, E. 2003. Financial Deregulation in Japan. *Japan and the World Economy* 15(1): 135–140.
Hoschka, T.C. 2005. Local Currency Financing – The Next Frontier for MTBs. Economic and Research Department Working Paper 078. Manila: ADB.
Inoguchi, M. 2007. Influence of ADB Bond Issues and US Bonds on Asian Government Bonds. *Asian Economic Journal* 21: 387–404.
Jiang, G. and R. McCauley. 2004. Asian Local Currency Bond Markets. *BIS Quarterly Review* June: 67–79.
Kim, K. 1999. Creating Long-Term Mortgage-Backed Bond Markets in Asian Developing Economies – A Post Crisis Agenda. Manila: ADB.
Lejot, P., D. Arner and Q. Liu. 2006. Missing Links: Regional Reforms for Asia's Bond Markets. *Asia Pacific Business Review* 12(3): 309–331.
Leung, J. 2006. Developing Bond Markets in Asia: Experience with ABF2. In *Developing Corporate Bond Markets in Asia*. BIS Papers 26. Basel: BIS.
McCauley, R. and Y. Park. 2006. Developing the Bond Market(s) of East Asia: Global, Regional or National? In *Asian Bond Markets: Issues and Prospects*. BIS Papers 30. Basel: BIS.
Nestor, S. and J. Thompson. 1999. Corporate Governance Patterns in OECD Economies: Is Convergence Under Way? Presentation at the Conference on Corporate Governance in Asia: A Comparative Perspective, OECD and Korea Development Institute, Seoul, 3–5 March.
Park, D. and Y. Park. 2005. Toward Developing Regional Bond Markets in East Asia. *Asian Economic Papers* 3: 183–211.
Rhee, S.G. 2000. Rising to Asia's Challenge: Enhanced Role of Capital Markets. In *Rising to the Challenge in Asia: A Study of Financial Markets Vol. 1*. Manila: ADB.
Rhee, S.G. 2004. The Structure and Characteristics of East Asian Bond Markets. In *Developing Regional Bond Markets in East Asia,* edited by Y. Park and T. Ito. Canberra: Australian National University Asia Pacific Press.
Schinasi, G.J. and R.T. Smith. 1998. Fixed Income Markets in the United States, Europe and Japan: Some Lessons for Emerging Markets. International

Monetary Fund Working Paper 98/173. Washington, DC: International Monetary Fund.
Tan, K., T. Karigane and T. Yoshitomi. 2001. Avoiding Double Mismatches and Withstanding Regional Financial Crisis: The Singapore Experience. ADBI Research Paper 30. Tokyo: ADBI.
Thompson, E.R. and J.P. Poon. 2000. ASEAN After the Financial Crisis: Links Between Foreign Direct Investment and Regulatory Change. *ASEAN Economic Bulletin* 17: 1–15.
Thompson, J. 1999. Alternative Systems of Corporate Governance in OECD Countries: Strengths and Weaknesses. Paper presented at the Capacity Building Workshop on Corporate Governance in Asia, ADB and ADBI, Manila, 22–26 November.
Tovar, C. and M. Quispe-Agnoli. 2008. New Financing Trends in Latin America: An Overview of Selected Issues and Policy Challenges. Federal Reserve Bank of Atlanta *Economic Review* 3: 1–16.
US Securities and Exchange Commission. 1933. *Securities Act of 1933*. http://www.sec.gov/about/laws/sa33.pdf.
Walter, I. 1993. High Performance Financial Systems: Blueprint for Development. *ISEAS Current Economic Affairs Series*. Singapore: Institute of Southeast Asian Studies.
Worzala, E., R.D. Johnson and C.M. Lizieri. 1997. Currency Swaps as a Hedging Technique for an International Real Estate Investment. *Journal of Property Finance* 8(2): 134–151.

Index

Titles of publications are shown in *italics*.